I0011584

Excel with VBA

For Engineers and Mathematicians

From the ABCs of VBA,
through Eigenvalues, Transfer Functions,
Root Locus, Frequency Response,
and
the Simplex Method for Optimization

(PC and Mac)

Francis D. Hauser
PhD

Excel with VBA for Engineers and Mathematicians by Francis Hauser

Copyright © 2015 Francis Hauser. All rights reserved.

Createspace, an Amazon.com Company

Excel ® is a registered trademark of Microsoft Corporation.

ISBN-13: 978-1511820080
ISBN-10: 151182008X

Library of Congress Control Number: 2015906434

About the Cover

The following figures appear on the cover. These figures are used during launch vehicle autopilot design to demonstrate performance and stability. The programs, the math model, and the data used to generate them are in Appendices A and B.

The following figure is a Nichols plot, which is the frequency response of an open-loop transfer function, plotted as gain in decibels versus phase in degrees.

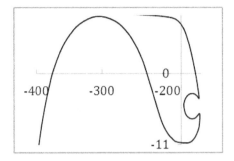

The following figure is a Bode plot of amplitude versus frequency of the same open-loop transfer function.

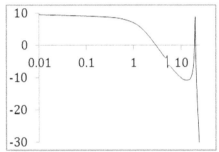

The following is a closed-loop root locus plot of the same open-loop transfer function.

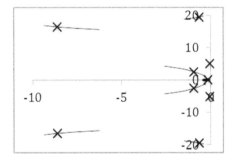

The following is a time response of vehicle angle due to an impulse on the engine angle.

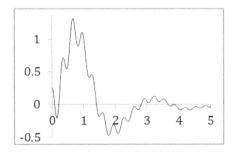

Synopsis

The reader can expect to be writing computer programs using **Microsoft Office Excel** with **VBA**. Virtually all of the **VBA** language that is pertinent to engineers and mathematicians (including students) is illustrated using listings of complete working programs that are applied to numerous examples. Topics include roots of polynomials, linear algebraic equations, Runge-Kutta numerical integration, 3-D object rotation, Newton-Raphson for nonlinear equality equations, linearizing equations, eigenvalues of general matrices with complex solutions, state variables, transfer functions, frequency response, Dantzig's Simplex algorithm, and the discrete Fourier transform. Tutorials on the theories behind the topics are also included. Methods of program checkout support the tutorials.

About the Author

Francis D. Hauser earned his PhD in electrical engineering from the University of Denver in 1972.

He is a *dynamic systems analyst* in the motions and control of launch and reentry vehicles, multibody spacecraft, fixed- and rotor-wing aircraft, large high-speed ocean-going watercraft, landcraft, and wind-driven turbines.

He is a *university and college lecturer* in graduate, undergraduate, and continuing-education courses on general optimization theory, Newtonian mechanics (statics and dynamics), linear algebra, Fourier analysis, and conventional, modern, and space-vehicle control.

Table of Contents

No New Syntax Is Presented in the Remaining Chapters

Introduction and Chapter Summaries

This book was born when I discovered Excel with VBA. I found out that I could do a complete *autopilot stability analysis of a large flexible launch vehicle* right on my laptop using Microsoft Office, which comes installed on virtually all PCs and Macs. This programming environment would have been so helpful through my years as a student in engineering school and as an aerospace engineer and university teacher.

I began converting into VBA (Visual Basic Applications) the programs I had written in the FORTRAN and MATLAB languages. As I was reprogramming, I began designing the book the same way I was learning. Starting with simple math and engineering programs, I learned the syntax incrementally. I became more and more aware that Excel/VBA is a very powerful programming platform. It is surrounded by the point-and-click menus and windows that have come to be associated with Microsoft.

- There are countless huge spreadsheets for input-output data.

- There are countless windows to hold program code.

- The Code Windows and spreadsheets can *talk to each other*.

- All of this is accompanied by a point-and-click menus-and-windows debugger.

- When you make a run, you see the results *immediately* on the spreadsheet. From these, you can make all kinds of plots. And of course, the printer is a point and click away.

- A reference library is right on the computer via the Internet.

- And it's *low cost*. VBA has been a part of Excel for more than ten years.

The book introduces Excel/VBA incrementally. The intended audience is students through practitioners, with some practitioners being VBA students.

- Each new type of syntax is demonstrated by programs with complete code listings.

- Tutorials and example problems accompany the theory. The tutorials are written from a practitioner's viewpoint. The theory includes linear algebra, numerical methods, calculus, and dynamic systems analysis. References are given.

- The programs are written to be easily modified for other problems. Many of the programs use a common format for inputting new problem equations and data.

- The programs have been thoroughly checked out. Many of them have worked in FORTRAN and MATLAB for years.

Checkout is a very important part of programming. Each program is demonstrated by several examples. The results of each example are checked out by at least one of the following methods:

- Using hand calculation
- Using examples that have known answers
- Writing a companion program specifically for checkout
- Solving some examples in more than one way

Chapter Summaries

1: The Programming Environment between Excel and VBA

VBA programs are written in Code Windows. There are two types, and each communicates differently with the spreadsheet. There is also a window that lists all of the VBA programs. Another window causes a selected program to be run.

In a step-by-step manner, Chapter 1 shows how to open and use these windows using a simple program. There are steps (or *mouse clicks*) needed to open a Code Window and write a program. There are steps needed to execute a program and link its input and output to particular spreadsheets. Programs can communicate with each other as well as with each spreadsheet.

There are slight differences in use between a PC and a Mac. Throughout this book, these differences are noted.

2: Making Graphs

This chapter contains three simple programs. Each program reads data from a spreadsheet, does simple arithmetic, and writes results to a spreadsheet. In each program, the VBA syntax is defined. The steps needed to graph the results are listed. Descriptions are given on how to output the data to the spreadsheets for 2-D and 3-D graphs.

3: Graphing Polynomials

This chapter contains two programs that graph polynomials in order to find their roots. One is for real roots and the other for complex roots. The VBA syntax is described in their listings.

4: Arrays and Data Types

Arrays are variables that contain multiple values. Data types include integer, floating point, character, et cetera. Several small programs illustrate the syntax for these very important topics.

5: Solving Linear Algebraic Equations

Three programs solve this type of equation and show the syntax for matrix algebra (multiplication, inversion, etc.).

6: Functions

Functions perform specific operations like the trigonometric functions, the logarithmic functions, the square root, et cetera. There are three types of functions: Excel, VBA, and user defined. The syntax for the common math and engineering functions are listed.

7: Looping and Branching and the Operators (Arithmetic, Comparison, Logical)

This chapter has five sections:
- Looping a definite number of times: For...Next
- Looping an indefinite number of times: Do...Loop
- Branching according to the *true/false* result of a condition test: If...Then...Else
- Branching by comparing values using the Select Case statement
- Using operators in arithmetic and in condition tests (comparison/logical)

Small programs show the syntax for each of these.

8: Frequency Response of a Transfer Function

A transfer function is a ratio of polynomials. Roots of polynomials can be complex numbers. Hence, computing the frequency response of a transfer function requires doing arithmetic with complex numbers. This chapter shows a program for this. Three examples are given, with plots of their responses.

9: 3-D Rotational Graphics

The task is to write a program that rotates a box in 3-D. The Euler angle transformation for this is derived. The discussion includes how to input the data so that the points can be connected and the lines in the back can be dashed.

10: The Call Statement

This chapter shows how to make one program call another to perform a task and return the results. Several small programs demonstrate the syntax.

11: Debugging

Debugging is fun. Point-and-click menus and windows make it easy. Execution can be stopped in several ways and at any line of code. Values of variables can be inspected in several ways. Execution can then be continued until the next stopping point. A simple program shows all of this.

12: The GoSub Statement

This operates like the `Call` statement. The `GoSub` statement causes execution to be transferred to a block of code within the same program. When this block is completed, execution continues at the statement following the `GoSub` statement.

Using this `GoSub` method of *program segmentation*, we will write a program to numerically integrate a set of nonlinear differential equations. Data is put in one segment. Equations are put in another. The *integrator* is put in a third. Another part of the program directs execution between these segments.

13: The GoTo Statement

This is like the `GoSub` statement without the return. A program using the `GoTo` statement is written to sort and interpolate a list of numbers.

No New Syntax Is Presented in the Remaining Chapters

14: The Newton-Raphson Method

A program is written that uses the Newton-Raphson method to solve a general set of nonlinear equality equations. A tutorial discusses this method, which centers around describing the equations to be solved with first-order Taylor series expansions of each. The first derivatives are computed using the *method of differences*.

The part of the program that computes the first derivatives uses the *program segmentation* described in Chapter 12. Data is put in one segment. Equations are put in another. The *method of differences* is put in a third. Around this is the main part of the program that uses these first derivatives in order to iteratively reach a solution.

The examples used for demonstration include finding real and complex roots of polynomials and solving general sets of nonlinear equations.

15: Eigenvalues of General Matrices with Complex Solutions

A program is written to compute eigenvalues of general matrices that can have complex solutions. A tutorial begins with the definition of the *eigenvalue problem*, the solutions of which are eigenvalues. A prominent method of obtaining these eigenvalues is the *QR method*. The tutorial demonstrates the iterative aspect of this method, including techniques that are used to reduce the number of iterations. The discussion includes methods to put differential equations into the form of the *eigenvalue problem*, which requires linearizing nonlinear equations.

The first program in this chapter linearizes nonlinear differential equations using the *method of differences* from Chapter 14. This program uses the programming segmentation described in Chapter 12.

The second program in this chapter computes eigenvalues of general matrices using the *QR method*. This program is checked out using two eigenvalue theorems:

- The trace of a matrix equals the sum of its eigenvalues.
- The determinant of a matrix equals the product of its eigenvalues.

A third program extends the QR program to generate the locus of eigenvalues as equation parameters vary. This locus is called a *root-locus*.

The examples that demonstrate these programs find roots (eigenvalues) of polynomials and eigenvalues of general nonlinear differential equations, which of course must be linearized.

16: Differential Equations Converted to State Variable Form

A program is written to put a set of nonlinear differential equations into *state variable form*. These equations are restricted to be *single input, single output*.

The *state variable form* is achieved by expanding the equations in first-order Taylor series. The first derivatives are computed using the *method of differences* as in Chapter 14. The equations and data are input using the *programming segmentation* introduced in Chapter 12. The program is demonstrated with five examples, each of which is checked out manually.

17: Transfer Functions Computed from the State Variable Form

A transfer function is a ratio of polynomials. The roots (eigenvalues) of the numerator are called *zeros*. The roots (eigenvalues) of the denominator are called *poles*.

A tutorial begins by manually computing the output transfer function from the *state variable form*. The resulting denominator is in the form of the *eigenvalue problem*. Hence, its roots can be computed using the *QR* program in Chapter 15. Computing the numerator is not as straightforward. If the number of *poles* is greater than the number of *zeros*, the numerator cannot directly be put into the form of the *eigenvalue problem*. The *state variable* form must be transformed into the *eigenvalue problem*. The *zeros* can then be computed by the *QR* program of Chapter 15.

A program implementing this transformation is written and demonstrated using the state variable forms that were computed in the five examples of Chapter 16.

18: Frequency Response Computed from the State Variable Form

Using the *three elementary matrix row* operations, the *state variable form* from Chapter 16 is put into *upper triangular form* at each frequency. The frequency response of the output is then given by the element in the lower right-hand corner.

A program implementing this is written and demonstrated using the state variable forms that were computed in the five examples of Chapter 16.

19: The Simplex Method of Optimization

A program is written that implements Dantzig's Simplex algorithm. This solves the general linear programming problem. Examples demonstrate this program and show that it can also solve linear algebraic equations like those in Chapter 5.

20: The Discrete Fourier Transform

A program is written to compute the *discrete Fourier transform* of a series of equally-spaced points. In an example, the series of points are the impulse response that was output by the numerical integrator in the example of Chapter 12. The *continuous Fourier transform* corresponding to this same series of points was computed in an example in Chapter 8. This allows a comparison between the *continuous* and *discrete Fourier transforms*.

Appendix A: Code Listings

This appendix contains complete listings of several large programs that were written in previous chapters.

Appendix B: The Launch Vehicle Example Shown on the Cover

This appendix contains the equations and data for the math model of a large launch vehicle. These equations and data comprise the input to programs that compute the time and frequency responses shown on the cover of this book.

Chapter 1: The Programming Environment between Excel and VBA

Open the **Excel** program and create a new workbook. Then **Save As.**

To facilitate this discussion, enter the following:
Filename: First   Where: Desktop   Type: Excel Macro-Enabled Workbook (.xlsm)
When the file named **First** is reopened, *click* the **Enable Macros** button if required.

Note: On a tab near the bottom left of the screen, the spreadsheet is called **Sheet1**. The + next to this tab is for adding more spreadsheets. We will do this later. For now, leave it at Sheet1.

The rows of the spreadsheets are given **numbers**. The columns are given **letters**. It is desirable, though not required, to change the **letters** to **numbers**. See the following table.

How to Switch the Columns from Letters to Numbers
On a PC with Excel 2013: File >>> Options >>> Formulas >>> R1C1 Reference Style.   On a Mac with Excel 2011: Excel >>> Preferences >>> General >>> R1C1 Reference Style.   If these instructions don't work on your system, Google   *How to switch to R1C1 reference style in Excel (your version).*

If the **Developer Tab** is not shown, it must be activated. See the following table:

How to Activate the Developer Tab
On a PC with Excel 2013: File >>> Options >>> Customize Ribbon >>> Developer.   On a Mac with Excel 2011: Excel >>> Preferences >>> Ribbon >>> Developer.   If these instructions don't work on your system, Google   *How to activate the developer tab in Excel (your version).*

The following is a step-by-step discussion of how to write and execute a **VBA** program.

Click the **Developer** tab. On its ribbon, click **Editor** (or **Visual Basic**). Two things happen.

1) The <u>Project</u> Window Opens.	2) The Category <u>Run</u> Appears in the Menu Bar.
Project **VBA Project (First.xlsm)** • **Sheet1 (Sheet1)** • **ThisWorkbook** Sheet1(Sheet1) and This Workbook are names of two windows that can contain VBA code.	Selecting Run and then Run Macro opens the Macros Window. It lists the names of programs that, right now, can be run. **Macros** *Initially Empty*

We will now write a program in the Code Window called **ThisWorkbook**.

1) In the **Project** Window, double-click **ThisWorkbook**. This Code Window will open.

2) At the cursor in the empty window, enter the following six lines of **VBA** code:

First.xlsm: ThisWorkbook (Code)	
Code	**Comments**

Sub one()
  x = 1
  Cells(1, 1) = 4 * Atn(x)
  pie = Cells(1, 1)
  Cells(1, 3) = 2 * pie
End Sub
	The empty parentheses are necessary. More in Chapter 10.
	
	Write the value of $\pi = 4*\tan^{-1}(1)$ into spreadsheet cell row 1, column 1.
	
	Read the value of π from cell row 1, column 1.
	
	Write the value of $2*\pi$ into cell row 1, column 3.

3) File >>> Save and close the window.

4) Select Run >>> Run Macro. This opens the **Macros** Window. It will show an item called **ThisWorkbook.one**. Click on it, and then select Run.

5) Return to the spreadsheet, and see the following:
- π is written in row 1, column 1.
- 2π is written in row 1, column 3.

6) Prepare for the next run. Clear the spreadsheet by selecting (or highlighting) the data and Edit >>> Clear >>> All. (Selecting is done by holding-down-the-clicker and dragging.)

Another Program

1) Via the + at the bottom of the spreadsheet, add Sheet 2. *Click* **Editor** (**Visual Basic**). This opens the **Project** Window. Observe that **Sheet2(Sheet2)** has been added. The windows **Sheet1(Sheet1)** and **Sheet2(Sheet2)** are currently empty.

Project
VBA Project (First.xlsm)
• Sheet1(Sheet1)
• Sheet2(Sheet2)
• ThisWorkbook

2) Select Run >>> Run Macro. In the **Macros** Window, click **ThisWorkbook.one** and Run.

3) This time, π and 2π are written on **Sheet 2**. This shows that *Program one* in *ThisWorkbook reads and writes to the open or visible spreadsheet.*

More Programs

To facilitate this discussion, we will now add another Code Window. If the **Project** Window is not open, *click* **Editor** (or **Visual Basic**). In the top menu bar, Insert >>> Module.

The **Project** Window now contains four Code Windows.

Project
VBA Project (First.xlsm)
• Module1
• Sheet1(Sheet1)
• Sheet2(Sheet2)
• ThisWorkbook

We will now copy **Program one** from **ThisWorkbook** to the other three Code Windows.

- *Double-click* ThisWorkbook, Edit >>> Select All >>> Copy, close the window.

- *Double-click* Module1, Edit >>> Paste, File >>> Save, close the window.

- *Double-click* Sheet1, Edit >>> Paste, File >>> Save, close the window.

- *Double-click* Sheet2, Edit >>> Paste, File >>> Save, close the window.

Now in the top menu, select Run >>> Run Macro. This opens the **Macros** Window.

Macros
• one
• Sheet1.one
• Sheet2.one
• ThisWorkbook.one

Discussion of the programs in the **Macros** Window:

- **ThisWorkbook.one** has already been shown to communicate with the *open* (or *visible)* sheet.

- **one**, which is in **Module1,** also communicates with the *open* sheet.

- **Sheet1.one** will communicate only with **Sheet1**.

- **Sheet2.one** will communicate only with **Sheet2**.

Summary and Notes

- The Code Window **ThisWorkbook** communicates with the *open* sheet.

- The Code Windows **Module*j*** communicate with the *open* sheet.

- The Code Windows **Sheet*j*** communicate ***only with* Sheet*j*.**

- By using **ThisWorkbook** and the **Module*j*** Code Windows, a program can run many cases, changing only the spreadsheets between cases.

- All programs in this book use the read-write statements that have been shown thus far. There is another way which will be defined at the end of this chapter.

- Code Windows can contain more than one program.

- Programs in *different* Code Windows communicate with each other through the spreadsheet.

- Programs in the *same* Code Window can also communicate with each other through the spreadsheet. But as will be shown in Chapter 10, they can also communicate with each other directly.

- **Tip:** It is good practice to close the Code Windows before selecting Run >>> Run Macro.

Printing the Spreadsheet Data

Spreadsheet data can be printed directly from **Excel**. Data can also be pasted from **Excel** into **Word** and **Powerpoint** and can be printed from these. In that way, the data can be further annotated. One way to *paste* the data into **Word** without gridlines is this:

- Select (highlight) the data and Copy.
- Paste into Powerpoint and annotate if desired. Pasting into Powerpoint removes the gridlines.
- Copy from Powerpoint.
- Paste into Word via Paste Special >>> PDF or Paste Special >>> Bitmap.
- *Note:* Printing Excel graphs (a.k.a. charts or plots) will be discussed in Chapter 2.

More about Code Windows and Spreadsheets

- Programs read and write to *specific cells*. Cutting and pasting data from these cells to others can keep the *specific cells* free for subsequent runs.

- One attractive feature of the spreadsheet is that, after a run, clarifying comments can be manually added to the data on the spreadsheet.

- To select two or more areas on the spreadsheet:
  - 1st area: hold-down-clicker and drag.
  - Subsequent areas: hold-down-command-key while holding-down-clicker and dragging, or hold-down-ctrl-key while holding-down-clicker and dragging.

Another Way to Read-Write

This way allows **any** program in **any** Code Window to read and write to **any** spreadsheet. Since this way is not used in any programs in this book, the reader may skip to the next chapter.

We will write two programs in the **Sheet1** Code Window below. **Program one** will be repeated. **Program two** will define these new read and write statements.

First.xlsm: Sheet1 (Code)	
Code	Comments
```\nSub one()\n x = 1\n Cells(1, 1) = 4 * Atn(x)\n pie = Cells(1, 1)\n Cells(1, 3) = 2 * pie\nEnd Sub\n```	• Sub one reads and writes only to Sheet1.
```\nSub two()\n x = 1\n Worksheets("Sheet4").Cells(1, 1) = 4 * Atn(x)\n pie = Worksheets("Sheet4").Cells(1, 1)\n Worksheets("Sheet5").Cells(1, 3) = 2 * pie\n Cells(1, 5) = 2 * pie\nEnd Sub\n```	• Sub two reads and writes to Sheet4 and Sheet5. *Note:* Sub two also writes to Sheet1 by default.
The prefix Worksheets("Sheet *j* ") directs the Cells statement to Sheet *j*, only if Sheet *j* has been added to the **Project** Window.	

Chapter 2. Making Graphs

This chapter describes three programs and how to graph their outputs.

Program one2

The first program computes y^2 and y^3 from values of y that are listed on the spreadsheet. This involves repeating a sequence of statements a predetermined number of times. Hence, it will use the VBA statements for looping known as **For...Next**.

Syntax for Looping via For...Next
For index = start-value **To** end-value [**Step** step-value]   {statements in the loop} **Next** index
Notes: • index is a variable (integer or floating point). • start-value, end-value, and step-value may be integers or floating points and positive or negative. • **Step** is optional. **Step 1** is the default.

The following is a listing of the program and its output:

one2.xlsm: ThisWorkbook (Code)
| ```
Sub one2()
For i = 1 To 9
   y = Cells( i, 1 )
   Cells( i, 2 ) = y
   Cells( i, 3 ) = y ^ 2
   Cells( i, 4 ) = y ^ 3
Next i
End Sub
``` |

The Spreadsheet from one2.xlsm			
Y (user input) Column 1	Y (series 1) Column 2	Y^2 (series 2) Column 3	Y^3 (series 3) Column 4
-1.5	-1.5	2.25	-3.375
-1.2	-1.2	1.44	-1.728
-0.8	-0.8	0.64	-0.512
-0.4	-0.4	0.16	-0.064
0	0	0	0
0.4	0.4	0.16	0.064
0.8	0.8	0.64	0.512
1.2	1.2	1.44	1.728
1.5	1.5	2.25	3.375

Values of y are input by the user in column 1. The program reads and writes these values into column 2. When graphed, this column is called **Series1**. The program also computes y^2 and y^3 and writes these values into columns 3 and 4.
```

The following is the plot of the output and how the plot was made.

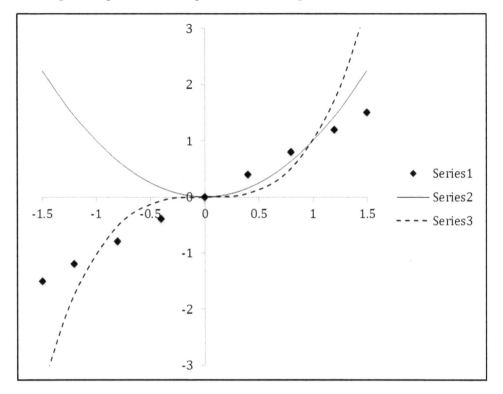

Excel refers to this plot as a **Scatter chart** or **X-Y chart**. Data for the horizontal (or **X**) axis is the first column that is selected. All of the other columns are for the vertical axis and are labeled **Series 1, 2, 3,** et cetera. All of the **series** share the single horizontal axis. Each series has its own **format**. One may be a solid line, another may be a dashed line, et cetera.

If the points are to be connected by a line or a dash, the horizontal-axis data must be in increasing or decreasing order. Otherwise, the horizontal axis data can be out of order. Each **axis** has its own **scaling** (i.e., minimum, maximum, increment). The scales for either or both axes can be logarithmic.

The following two tables show how to make a **Scatter chart**. One is for a PC. The other is for a Mac.

One Way to Make Scatter Charts on a PC with Excel 2013

Step 1: Select (highlight) the data to be plotted. For Program one2, this area is from cell(1,1) to cell(9,4).

Step 2: Select the Insert Tab. In the chart area of the ribbon, insert a Scatter chart with Smooth Lines.

Step 3: Click on the chart. This adds chart tool tabs Design and Format. Select Design. On this ribbon, select Add Chart Elements. Select Chart and Axis Titles, which adds *text boxes*. Select Gridlines.

Step 4: Click on the chart, and select the Format Tab. On the chart itself, do the following:

- Double-click on the vertical axis. In the *pop-up window*, select the *three-bars icon* for Axis Options. Enter range, increments, horizontal axis crossing, and maybe log scale. Repeat for horizontal axis.

- Double-click on series 1 plot (or 2, etc.). In the *pop-up window*, select *paint bucket icon* for Fill & Line.

  - If the plot is a *line*, select Line and then color, dash type, and width.

  - If the plot is *points*, select Marker and then Marker Options for type and size and Fill for color.

  - *Note:* To change a series from a *line* to *points* (or vice versa), select the series. Then again, select Insert Tab, Scatter chart, and this time, the Scatter Points icon.

Step 5: Size the chart.
  - Select the Format Tab and on this ribbon, type in the size (height and width).
or, - With the *cursor* on the borders of the chart, click and drag the chart area adjusters.

One Way to Make Scatter Charts on a Mac with Excel 2011

Step 1: Select (highlight) the data to be plotted. For Program one2, this area is from cell(1,1) to cell(9,4).

Step 2: Select the Charts Tab. On this ribbon, insert a Scatter chart with Smooth Lined Scatter.

Step 3: Select Chart Layout tab. Select Chart and Axis Titles to add *text boxes*. Select Gridlines.

Step 4: Click on the chart, and select the Format Tab. On the chart itself, do the following:

- Double-click on the vertical axis. In the *pop-up window*, select Scale. Enter the range, increments, and horizontal axis crossing. Note the option for log scale. Repeat for the horizontal axis.

- Double-click on the series 1 plot (or 2, etc.). In the *pop-up window*:

  - If the plot is a *line*, select Line. Then Solid for color and Weights & Arrows for dash and width.

  - If the plot is *points*, select Marker Fill and Solid for color and Marker Style for style and size.

  - *Note:* To change a series from a *line* to *points* (or vice versa), select the series. Then again, select the Charts Tab, Scatter, and this time, Marked Scatter.

Step 5: Size the chart.
  - Select the Format Tab, and on this ribbon, type in the size (height and width).
or, - With the *cursor* on the borders of the chart, click and drag the chart area adjusters.

Program two2

The second program computes e^x and **ln(x)** over a range of **X** from -2 to +3. This program will show how to plot several *series* when each has a different x-axis value. The following table introduces more VBA statements:

Function	Syntax
$y = e^x$	y = Exp(x)
$y = \ln(x)$	y = Log(x)
y = x rounded to a specified number of decimal places	y = Application.Round(x, nd)
y = a list of numbers assigned to y	y = Array(number 1, number 2, ...)
y(1) refers to the first number in the array	Option Base 1
y(0) refers to the first number in the array	Option Base 0
Option Base 0 is the default (see Chapter 4).	

The following is the program code:

two2.xlsm: ThisWorkbook (Code)	
``Option Base 1

Sub two2()

Xa = Array(-2, -1.5, -1, -0.75, -0.5, -0.25, 0, 0.6, 1.25)
For i = 1 to 9
  Y = Exp(Xa(i))
  Cells(i, 1) = Xa(i)
  Cells(i, 2) = Application.Round(Y, 2)
Next i

Xb = Array(0.01, 0.05, 0.1, 0.2, 0.5, 0.75, 1, 1.25)
For i = 1 to 8
  Y = Log(Xb(i))
  Cells(i + 9, 1) = Xb(i)
  Cells(i + 9, 3) = Application.Round(Y, 2)
Next i

Xc = Array(0.5, 1, 2, 3, 1.5, 2.5)
For i = 1 to 6
  Y = Log(Xc(i))
  Cells(i + 9 + 8, 1) = Xc(i)
  Cells(i + 9 + 8, 4) = Application.Round(Y, 2)
Next i

End Sub``` | **Option Base 1** allows Xa(1) = -2 (see above table or Chapter 4).

The function e^x is computed from the numbers in the Xa array. Since this is a list of monotonic numbers with uneven intervals, it can be formatted with a dashed line. It is printed in column 2 and plotted as *Series1*.

The function **y = ln(x)** is computed from the numbers in the Xb array. Since it is a list of monotonic numbers with uneven intervals, it can be formatted with a solid line. It is printed in column 3 and plotted as *Series2*.

The function **y = ln(x)** is computed from the Xc array. This is a list of nonmonotonic numbers with uneven intervals. Hence it must be formatted with points. It is printed in column 4 and plotted as *Series3*.

The arrays Xa, Xb, and Xc are printed consecutively in column 1, in the rows that correspond to their individual functions.

Note that arithmetic can be done in the *Cells* statements. |

The following is the spreadsheet output:

The Spreadsheet from two2.xlsm			
x axis Column 1	$y = e^{X_a}$ Column 2	$y = \ln(X_b)$ Column 3	$y = \ln(X_c)$ Column 4
X_a			
-2.00	0.14		
-1.50	0.22		
-1.00	0.37		
-0.75	0.47		
-0.50	0.61		
-0.25	0.78		
0	1.00		
0.60	1.82		
1.25	3.49		
X_b			
0.01		-4.61	
0.05		-3.00	
0.10		-2.30	
0.20		-1.61	
0.50		-0.69	
0.75		-0.29	
1.00		0	
1.25		0.22	
X_c			
0.50			-0.69
1.00			0
2.00			0.69
3.00			1.10
1.50			0.41
2.50			0.92

The following is the plot. The data field selected for the plot is the rectangular area from **(1, 1) to (23, 4)**. The step-by-step process for this scatter chart is the same as in **Program one2**.

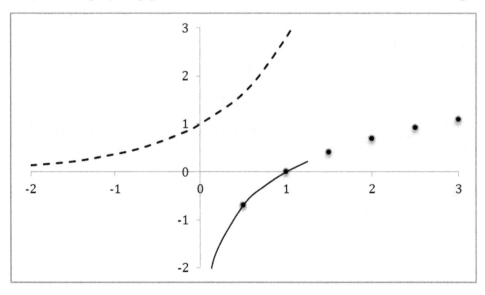

Final note on **Scatter Charts**: empty cells do not disturb plotting. They are used to separate groups in the same **Series**. An empty cell is like *lifting the pen* between the groups.

Program three2

Excel has another type of chart. It's called a Surface chart, and is like a topographic map. Its three axes are called vertical, horizontal, and depth. The vertical axis is a **value** axis, having a minimum and maximum value and increments. The horizontal and depth axes are **category** axes (i.e., each axis is a list of items). But these lists can be numbers and, though nonscalable, can be used to simulate values. If these *simulated values* correspond to the *actual values* used to compute the function on the vertical axis, the Surface chart simulates a 3-D chart that can be rotated. This is demonstrated in Program three2.

Program three2 computes $f(i,j) = \sqrt{(i-2)^2 + (j-2)^2}$ for i = 0 to 4 and j = 0 to 4. The values of $f(i,j)$ are output in matrix form to be used for the **Vertical** axis. The values of **i** and **j** are output to be used as categories for the **Depth** and **Horizontal** axes.

The following is a listing of the code and the spreadsheet. The code illustrates the syntax for the following:

- use of nested **For...Next** loops
- use of **sqr(x)** for the square root of x

three2.xlsm: ThisWorkbook (Code)
| ```
Sub three2()
For i = 0 To 4
  For j = 0 To 4
    f = Sqr( ( i − 2 )² + ( j − 2 )² )
    Cells( 2 + i, 2 + j ) = Application.Round( f, 2 )
    Cells ( 1, 2 + j ) = j
  Next j
  Cells( 2 + i, 1 ) = i
Next i
End Sub
``` |

The Spreadsheet from three2.xlsm

	Column 1	Values of *j* Used as Horizontal Axis Categories				
		Column 2	Column 3	Column 4	Column 5	Column 6
Row 1		0	1	2	3	4
Values of *i*	0	2.83	2.24	2	2.24	2.83
Used as	1	2.24	1.41	1	1.41	2.24
Depth Axis	2	2.00	1.00	0	1.00	2.00
Categories	3	2.24	1.41	1	1.41	2.24
	4	2.83	2.24	2	2.24	2.83
```

The following is a **Surface chart** of this data. The rectangular area selected for the chart is **(1, 1) to (6, 6)**. Note that cell(**1,1**) is blank.

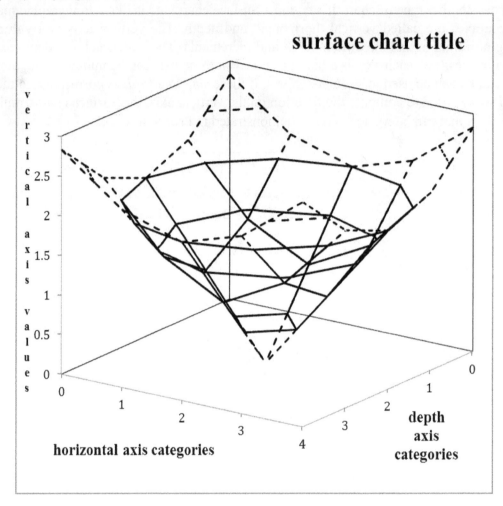

The following two tables show how to make a **Surface chart**. One is for a PC. The other is for a Mac.

One Way to Make Surface Charts on a PC with Excel 2013

Step 1: Highlight the rectangular area of data to be plotted. For Program three2, from blank cell(1,1) to cell(9,4).

Step 2: Select the Insert Tab. On this ribbon, insert Surface chart with a Wireframe 3-D Surface.

Step 3: Click on the chart. Select Design Tab and Add Chart Elements. Select Titles for the chart and for the horizontal, vertical, and depth axes. Select Gridlines for these axes.

Step 4: Click on the chart, and select the Format Tab. Then on the chart itself, do the following:

- Double-click on the vertical axis. In the *pop-up window*, select the *three-bars icon* for Axis Options. Enter range, increments, and Floor Crosses At.

- Double-click only Legend Entry 1 (or 2, etc.). In the *pop-up window*, select the *paint bucket icon* for Fill and Line. Then select Border for color, width, and dash.

- Double-click on the depth axis. In the *pop-up window*, select the *three-bars icon* for Axis Options. Then select Axis Options for *series in reverse order*.

- Double-click on the plot area of the chart. In the *pop-up window*, select the *pentagon icon* for Effects. Then 3-D rotation.

Step 5: Size the chart. Same as Scatter chart.

One Way to Make Surface Charts on a Mac with Excel 2011

Step 1: Highlight the rectangular area of data to be plotted. For Program three2, from blank cell(1,1) to cell(9,4).

Step 2: Select the Charts Tab. On this ribbon, select Other and Wireframe 3-D Surface.

Step 3: Click on the chart. Select the Chart Layout Tab. Select Titles for the chart and for the horizontal, vertical, and depth axes. Select Gridlines for these axes.

Step 4: Click on the chart, and select the Format Tab. Then on the chart itself, do the following:

- Double-click on the vertical axis. In the *pop-up window*, select Scale, and then enter range, increments, and Floor Crosses At.

- Double-click only Legend Entry 1 (or 2, etc.). In the *pop-up window*, select Line and Solid for color and Weights & Arrows for width and dash.

- Double-click on the depth axis. In the *pop-up window*, select Scale, and then maybe select *series in reverse order*.

- Double-click on the plot area of the chart. In the *pop-up window*, select 3-D Rotation.

Step 5: Size the chart. Same as Scatter chart.

Printing a Chart

A chart can be printed directly from **Excel**. A chart can also be pasted from **Excel** into **Word** and **Powerpoint** and can be printed from these. In that way, it can also be resized, reformatted, and annotated. One way to *paste* a chart into **Word** without the border is this:

- Click on the chart and copy.
- Paste into **Powerpoint** and resize, reformat, and annotate if desired.
- Copy from **Powerpoint**.
- Paste into **Word** via Paste Special >>> PDF or Paste Special >>> Bitmap.
- *Note:* The use of **Powerpoint** removes the border.

Chapter 3: Graphing Polynomials

One way to find the roots of a polynomial is to graph it. This is the polynomial used in this chapter:

$$f = s^3 + s^2 - 2$$

Program four (Real Roots)

This program graphs f to find its real roots between s=-3 and s=+3. The values used for s are input via the **Array** function.

four.xlsm: ThisWorkbook (Code)	Spreadsheet four.xlsm	
	s in Column 1	**f in Column 2**
	-3	-20
	-2.5	-11.38
	-2	-6
Option Base 1 ' This Option allows s(1) = -3	-1.75	-4.3
Sub four()	-1.5	-3.13
s = Array(-3, -2.5, -2, -1.75, -1.5, -1.25, _ ' Line Continue	-1.25	-2.39
-1, -0.75, -0.5, 0, 0.5, 1, 1.5, 2, 2.5, 3)	-1	-2
For i = 1 To 16	-0.75	-1.86
f = s(i) ^ 3 + s(i) ^ 2 - 2	-0.5	-1.88
Cells(i, 1) = s(i)	0	-2
Cells(i, 2) = Application.Round(f, 2)	0.5	-1.63
Next i	1	0
End Sub	1.5	3.63
	2	10
	2.5	19.88
	3	34
New Syntax		
• An *apostrophe* causes the rest of a line to be a *comment*.		
• A space followed by underscore (_) allows a line to continue.		

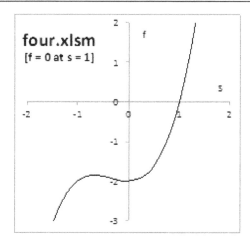

four.xlsm
[f = 0 at s = 1]

The scatter plot was drawn using the instructions in Chapter 2. The selected area is from cells(1, 1) to (16, 2). The plot shows one root at s = 1. It also shows that the other two roots are complex.

21

Program five (Complex Roots)

This program will plot the magnitude of f and show all three of its roots by allowing **s** to be a complex number. When $s = a + jb$ is substituted into f, the following results:

$$f = real\ part\ +\ j * imaginary\ part\ = \text{Re} + j * \text{Im}$$

The equations for **Re** and **Im** are now derived. In general, this is true:

$$f = c_n s^n + c_{n-1} s^{n-1} + ... + c_1 s + c_0$$

Substituting the polar form $s = re^{j\theta}$, this occurs:

$$f = c_n r^n e^{jn\theta} + c_{n-1} r^{n-1} e^{j(n-1)\theta} + ... + c_1 r e^{j\theta} + c_0$$

Now this is true:

$$s^0 = 1$$
$$s^1 = re^{j\theta} = r(\cos\theta + j\sin\theta)$$
$$s^2 = r^2 e^{j2\theta} = r^2(\cos 2\theta + j\sin 2\theta)$$
$$\bullet$$
$$\bullet$$
$$s^n = r^n e^{jn\theta} = r^n(\cos n\theta + j\sin n\theta)$$

Gathering parts and including the coefficients results in this:

$$\text{Re} = c_0 + \sum_{i=1}^{n} c_i r^i \cos i\theta \quad \text{and} \quad \text{Im} = \sum_{i=1}^{n} c_i r^i \sin i\theta$$

The magnitude of f is the following:

$$|f| = \sqrt{\text{Re}^2 + \text{Im}^2}$$

Specifically, **Program five** will compute the magnitude of this equation:

$$f = c(3)s^3 + c(2)s^2 + c(1)s + c0$$

for $s = a_i + jb_j$, as a_i ranges from -8 to 5, and b_j ranges from -4 to 4. The results will be printed out for a **Surface Chart.** Note that $c(3) = 1$, $c(2) = 1$, $c(1) = 0$ and $c0 = -2$.

New Syntax Needed to Compute $\theta = \tan^{-1}(b/a)$

To prevent division by zero, the following code is put in Program five:

```
If a = 0 Then
    thetar = 90/57.296
Else
    thetar = Application.Atan2( a, b )
Endif
```

---

five. xlsm-ThisWorkbook (Code)

Code	Comments
| ```
Option Base 1
Sub five()
c0 = -2
c = Array(0, 1, 1)
na = 14
a = Array(-8, -6, -4, -2, -1.5, -1, -0.5, 0, 0.5, _
        1, 1.5, 2, 2.5, 5)
nb = 11
b = Array(-4, -3, -2, -1, -0.5, 0, 0.5, 1, 2, 3, 4)

For i = 1 To na        ' FOR EACH VALUE OF a( I )

  For j = 1 To nb      ' FOR EACH VALUE OF b( j )

   r = Sqr(a(i) ^ 2 + b(j) ^ 2)
   If a(i) = 0 Then
    thetar = 90 / 57.296
   Else
    thetar = Application.Atan2(a(i), b(j))
   End If
   Re = c0: Im = 0   ' BEGIN THE SUMMATIONS
   For k = 1 To 3
     Re = Re + c(k) * r ^ k * Cos(k * thetar)
     Im = Im + c(k) * r ^ k * Sin(k * thetar)
   Next k
   Amp = Sqr(Re ^ 2 + Im ^ 2)
   Cells(j + 1, i + 1) = Application.Round(Amp, 2)

  Next j

Next i

For i = 1 To na
  Cells(1, i + 1) = a(i)
Next i
For j = 1 To nb
  Cells(j + 1, 1) = b(j)
Next j
End Sub
``` | • coefficients of $f$<br><br>• values of a( $i$ )<br><br>• values of b( $j$ )<br><br>• **For** each value of a( $I$ )<br><br>  • **For** each value of b( $j$ )<br><br>    • convert each s to polar form.<br>      • $r = \sqrt{a(i)^2 + b(j)^2}$      • $\theta = \tan^{-1}(b(j)/a(i))$<br><br>    • For...Next loop performs the summations.<br>      • $\mathrm{Re} = c0 + \sum_{k=1}^{3} c_k r^k \cos(k\theta)$    • $\mathrm{Im} = \sum_{k=1}^{3} c_k r^k \sin(k\theta)$<br>    • $\lvert f \rvert = \sqrt{\mathrm{Re}^2 + \mathrm{Im}^2}$<br><br>    • Print out $\lvert f \rvert$ in a rectangular array for vertical axis values.<br><br>  • **Next** b( $j$ )<br><br>• **Next** a( $I$ )<br><br>• Print out a( $i$ ) in row 1 for the horizontal axis categories.<br><br>• Print out b( $j$ ) in column 1 for the depth axis categories. |

Syntax:

In VBA, the *equal sign (=)* means *is replaced by*. This is shown by the statement in the above program,

Re = Re + c(k)*r^k*cos(k*thetar).

The Spreadsheet from five.xlsm

1	2	3	4	5	6	7	8	9	10	11	12	13	14	15
	-8	-6	-4	-2	-1.5	-1	-0.5	0	0.5	1	1.5	2	2.5	5
-4	645.2	332.4	158.4	80.6	72.1	67.1	65.3	66.5	70.6	77.7	88.0	102.0	120.2	296.4
-3	556.8	262.6	105.1	39.1	32.5	28.8	27.9	29.2	32.5	38.0	45.9	57.0	71.9	228.0
-2	496.5	216.5	75.3	16.1	10.9	8.5	8.5	10.0	12.5	16.1	21.7	30.0	42.0	182.5
-1	461.5	190.4	55.2	7.1	2.8	0	1.9	3.2	4.2	5.7	9.0	15.3	25.4	156.5
-0.5	452.9	184.1	51.3	6.1	2.9	1.6	1.8	2.3	2.4	2.6	5.3	11.4	21.3	150.1
0	450.0	182.0	50.0	6.0	3.1	2.0	1.9	2.0	1.6	0	3.6	10.0	19.9	148.0
0.5	452.9	184.1	51.3	6.1	2.9	1.6	1.8	2.3	2.4	2.6	5.3	11.4	21.3	150.1
1	461.5	190.4	55.2	7.1	2.8	0	1.9	3.2	4.2	5.7	9.0	15.3	25.4	156.5
2	496.5	216.5	75.3	16.1	10.9	8.5	8.5	10.0	12.5	16.1	21.7	30.0	42.0	182.5
3	556.8	262.6	105.1	39.1	32.5	28.8	27.9	29.2	32.5	38.0	45.9	57.0	71.9	228.0
4	645.2	332.4	158.4	80.6	72.1	67.1	65.3	66.5	70.6	77.7	88.0	102.0	120.2	296.4

23
```

The following three charts are obtained by:

- Selecting the spreadsheet area (1, 1) to (12, 15)
- Clicking **Wireframe 3-D Surface** (see Chapter 2)

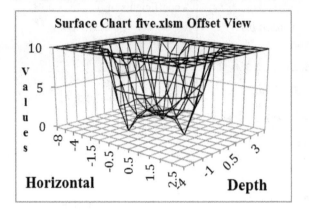

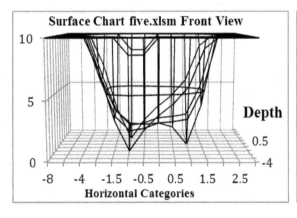

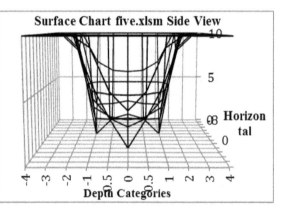

From these **Surface Charts**, the roots are as follows:

$$s_1 = \ \ 1$$
$$s_2 = -1 + j\ 1$$
$$s_3 = -1 - j\ 1$$

Chapter 4: Arrays and Data Types

Variables that are assigned multiple values are called arrays. Indices are used to reference a particular value in an array. For example, if 5 values are assigned to variable X, then X appears in code as X(i), and i can range from 1 to 5. Then the statement Y = X(3) assigns to Y the value in the X array for i = 3.

Array variables can have more than one index. Consider the variable beta(i, j, k).
If i ranges from 1 to 2, j ranges from 1 to 4, and k ranges from 1 to 5, then beta can have 40 values.

The Dim Statement

The program compiler (interpreter) must know, in advance, how much space in memory to set aside for each array variable. This is done via the **Dim** statement. All arrays must be sized in a **Dim** statement. *The one exception will be discussed later in the* **Final Notes**. Here is an example of a **Dim** statement: Dim u(10,10), v(5) allocates a ten-by-ten space for **u** and five spaces for **v**.

Additional comments:

- The **Dim** statement usually allocates more spaces than are actually needed.
- There may be multiple **Dim** statements.
- A **Dim** statement can be placed anywhere in the code, *but it must appear before each of its variables are used.*

Another Use of the Dim Statement

There is an option called **Explicit**. When this is used, all variables (scalars and arrays) *must* appear in a **Dim** statement. Hence, with the statement **Option Explicit** at the top of the code, variable names must use the spelling that is used in a **Dim** statement. This spelling includes the case (upper or lower). This option is useful when a program is under development.

A Third Use of the Dim Statement

The **Dim** statement is also used to declare the data type of each variable (i.e., whether it is an integer, floating point, character, etc.). VBA has a *smart data type* called *variant*. It's the default type for all variables. The program in the following table illustrates the *variant* data type.

Program Illustrating the Variant Data Type	
Notes:	
• If the type is not specified, type *variant* is assumed. Hence, in this program, variable b is a *variant*.	
• The data type of a variant automatically adapts during the program.	
• *Variant* is the only data type that is used in any program in this book.	
Code	**Comments**

Sub variant_study_1()
  b = " first "
    Cells(1, 1) = b
  b = 11
    Cells(2, 1) = b
  b = 77.5
    Cells(3, 1) = b
  b = Array(" second ", 33, " third ", 3.14159)
    For i = 0 To 3
      Cells(4, i + 1) = b(i)
    Next i
  b = 55
    Cells(5, 1) = b
End Sub
	• b is a character variable whose value is specified within quotes.
	• b automatically becomes an integer.
	
	• b becomes a floating point number.
	
	• b becomes an array of dimension *four*.
	    • By default [Option Base 0], first item is b(0).
	    • When $I = 0$, Cells(4, I + 1) = Cells(4, 1).
	
	• b becomes a floating point or integer number.
	(The array function has been overridden.)

Spreadsheet From Program variant_study_1			
Column 1	Column 2	Column 3	Column 4
first 11 77.5 second 55	 33	 third	 3.14159

The following program further illustrates the **Dim** statement. It yields the same result as the above program.

Second Program Illustrating the Variant Data Type	

Sub variant_study_2()
Dim b(10)
  b(0) = " first "
    Cells(1, 1) = b(0)
  b(0) = 11
    Cells(2, 1) = b(0)
  b(0) = 77.5
    Cells(3, 1) = b(0)
  b(0) = "second": b(1) = 33: b(2) = "third": b(3) = 3.14159
    For i = 0 To 3
      Cells(4, i + 1) = b(i)
    Next i
  b(0) = 55
    Cells(5, 1) = b(0)
End Sub
	• The Dim statement has been added.
	
	• b(0) is a character variable.
	
	• b(0) automatically becomes an integer.
	
	• b(0) becomes a floating point number.
	
	• Data types in the **b** array can differ.
	
	Note: Multiple statements on a line are separated by colons.
	
	• b(0) becomes a floating point or integer number.

Option Base

VBA has an option called **Base**. With **Option Base 1**, the indices for arrays start at *unity*. With **Option Base 0**, the indices start at *zero*. **Option Base 0** is the default. The following programs illustrate this. Both programs produce the same result.

Program Sub one	Program Sub two

Sub one()
alpha = Array(-25, 25, "four", 0, -10)
  For i = 0 To 4
    Cells(1 , i + 1) = alpha(i)
  Next i
End Sub
	Option Base 1
	Sub two()
	alpha = Array(-25, 25, "four", 0, -10)
	  For i = 1 To 5
	    Cells(1 , i) = alpha(i)
	  Next i
	End Sub

Note the *arithmetic* required in the Cells statement. When i = 0 , Cells(1 , i + 1) = Cells(1 , 1)	

Final Notes

• **This is the exception in the Dim statement that was mentioned earlier.** A variable set by the **Array** function may be declared in a **Dim** statement but must not be dimensioned in a **Dim** statement. In other words, If **X = Array(1, 2, 3)**, it is permissible to have the statement **Dim X**. But it is not permissible to have **Dim X(3)**.

• The **Array** function is a convenient way of assigning values to a variable that has a single index. It is awkward to use for a variable that has multiple indices. Also, it can only assign values *in the program code itself*. That is, values cannot be assigned from *the spreadsheet*.

• The storage space for the *variant* data type is twice that for double precision. The numeric range is the same as that for double precision. From Lomax[*], use of the *variant* data type does *slightly* increase program run time.

• *Variant* is the default type for all numeric and character variables. No other data type is used in any program in this book.

• When an option (**Base** and/or **Explicit**) is used, it applies to all programs in that Code Window.

• The **Dim** statement *zeros its variables*.

---

[*] Lomax, P. *VB & VBA in A Nutshell*. O'Reilly, 1998.

Chapter 5: Solving Linear Algebraic Equations
Matrices and Dynamic Arrays

There are several *Excel functions* for matrices (rectangular arrays). These will be demonstrated while solving simultaneous linear algebraic equations. Two of the functions are the following:

- **Minverse** for matrix inversion
- **MMult** for the product of two matrices

There are two rules for using these:

1. The array that is input to **Minverse** and the arrays that are input to **MMult** must be dimensioned to their exact size. If these arrays are themselves outputs from **Minverse** and/or **MMult**, this sizing is automatic.

2. The arrays that are output by **Minverse** and **MMult** *must not be sized* in a **Dim** statement. This rule is the same as the one for a variable that is set by the **Array** function (see Final Notes in Chapter 4).

Programs using **Minverse** in this book will use **Option Base 1** because it is better suited for matrices and because the spreadsheet begins with row 1 column 1.

Dynamic Arrays

The **Dim** statement is for fixed arrays—for example, A(10, 10). But sometimes, like when using **Minverse**, it is necessary to specify dimensions while the program is running. The **ReDim** statement allows this.

Syntax for the ReDim Statement	
Dim A( )	• The empty parentheses declares **A** to be a dynamic array.
•	
•	
•	
n=3	• Later in the program, the size of the **A** matrix becomes known.
ReDim A(n, n)	• This statement *true-sizes* the **A** matrix.
•	
•	
•	

> **Notes:** • The statement Dim A(n, n) is not allowed.
> • The statement ReDim A(n, n) is allowed.
> • Both the Dim statement and the ReDim statement set their variables to zero.
> • The ReDim statement can be used only in the subprogram wherein its Dim statement appears.

The following two programs illustrate the use of **Minverse** and **MMult** and the **ReDim** statement.

Program inverse

This program inverts the Hilbert matrix. Each of its i and j elements is formed by the following equation:

$$\frac{1}{(i+j-1)}$$

Each element of the inverse of the Hilbert matrix is an integer.

<table>
<tr><th colspan="2">Program inverse</th></tr>
<tr><th>Code</th><th>Comments</th></tr>
<tr><td>

```
Option Base 1
Sub inverse()
Dim A()
 n = 6
 ReDim A(n, n)
 For i = 1 To n
  For j = 1 To n
   A(i, j) = 1 / (i + j - 1)
   Cells(i, j) = Application.Round(A(i, j), 6)
  Next j
 Next i
 Ainv = Application.MInverse(A)
 ident = Application.MMult(Ainv, A)
 For i = 1 To n
  For j = 1 To n
   Cells(i, j + n) = Ainv(i, j)
   Cells(i + n, j) = Application.Round(ident(i, j), 1)
  Next j
 Next i
End Sub
```

</td><td>

• Declare **A** to be a dynamic matrix.
• **n** is the size of the **A** matrix.
• The **A** matrix is sized exactly (required by Minverse).

• Compute and print out the **A** matrix.

• Ainv = A^{-1}
• ident = A^{-1}*A (This provides an accuracy check.)

• Print out the results.

</td></tr>
</table>

<table>
<tr><th colspan="12">Program inverse Spreadsheet Results</th></tr>
<tr><th colspan="6">Hilbert Matrix (n = 6)</th><th colspan="6">Hilbert Matrix Inverse</th></tr>
<tr><td>1</td><td>1/2</td><td>1/3</td><td>1/4</td><td>1/5</td><td>1/6</td><td>36</td><td>-630</td><td>3360</td><td>-7560</td><td>7560</td><td>-2772</td></tr>
<tr><td>1/2</td><td>1/3</td><td>1/4</td><td>1/5</td><td>1/6</td><td>1/7</td><td>-630</td><td>14700</td><td>-88200</td><td>211680</td><td>-220500</td><td>83160</td></tr>
<tr><td>1/3</td><td>1/4</td><td>1/5</td><td>1/6</td><td>1/7</td><td>1/8</td><td>3360</td><td>-88200</td><td>564480</td><td>-1411200</td><td>1512000</td><td>-582120</td></tr>
<tr><td>1/4</td><td>1/5</td><td>1/6</td><td>1/7</td><td>1/8</td><td>1/9</td><td>-7560</td><td>211680</td><td>-1411200</td><td>3628800</td><td>-3969000</td><td>1552320</td></tr>
<tr><td>1/5</td><td>1/6</td><td>1/7</td><td>1/8</td><td>1/9</td><td>1/10</td><td>7560</td><td>-220500</td><td>1512000</td><td>-3969000</td><td>4410000</td><td>-1746360</td></tr>
<tr><td>1/6</td><td>1/7</td><td>1/8</td><td>1/9</td><td>1/10</td><td>1/11</td><td>-2772</td><td>83160</td><td>-582120</td><td>1552320</td><td>-1746360</td><td>698544</td></tr>
</table>

• On the actual spreadsheet, the Hilbert matrix is printed using decimal-point numbers.
• Program inverse will run without the ReDim statement if Dim A()
  is replaced by Dim A(6, 6).
• The identity matrix is not shown, but it was indeed the identity matrix.

Program lineq1

This program solves this linear algebraic equation:

$$A * x = b \quad \text{where} \quad A = \begin{bmatrix} 1 & -1 & 3 \\ 1 & 2 & -2 \\ 3 & -1 & 5 \end{bmatrix} \quad \text{and} \quad b = \begin{bmatrix} 4 \\ 10 \\ 14 \end{bmatrix}$$

The program finds **x** from this equation:

$$x = A^{-1} * b$$

Program lineq1	
Code	Comments
Option Base 1 Sub lineq1() Dim A(), b() n = Cells(1, 1) ReDim A(n, n), b(n, 1) For i = 1 To n For j = 1 To n A(i, j) = Cells(i, j + 1) Next j Next i	• Declare **A** and **b** to be dynamic matrices. • n is the size of the **A** matrix. • **A** and **b** can now be sized exactly (**b** *is sized as a column matrix*).
For i = 1 To n b(i, 1) = Cells(i, n + 2) Next i	• **A** and **b** are read from the spreadsheet.
Ainv = Application.MInverse(A)	• Ainv = A^{-1}
x = Application.MMult(Ainv, b)	• x = A^{-1}*b

bcheck = Application.MMult(A, x)
For i = 1 To n
  Cells(i, 6) = x(i, 1)
  Cells(i, 7) = bcheck(i, 1)
Next i
End Sub
	• bcheck = A*x This checks the answer.
	
	• **x** and bcheck are printed to the spreadsheet.

Program lineq1 Spreadsheet Results						
Input					Output	
n	A(i , j)			b(i , 1)	x(i , 1)	bcheck(i , 1)
	1	-1	3	4	2	4
3	1	2	-2	10	7	10
	3	-1	5	14	3	14

Program lineq2

This program also solves linear algebraic equations:

$$x = A^{-1} * b \quad \text{where} \quad A = \begin{bmatrix} 1 & 1/2 & 1/3 \\ 1/2 & 1/3 & 1/4 \\ 1/3 & 1/4 & 1/5 \end{bmatrix} \quad \text{and} \quad b = \begin{bmatrix} 1 \\ 1 \\ 1 \end{bmatrix}$$

But for this program, **b** is specified by the **Array** function, making it a row matrix. It will have to be transposed by the **Transpose** function. The program will also demonstrate the **MDeterm** function, which computes matrix determinants.

Program lineq2	
Code	Comments
| ```
Option Base 1
Sub lineq2()
Dim A()
n = 3:              Cells(1, 1) = n
ReDim A(n, n)
For i = 1 To n
  For j = 1 To n
    A(i, j) = 1 / (i + j - 1): Cells(i, j + 1) = A(i, j)
  Next j
Next i
b = Array(1, 1, 1)
For i = 1 To n
              Cells(i, n + 2) = b(i)
Next i
bT = Application.Transpose(b)

Ainv = Application.MInverse(A)

x = Application.MMult(Ainv, bT)

bcheck = Application.MMult(A, x)

deter = Application.MDeterm(A)
For i = 1 To n
    Cells(i, 6) = x(i, 1)
    Cells(i, 7) = bcheck(i, 1)
Next i
    Cells(1, 8) = deter
End Sub
``` | • Declare **A** to be a dynamic matrix.<br>• **n** is the size of **A**.<br>• **A** can now be dimensioned exactly per the requirements of Minverse.<br><br>• Compute and print out the **A** matrix.<br><br><br>• Set the values of **b**. Since this is done with the Array function, **b** is a row matrix.<br><br><br>• Transpose **b** to allow multiplication by the $A^{-1}$ matrix.<br><br>• Ainv = $A^{-1}$<br><br>• x = $A^{-1}*b^T$<br><br>• bcheck = A*x<br><br>• deter is the determinant of the **A** matrix.<br><br><br>• Print out **x**, bcheck, and deter. |

Program lineq2 Spreadsheet Results						
n	A			b	x	bcheck	determinant
3	1	1/2	1/3	1	3	1	
	1/2	1/3	1/4	1	-24	1	.000463
	1/3	1/4	1/5	1	30	1	
```

Chapter 6: Functions

Chapter 5 introduced the functions **Minverse**, **MMult**, **MDeterm**, and **Transpose**. More functions are defined in this chapter. There are three types of functions:

- Excel functions
- VBA functions
- User-defined functions

All of Excel's functions are accessible to VBA programs. But there is overlap. If a VBA function is the same as an Excel function, the VBA function must be used.

- The syntax for an Excel function: y = Application.name(argument list)
- The syntax for a VBA function: y = name(argument list)
- The syntax for a user-defined function: y = name(argument list)

The following four tables list common Excel and VBA functions. For more, see these resources:

- Lomax, Paul. *VB and VBA in a Nutshell*. O'Reilly, 1998.
- The *Help Window* for Excel functions (denoted fx).

Trig and Math Functions	
$y=\sin(\theta)$ with θ in radians	y = Sin(x)
$y=\cos(\theta)$ with θ in radians	y = Cos(x)
$y=\tan(\theta)$ with θ in radians	y = Tan(x)
$\theta = \sin^{-1}(x)$ with θ in radians	y = Application.Asin(x)
$\theta = \cos^{-1}(x)$ with θ in radians	y = Application.Acos(x)
$\theta = \tan^{-1}(x)$ with θ in radians	y = Atn(x)
$\theta = \tan^{-1}(x2/x1)$ with θ in radians	y = Application.Atan2(x1 ,x2)
y=square root of x	y = Sqr(x)
$y = e^x$	y = Exp(x)
y=log x to base 10	y = Application.Log10(x)
y=natural log of x	y = Log(x)
y=log x to base a	y = Application.Log(x, a)
y=absolute value of x	y = Abs(x)
y=sign of x (+1, 0 or -1)	y = Sgn(x)

Functions That Place the Decimal Point	
y = integer by truncating x after the decimal point	y = Fix(x)
y = nearest integer to x in negative direction	y = Int(x)
y = nearest integer to x by rounding up or down	y = Round(x)
y = x rounded (up or down) to nd decimal places	y = Application.Round(x, nd)
y = x rounded up to nd decimal places	y = Application.RoundUp(x, nd)
y = x truncated to nd decimal places	y = Application.RoundDown(x, nd)
Note: nd may be positive, zero, or negative.	

Array Functions	
• These are **Excel** functions. Their input arrays must be dimensioned exactly, and the output array must not be dimensioned (see Chapter 5). • By default, all array indices start at 0. To change to 1, use **Option Base 1**.	
y = maximum value of a general array	y = Application.Max(x)
y = minimum value of a general array	y = Application.Min(x)
y = inverse of x matrix	y = Application.Minverse*(x)
y = product of two matrices	y = Application.MMult(x1, x2)
y = determinant of x matrix	y = Application.MDeterm(x)
y = transpose of x matrix	y = Application.Transpose(x)
y = list of numbers assigned to a row array	y = Array(x1, x2, x3,...., xn)
* **Minverse** returns a scalar when its input is a 1x1 matrix.	

Complex Functions	
$y = (a + j\, b)$ combined into a single complex number	y = Application.Complex(a, b)
y = real coefficient of a complex number	y = Application.ImReal(x)
y = imaginary coefficient of a complex number	y = Application.Imaginary(x)
y = magnitude of a complex number	y = Application.ImAbs(x)
y = angle (in radians) of a complex number	y = Application.ImArgument(x)
y = quotient of two complex numbers	y = Application.ImDiv(x, z)
y = product of two or more complex numbers	y = Application.ImProduct(x, z, w)
y = complex number raised to an integer power	y = Application.ImPower(x, n)
$y = e^x$ where x is a complex number	y = Application.ImExp(x)

Syntax for a User-Defined Function
Sub main()
.
y = *fname*(argument list)
.
End Sub
Function *fname*(argument list)
.
Exit Function   ' Optional
.
fname = *expression*
End Function

●**Example *nfactorial*:** This user-defined function returns nfactorial (n!) for a positive integer.

Example *nfactorial*	

Sub main()
  n = Cells(1, 1)
  X = nfactorial(n)
  Cells(1, 2) = X
End Sub
Function nfactorial(n)
  nfactorial = 1
  For i = 1 To n
    nfactorial = nfactorial * i
  Next i
End Function
	<u>Comment</u>
	
	·If n = 0, statements in **For … Next** loop are not executed. That achieves the result
	0 ! = 1 ! = 1

34

Chapter 7

Looping and Branching,
and
the Operators (Arithmetic, Comparison, and Logical)

This chapter is divided into the following sections:
- Section A: Looping a definite number of times via For...Next
- Section B: Looping an indefinite number of times via Do...Loop
- Section C: Branching according to the *true/false* result of a condition test If...Then...Else
- Section D: Branching by comparing values using the Select Case statement
- Section E: The operators used in the following:
  - Arithmetic (addition, subtraction, etc.)
  - Condition tests (comparison and logical)

Section A: Looping via For...Next

Looping a definite number of times has been introduced in previous chapters. It's appropriate to repeat it here.

Syntax for **For...Next**

For index = start-value **To** end-value [**Step** step-value]
    {statements in the loop that may include the **Exit For** statement}
Next index
 	
where: 1. index is an integer or floating point variable.
    2. start-value, end-value, and step-value may be integer or floating point and positive or negative.
    3. **Step** is optional. **Step 1** is the default.
    4. If end-value is less then start-value, execution transfers to after the **For...Next** loop.
    5. **Exit For** is a way to exit the loop before completion. It causes the program to branch
       to the statement after **Next** index. It is useful for program checkout. **Exit For** is optional.

•Section B: Looping via Do...Loop

The **Do...Loop** statement repeatedly executes a block of code *while* or *until* some condition is satisfied. Section E of this chapter discusses these condition tests. **Do...Loop** has five types.

• **Do While...Loop**: This executes the statements in the loop **while** some condition is true, and the condition is tested **before** the loop starts.

Syntax for Do While...Loop
Do While { *condition test* }   {statements which may include **Exit Do**} **Loop**
Note: • If the *condition* test fails the first time, the statements in the loop will not be executed at all. • **Exit Do** is optional.

The following is a program demonstrating the **Do While...Loop**. This program estimates a computer's precision. The program determines the *smallest difference between two numbers* that the host computer can detect. Starting with an initial value of epsilon = 1, the program repeatedly divides epsilon by 2 until (1+epsilon = 1).

The VBA Code for *the Machine Epsilon Test* Using a Do While...Loop	

Sub epsilon_test()
  epsilon = 1
  Do While (1 + epsilon) > 1
    epsilon = epsilon / 2
  Loop
  epsilon = 2 * epsilon
End Sub
	Important Note: This program shows a lesson about using **While**. Since the test fails inside the **Do...Loop**, an adjustment must be made outside the loop. That's the reason for the last line of code: epsilon = 2 * epsilon.
	Conclusion: A computer can detect a *difference between numbers* as small as this value of epsilon. For the Macbook OSX and the Hewlett-Packard 15 with Windows 8.1, $epsilon = 2^{-52}$.

• **Do...Loop While**: This executes the statements in the loop **while** some condition is true, but the condition is tested **after** the loop is done.

Syntax for Do...Loop While
Do   {statements that may include **Exit Do**} **Loop While** { *condition test* }
Note: • The statements in the loop will be executed at least once. • **Exit Do** is optional.

• **Section B (cont.):**

The word **While** can be replaced by **Until**. To make this replacement, adjustments must be made to the *condition test*. This will be shown in a sample program below.

• **Do Until...Loop**: This executes the statements in the loop **until** some condition is true, where the condition is tested **before** the loop starts.

Syntax for Do Until...Loop
Do Until { *condition test* }   {statements that may include **Exit Do**} **Loop** *Note:* • If the *condition test* fails the first time, the statements in the loop will not be executed at all. • **Exit Do** is optional.

The following is a program demonstrating the **Do Until...Loop**. This is done by modifying the previous program that used the **Do While...Loop**. The *condition test* must be changed. The change is seen in the line of code **Do Until (1 + epsilon) = 1**.

The VBA code for *The Machine Epsilon Test* using a **Do Until...Loop**	

Sub epsilon_test()
   epsilon = 1
   Do Until (1 + epsilon) = 1
      epsilon = epsilon / 2
   Loop
   epsilon = 2 * epsilon
End Sub
	Important Note: This program demonstrates a lesson about using **Until**. Since the *condition test* fails inside the **Do...Loop**, an adjustment must be made outside the loop. That's the reason for the last line of the code:
	
	epsilon = 2 * epsilon

• **Do...Loop Until**: This executes the statements in the loop **until** some condition is true, but the condition is tested **after** the loop is done.

Syntax for Do...Loop Until
Do   {statements that may include **Exit Do**} **Loop Until** { *condition test* } *Note:* • The statements in the loop will be executed at least once. • **Exit Do** is optional.

• **Do...Loop** (test not included):

Syntax for Do...Loop

Do
   {statements that must include how the loop is terminated
      and may include **Exit Do**}
Loop

•Section C: Branching via If ... Then ... Else

This statement allows branching according to a *true* or *false* result of a condition test. Section E of this chapter discusses these condition tests. Five types of **If ... Then ... Else** are shown.

•Branching to a single statement:

```
If { condition } Then { single statement if condition is true }
```

•Branching to a block of statements:

```
If { condition } Then
    { statements if condition is true }
End If
```

•Branching at a *fork*:

```
If { condition } Then
    { statements if condition is true }
Else
    { statements if condition is false }
End If
```

•Branching at a *multiple-condition fork*:

```
If { condition 1 } Then
    { statements if condition 1 is true }
ElseIf { condition 2 } Then
    { statements if condition 1 is false and condition 2 is true }
    Else
    { statements if condition 1 is false and condition 2 is false }
End If
```

•Another type of branching at a *multiple-condition fork*:

```
If { condition 1 } Then
    { statements if condition 1 is true }
ElseIf { condition 2 } Then
    { statements if condition 1 is false and condition 2 is true }
End If
```
Note: Nothing is done if *conditions 1* and *2* are both false.

Notes:

- **ElseIf** doesn't have its own **End If**.
- There can be many **ElseIfs** and **Elses**.

• **Section D: Branching via Select Case:**

This is branching by comparing the value of a variable to **tags** on several cases. For example, when the variable **whichcase = 10**, the program branches to **Case 10**. The following is the syntax.

Syntax for Select Case

Select Case *whichcase*
   Case *tag1*
     {statements when *whichcase* = *tag1*, after which control transfers to End Select}
      .
      .
      .
   Case *tagn*
     {statements when *whichcase* = *tagn*, after which control transfers to End Select}
   Case Else
     {statements to execute when there is no match}
 End Select

Notes: • *whichcase* is a variable whose value is compared to *tagn*. *whichcase* can be a number (integer or floating point, positive or negative), or it can be a character string.   • *tagn* is a constant.

In **Select Case**, VBA proceeds down the list of **tags** until it finds a match. After executing the statements in that block, control transfers to End Select, even though other **tags** farther down the list would also match. Hence, the order and the content of the **tags** is very important.

The following program shows the three forms that the **tags** can have. The program shows that **tag** can be a number, a range of numbers, or the *Is form*. The program determines the value of **grade** from the input value of **score**.

Three Forms of *Tags*	
Code	Explanation

Select Case score
   Case 100
     grade = " excellent "
   Case 90 To 99
     grade = " A "
   Case 80 To 89
     grade = " B "
   Case 70 To 79
     grade = " C "
   Case Is >= 60
     grade = " D "
   Case Else
     grade = " F "
 End Select
	1) *tag* can be a **number (or string)**.
	
	 2) *tag* can be a **range of numbers (or strings)**, from *lower* to *upper*.
	
	 3) *tag* can be the *Is form* and can use any of the *comparison operators* described in Section E of this chapter.

•Section D (cont.):

The following table shows more examples for *tag*.

tag	Value of *whichcase*
Case 1	1
Case -1	-1
Case 1, 1.5	1 or 1.5 *The comma means **or***
Case 1 To 2	(from 1 to 2)
Case 1 To 2, 4 To 5	(from 1 to 2) or (from 4 to 5)
Case Is = 1	1
Case Is = -1	-1
Case Is = 1, Is = 1.5	1 or 1.5
Case Is >= 1, Is <= 2	Any real number. Since this obviously is not intended, care must be taken.
Case Is < 1	< 1 including the negative numbers
Case "aA a "	"aA a " including spaces between the quotes

This is a reminder. If the statements following a *tag* are executed, control will transfer to End Select even though other *tags* further down the list would also match.

•Section E: Operators (Arithmetic, Comparison, and Logical)

Equations use arithmetic operators for addition, subtraction, et cetera. In looping and branching, *condition tests* that evaluate as *true* or *false* determine the paths through the code. These *condition tests* use what are called comparison and logical operators. This section illustrates the syntax for all of these operators as they apply to numbers. Refer to Lomax* for how they apply to character strings.

Arithmetic Operators

The following is a list of the standard **arithmetic operators**.

Operator for...	VBA Code
addition	+
subtraction and negation	-
multiplication	*
division	/
exponentiation	^

Refer to **Lomax*** for the syntax of integer division (\) and integer division remainder (Mod).

Comparison Operators

Whereas the result of an **arithmetic expression** is a number, the result of a **comparison expression** is *true* or *false*.

Comparison Expression in Words	VBA Syntax	Result of Comparison
3 is greater than 2	3 > 2	true
3 is less than 2	3 < 2	false

The following is a list of all of the **VBA comparison operators**.

Operator for the Comparison	VBA Syntax
greater than	>
less than	<
greater than or equal to	> =
less than or equal to	< =
equal to	=
not equal to	<>

---

* Lomax, P. *VB and VBA in a Nutshell*. O'Reilly, 1998.

Logical Operators

Like a comparison expression, the result of a logical expression is true or false. The following table illustrates logical expressions using the logical operator called **And**:

Logical Expression in Words	VBA Syntax	Result of Comparison
3 is greater than 2 **And** 1 is greater than 0	3 > 2 **And** 1 > 0	true
3 is greater than 2 **And** 1 is less than 0	3 > 2 **And** 1 < 0	false

The following table illustrates four VBA logical operators. In the table, **A** is true or false, and **B** is true or false.

VBA Syntax	Logical Result
A And **B**	**true** if both **A** and **B** are **true**. Otherwise **false**.
A Or **B**	**true** if either or both **A** and **B** are **true**. Otherwise **false**.
A Xor **B**	**true** if **A** and **B** are different. Otherwise **false**.
A Eqv **B**	**true** if **A** and **B** are the same. Otherwise **false**.

Another VBA logical operator is called **Not**. Not false is true. Not true is false.

The Rules for Operator Precedence

- First, the **arithmetic** is done. Within the arithmetic itself, there is also a precedence.

> - All exponentiation is done first.
> - All multiplication and division are done next and from left to right (e.g., 4 / 2 * 2 = 4).
> - All addition and subtraction are done last, from left to right.

- Second, the **comparisons** are done.

- Third, the **logical expressions** are evaluated in the following order:

```
Not
And
Or
Xor
Eqv
```

When the same operator appears multiple times on the same line, evaluation is from left to right.

Example Demonstrating Operator Precedence

Consider the following valid VBA statement:

b = Not 2^2 + 1 > 4 - 2 * 2 / 3 * 3 And 1 < 0 Or 3 > 2   **Equation 1**

This statement is from bad programming, but it is valid. To evaluate it, the obvious first step is to do the arithmetic. The statement becomes the following:

b = Not 5 > 0 And 1 < 0 Or 3 > 2

This statement starts with **Not 5**, which by itself doesn't make sense. However, by using parentheses for grouping, b = Not (5 > 0) And (1 < 0) Or (3 > 2). Rewritten, it becomes this:

b = *false* And *false* Or *true*

Now comes a dilemma. Evaluating **b** from left to right, this results:

b = *false* Or *true* = *true*

Evaluating **b** from right to left, this results:

b = *false* And *true* = *false*

There must be a rule to tell which one. There is! **And** is evaluated before **Or**. Hence, the following is accurate:

b = *false* Or *true* = true

Is that what the programmer wants?

Tip: Expressions within a parentheses are evaluated first.

So, rather than memorize rules, the programmer can and should use parentheses to organize the conditions to get the right answer.

For example, b = TRUE if the parentheses in **Equation 1** are as follows:

b = (Not((2^2 + 1) > (4 - 2 * (2 / 3) * 3)) And 1 < 0) Or (3 > 2)

Also, b = FALSE if the parentheses in **Equation 1** are as follows:

b = (Not((2^2 + 1) > (4 - 2 * (2 / 3) * 3))) And (1 < 0 Or 3 > 2)

Final Note: The following VBA statements are valid:

b = True
Cells(1, 1) = b

The logical variable TRUE is printed in cell(1, 1).

Chapter 8: Frequency Response of a Transfer Function

This chapter presents a program to compute the frequency response of a transfer function. A transfer function is a ratio of polynomials and can be written in the following form:

$$[\text{gain}]\frac{(s+\text{nRe}_1+j\text{nIm}_1)(s+\text{nRe}_2+j\text{nIm}_2)...(s+\text{nRe}_{num}+j\text{nIm}_{num})}{(s+\text{dRe}_1+j\text{dIm}_1)(s+\text{dRe}_2+j\text{dIm}_2)...(s+\text{dRe}_{den}+j\text{dIm}_{den})}$$

To compute the frequency response, let $s = j\omega_i$, where ω_i (in rad/sec) varies over a desired interval. With this substitution, the transfer function can now be written this way:

$$[\text{gain}+j0]\frac{(\text{nRe}_1+j(\omega_i+\text{nIm}_1))(\text{nRe}_2+j(\omega_i+\text{nIm}_2))...(\text{nRe}_{num}+j(\omega_i+\text{nIm}_{num}))}{(\text{dRe}_1+j(\omega_i+\text{dIm}_1))(\text{dRe}_2+j(\omega_i+\text{dIm}_2))...(\text{dRe}_{den}+j(\omega_i+\text{dIm}_{den}))}$$

For each value of ω_i, the magnitude and phase of this transfer function are computed by multiplying and dividing complex numbers. The functions for doing this were shown in Chapter 6. See the table on the next page for the frequency response program.

Program fresp_TF	
Code	**Comments**
| ```
Option Base 1
Sub fresp_TF()
 Dim nRe(100), nImag(100), dRe(100), dImag(100)
 nW = 24
 W = Array(0.1, 0.2, 0.5, 0.7, 1, 2, 3, 4, 5, 6, 8, 9, _
     11, 12.6, 14, 16, 19, 22, 25, 28, 32, 40, 60, 100)
 gain = Application.Complex(Cells(1, 1), 0)
 num = Cells(1, 2)
 For i = 1 To num
   nRe(i) = -Cells(i, 3)
   nImag(i) = Cells(i, 4)
 Next i
 den = Cells(1, 5)
 For i = 1 To den
   dRe(i) = -Cells(i, 6)
   dImag(i) = Cells(i, 7)
 Next i


 For k = 1 To nW

   nT = Application.Complex(1, 0)
   If num > 0 Then
     For i = 1 To num
       nTi = Application.Complex(nRe(i), W(k) + nImag(i))
       nT = Application.ImProduct(nT, nTi)
     Next i
   End If

   dT = Application.Complex(1, 0)
   For i = 1 To den
     dTi = Application.Complex(dRe(i), W(k) + dImag(i))
     dT = Application.ImProduct(dT, dTi)
   Next i


   result = Application.ImDiv(nT, dT)
   result = Application.ImProduct(gain, result)

   amp = Application.ImAbs(result)
   ampdb = 20 * Application.Log10(amp)
   phasedeg = Application.ImArgument(result) * 57.296


   Cells(k, 10) = W(k)
   Cells(k, 11) = Application.Round(ampdb, 2)
   Cells(k, 12) = Application.Round(phasedeg, 2)


 Next k
End Sub
``` | • Response is computed at these frequencies, **W(k)** (rad/sec). These frequencies are those for Examples fresp 1 and fresp 2.<br><br>• Read in and convert gain to a complex number.<br><br><br><br>• Read in the numerator and denominator roots.<br><br><br><br>• **For** each frequency **W(k)**<br><br><br><br>• Multiply the numerator roots (if any).<br><br><br><br>• Multiply the denominator roots.<br><br><br><br>• result = gain * numerator/ denominator<br><br>• amp = magnitude of result<br>• ampdb = 20 * log $_{10}$( amp )<br>• phasedeg = (angle of result ) * 57.296<br><br>• Print out to spreadsheet.<br><br>• **Next W(k)** |
```

Example fresp 1: The transfer function of a ***damped sin*** is the following:

$$\left[\omega_n^2\right]\frac{1}{s^2+2\zeta\omega_n s+\omega_n^2}=\left[\omega_n^2\right]\frac{1}{(s+\zeta\omega_n+j\omega_n\sqrt{1-\zeta^2})\,(s+\zeta\omega_n-j\omega_n\sqrt{1-\zeta^2})}$$

For $\zeta = 0.158$ and $\omega_n = 12.65$ rad/sec:

$$[160]\frac{1}{(s+2+j12.49)\,(s+2-j12.49)}$$

The following table shows this transfer function on the spreadsheet:

Spreadsheet for Transfer Function of Example fresp 1						
		Numerator Roots (Rad/Sec)			Denominator Roots (Rad/Sec)	
gain	num	nRe(i)	nIm(i)	den	dRe(i)	dIm(i)
160	0			2	-2	12.49
					-2	-12.49
Column 1	Column 2	Column 3	Column 4	Column 5	Column 6	Column 7

The following table is a partial list of the frequency response from Program fresp_TF.

Frequency Response for Example fresp 1		
W(k) (Rad/Sec)	Ampdb	Phasedeg
0.1	0	-0.14
0.2	0	-0.29
.	.	.
.	.	.
.	.	.
60	-26.67	-176.01
100	-35.78	-177.67
Column 10	Column 11	Column 12

The following are the scatter charts of **ampdb** and **phasedeg** vs frequency W(k). These plots are called **Bode plots** and are made per the instructions in Chapter 2.

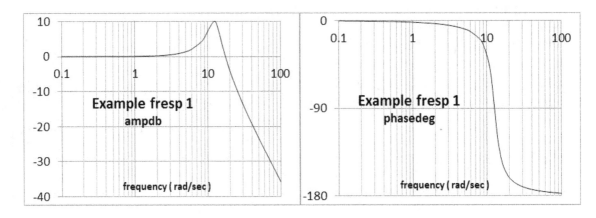

Example fresp 2: The transfer function of a *damped cos* is as follows:

$$\left[\frac{\omega_n}{\zeta}\right]\frac{s+\zeta\omega_n}{s^2+2\zeta\omega_n s+\omega_n^2}=\left[\frac{\omega_n}{\zeta}\right]\frac{s+\zeta\omega_n}{(s+\zeta\omega_n+j\omega_n\sqrt{1-\zeta^2})\,(s+\zeta\omega_n-j\omega_n\sqrt{1-\zeta^2})}$$

For $\zeta = 0.158$ and $\omega_n = 12.65$ rad/sec:

$$[79.9]\frac{s+2}{(s+2+j12.49)\,(s+2-j12.49)}$$

The following table shows this transfer function on the spreadsheet:

Spreadsheet for Transfer Function of Example fresp 2						
		Numerator Roots (Rad/Sec)			Denominator Roots (Rad/Sec)	
gain	num	nRe(i)	nIm(i)	den	dRe(i)	dIm(i)
79.9	1	-2	0	2	-2	12.49
					-2	-12.49
Column 1	Column 2	Column 3	Column 4	Column 5	Column 6	Column 7

The following table is a partial list of the frequency response from **Program fresp_TF**:

Frequency Response for Example fresp 2		
W(k) (Rad/sec)	Ampdb	Phasedeg
0.1	0	2.72
0.2	0.03	5.42
.	.	.
.	.	.
.	.	.
60	2.87	-87.92
100	-1.81	-88.82
Column 10	Column 11	Column 12

The following are the scatter charts of **ampdb** and **phasedeg** vs. frequency W(k). These were made per the instructions in Chapter 2.

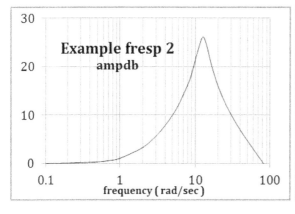

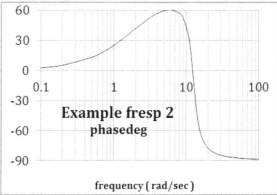

Example fresp 3: The following transfer function is from Greensite[*]:

$$\frac{\text{engine angle command}}{\text{engine angle}} = [2.346]\frac{(s + 4.1176)(s + 0.0642)}{(s + 1.9134)(s - 1.8266)(s - 0.0588)}$$

It is used here for the following reasons:
- as another example for Program fresp_TF
- to show another kind of plot that is available in Excel
- for comparison with results of Example *fr 5* (Chapter 18), which shows another way to compute a frequency response.

The following table shows the transfer function on the spreadsheet:

Spreadsheet Input for Example fresp 3						
		Numerator Roots (Rad/Sec)			Denominator Roots (Rad/Sec)	
gain	num	nRe(i)	nIm(i)	den	dRe(i)	dIm(i)
2.346	2	-4.1176	0	3	-1.9134	0
		-0.0642	0		1.8266	0
					0.0588	0
Column 1	Column 2	Column 3	Column 4	Column 5	Column 6	Column 7

In Program fresp_TF, the transfer function is a complex number called result.

$$\frac{\text{engine angle command}}{\text{engine angle}} = \text{result} = \text{WR} + j\ \text{WI}$$

The Syntax for Computing WR and WI
The following two statements are inserted in Program fresp_TF.
WR = Application.ImReal(result)
Wi = Application.Imaginary(result)

The following table is a partial list of the frequency response output on the spreadsheet:

Frequency Response for Example fresp 3		
W(k) (Rad/Sec)	WR	WI
0.01	2.85	0.96
0.02	2.41	1.78
.	.	.
.	.	.
.	.	.
15	-0.04	-0.15
20	-0.02	-0.12
Column 10	Column 11	Column 12
The desired frequencies listed in Program fresp_TF: nW = 21: W = Array(0.01, 0.02, 0.03, 0.04, 0.05, 0.06, 0.08, 0.09, _ 0.11, 0.13, 0.16, 0.2, 0.3, 0.5, 1, 1.5, 2, 3, 8, 15, 20)		

---

[*] Greensite, A. *Analysis and Design of Space Vehicle Flight Control Systems.* Spartan Books, 1970.

The following is a scatter chart of WR versus WI. This type of plot is called a Nyquist plot. The theory behind what this plot means is discussed in Example *fr* 5 of Chapter 18.

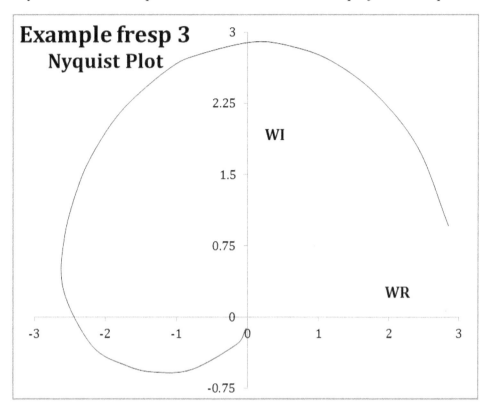

Chapter 9: 3-D Rotational Graphics

Consider the box in the following figure. The task is to write a program that rotates this box in three dimensions.

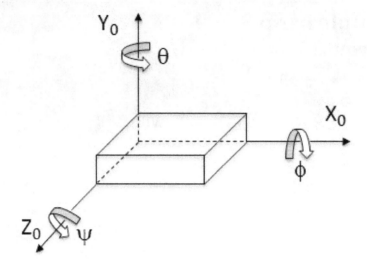

One way to draw the box is to connect its corners. Each corner, including the origin, can be thought of as a vector. The box can be rotated by rotating these vectors. Vectors are rotated by coordinate transformations. The following is a derivation of one of these.

The box is drawn in the X_0-Y_0-Z_0 coordinate system. ϕ is the angle of rotation about X_0. (When the thumb of the right-hand points in the X_0 direction, the fingers point in the positive direction for ϕ.) The above figure also defines the angles θ and ψ. The coordinate transformation will be derived by rotating the box by these angles, one at a time.

• The first rotation is about the *Z axis of the box*, which at the start is aligned with Z_0. The box rotates by the angle ψ, from the X_0-Y_0-Z_0 system to the X_1-Y_1-Z_1 system.

$$\begin{bmatrix} X_1 \\ Y_1 \\ Z_1 \end{bmatrix} = \Psi_M \begin{bmatrix} X_0 \\ Y_0 \\ Z_0 \end{bmatrix} \text{ where } \Psi_M = \begin{bmatrix} \cos\Psi & \sin\Psi & 0 \\ -\sin\Psi & \cos\Psi & 0 \\ 0 & 0 & 1 \end{bmatrix}$$

The ψ_M matrix projects X_1-Y_1-Z_1 back onto X_0-Y_0-Z_0.

● The second rotation is about the **Y** *axis of the box*, which at this point is aligned with **Y₁**. The box rotates by the angle **θ**, from the **X₁-Y₁-Z₁** system to the **X₂-Y₂-Z₂** system. (The figure shows rotation by [-θ] to facilitate visualizing the math.)

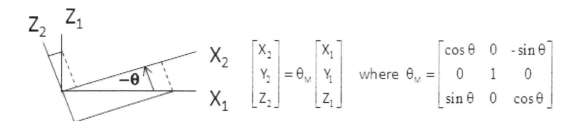

$$\begin{bmatrix} X_2 \\ Y_2 \\ Z_2 \end{bmatrix} = \theta_M \begin{bmatrix} X_1 \\ Y_1 \\ Z_1 \end{bmatrix} \quad \text{where} \quad \theta_M = \begin{bmatrix} \cos\theta & 0 & -\sin\theta \\ 0 & 1 & 0 \\ \sin\theta & 0 & \cos\theta \end{bmatrix}$$

The **θ**M matrix projects **X₂-Y₂-Z₂** back onto **X₁-Y₁-Z₁**.

● The third rotation is about the **X** *axis of the box*, which at this point is aligned with **X₂**. The box rotates by the angle **φ**, from the **X₂-Y₂-Z₂** system to its own **X-Y-Z** system.

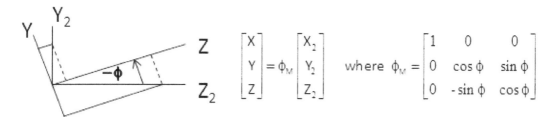

$$\begin{bmatrix} X \\ Y \\ Z \end{bmatrix} = \phi_M \begin{bmatrix} X_2 \\ Y_2 \\ Z_2 \end{bmatrix} \quad \text{where} \quad \phi_M = \begin{bmatrix} 1 & 0 & 0 \\ 0 & \cos\phi & \sin\phi \\ 0 & -\sin\phi & \cos\phi \end{bmatrix}$$

The **φ**M matrix projects **X-Y-Z** back onto **X₂-Y₂-Z₂**.

The **X-Y-Z** *vectors of the box* can now be projected back onto the **X₀-Y₀-Z₀** system by multiplying the three transformation matrices:

$$\begin{bmatrix} X \\ Y \\ Z \end{bmatrix} = [\phi_M * \theta_M * \psi_M] \begin{bmatrix} X_0 \\ Y_0 \\ Z_0 \end{bmatrix} = [C] \begin{bmatrix} X_0 \\ Y_0 \\ Z_0 \end{bmatrix}$$

Where:

$$C = \begin{bmatrix} \cos\theta\cos\psi & \cos\theta\sin\psi & -\sin\theta \\ \sin\phi\sin\theta\cos\psi - \cos\phi\sin\psi & \sin\phi\sin\theta\sin\psi + \cos\phi\cos\psi & \sin\phi\cos\theta \\ \cos\phi\sin\theta\cos\psi + \sin\phi\sin\psi & \cos\phi\sin\theta\sin\psi - \sin\phi\cos\psi & \cos\phi\cos\theta \end{bmatrix}$$

The following figure assigns a number to each corner. The reason for the numbering is that vectors to each of the corners are individually rotated by the **C** matrix. In order to connect adjacent corners in a Scatter chart, the order they are listed and transformed is important.

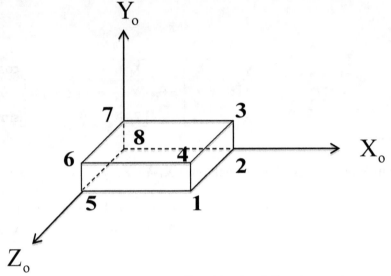

In the table below, the corners (or vectors) are listed in the following order:

1, 2, 3, 4, 1, 5, 6, 7, 3

The next row is left empty to simulate *pen lifting*. Then, **4** and **6** are listed. This completes the visible perimeter of the box. Point **8** is behind the box and will be connected by *dashed* lines. Therefore, following another empty row, three hidden vectors are listed, **5, 8, 2**. A final empty row is followed by **7** and **8**. The coordinates of these vectors are assigned the following lengths:

X length = 4 , Y length = 1 , Z length = 2.

The following table summarizes how these vectors are entered on the spreadsheet:

The Vectors on the Spreadsheet			
	X (Column 3)	Y (Column 4)	Z (Column 5)
row 1, point 1	4	0	2
row 2, point 2	4	0	0
row 3, point 3	4	1	0
row 4, point 4	4	1	2
row 5, point 1	4	0	2
row 6, point 5	0	0	2
row 7, point 6	0	1	2
row 8, point 7	0	1	0
row 9, point 3	4	1	0
row 10, empty			
row 11, point 4	4	1	2
row 12, point 6	0	1	2
row 13, empty			
row 14, point 5	0	0	2
row 15, point 8	0	0	0
row 16, point 2	4	0	0
row 17, empty			
row 18, point 7	0	1	0
row 19, point 8	0	0	0

The following table is a listing of the program.

Program zyx to Graph the Front View of the Rotated Box (i.e., X_0-Y_0 Plane)	
zyx Code	Comments
| ```
Sub main()
Dim C(3, 3), x(30), y(30), z(30), xo(30), yo(30), zo(30)

  psid = Cells(1, 1): thetad = Cells(2, 1): phid = Cells(3, 1)


  psi = psid / 57.3: theta = thetad / 57.3: phi = phid / 57.3
  C(1, 1) = Cos(theta) * Cos(psi)
  C(2, 1) = Sin(phi) * Sin(theta) * Cos(psi) - Cos(phi) * Sin(psi)
  C(3, 1) = Cos(phi) * Sin(theta) * Cos(psi) + Sin(phi) * Sin(psi)
  C(1, 2) = Cos(theta) * Sin(psi)
  C(2, 2) = Sin(phi) * Sin(theta) * Sin(psi) + Cos(phi) * Cos(psi)
  C(3, 2) = Cos(phi) * Sin(theta) * Sin(psi) - Sin(phi) * Cos(psi)
  C(1, 3) = -Sin(theta)
  C(2, 3) = Sin(phi) * Cos(theta)
  C(3, 3) = Cos(phi) * Cos(theta)


  n = Cells(1, 2)
For i = 1 To n
  xo(i) = Cells(i, 3): yo(i) = Cells(i, 4): zo(i) = Cells(i, 5)
  x(i) = C(1, 1) * xo(i) + C(2, 1) * yo(i) + C(3, 1) * zo(i)
  y(i) = C(1, 2) * xo(i) + C(2, 2) * yo(i) + C(3, 2) * zo(i)
  z(i) = C(1, 3) * xo(i) + C(2, 3) * yo(i) + C(3, 3) * zo(i)
Next i


For i = 1 To 9
  Cells(i, 6) = Application.Round(x(i), 2)
  Cells(i, 7) = Application.Round(y(i), 2)
Next i

  Cells(11, 6) = Application.Round(x(11), 2)
  Cells(11, 7) = Application.Round(y(11), 2)
  Cells(12, 6) = Application.Round(x(12), 2)
  Cells(12, 7) = Application.Round(y(12), 2)

  Cells(14, 6) = Application.Round(x(14), 2)
  Cells(14, 8) = Application.Round(y(14), 2)
  Cells(15, 6) = Application.Round(x(15), 2)
  Cells(15, 8) = Application.Round(y(15), 2)
  Cells(16, 6) = Application.Round(x(16), 2)
  Cells(16, 8) = Application.Round(y(16), 2)

  Cells(18, 6) = Application.Round(x(18), 2)
  Cells(18, 8) = Application.Round(y(18), 2)
  Cells(19, 6) = Application.Round(x(19), 2)
  Cells(19, 8) = Application.Round(y(19), 2)
End Sub
``` | • Read in the angles:<br>  $\psi$ = psid, $\theta$ = thetad, $\phi$ = phid<br><br><br>• Compute the matrix $C = \phi_M * \theta_M * \psi_M$<br><br><br><br>• Read in the number of vectors<br>  used to define the box.<br><br>**For Each Vector**<br>  • Read in the vector<br>  • Transform (or rotate) the vector<br>**Next Vector**<br><br><br>• To project the box onto the $X_0$-$Y_0$ plane,<br>  print the X-Y components of the rotated box.<br><br>**Note:**<br>• The points for the visible part of the box are<br>  in rows 1 to 12 and columns 6 and 7.<br>  These are plotted as **Series 1** with<br>  a solid line.<br><br>• The points for the back of the box are in<br>  rows 14 to 19 and columns 6 and 8. These<br>  are plotted as **Series 2** with a dashed line.<br><br>• The empty rows are for *pen lifting*<br>  during plotting.<br><br>• By altering the print statements,<br>  other views can be obtained. |
```

The results on the spreadsheet are shown in the following table:

Program zyx Spreadsheet Input and Results							
Angles of Rotation Column 1	Number of Points Column 2	Input Vectors			Output Vectors (X_0-Y_0)		
		X Column 3	Y Column 4	Z Column 5	X_0 Column 6	Y_0 Column 7	Y_0 Column 8
-45	19	4	0	2	0.29	-2.29	
-45		4	0	0	2	-2	
45		4	1	0	2.15	-1.15	
		4	1	2	0.44	-1.44	
		4	0	2	0.29	-2.29	
		0	0	2	-1.71	-0.29	
		0	1	2	-1.56	0.56	
		0	1	0	0.15	0.85	
		4	1	0	2.15	-1.15	
		4	1	2	0.44	-1.44	
		0	1	2	-1.56	0.56	
		0	0	2	-1.71		-0.29
		0	0	0	0		0
		4	0	0	2		-2
		0	1	0	0.15		0.85
		0	0	0	0		0

The following is the **Scatter Chart**.

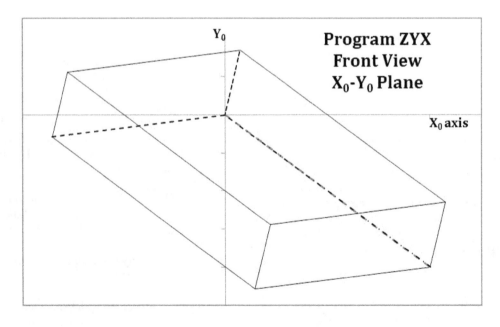

By altering the printout on the spreadsheet, other projections are possible.

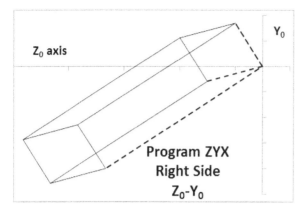
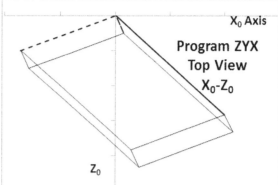

Chapter 10: The Call Statement

Up until this chapter, all of the programs have been written in the structure **Sub main()...End Sub.** This chapter shows how a program can be modularized by having a *main program* call a *sub program* to perform a certain task and return the results to the *main*. This will be illustrated by modifying Program **zyx** of Chapter 9.

The left-hand side of the following table describes the segments of Program zyx. The right-hand side of the table shows that *segment 2* has been replaced by a **Call** statement. The task of *segment 2* has been moved to a *sub program* called **Sub zyx**.

Program zyx	Program zyx Using the **Call** Statement
Sub main()	Sub main()
Segment 1: Read in the angles.	Segment 1: Read in the angles.
Segment 2: Compute the Z-Y-X coordinate-transformation matrix.	Segment 2: **Call zyx(C, psid, thetad, phid)** The **Call** statement sends these angles to the subprogram named **Sub zyx**. This subprogram computes and returns the C matrix. The rest of the program continues.

Segment 3: Read in the number of vectors.
 	
For Each Vector
   • Read in the vector.
   • Transform the vector.
Next Vector
	Segment 3: Read in the number of vectors.
	
	For Each Vector
	   • Read in the vector.
	   • Transform the vector.
	Next Vector

Segment 4: Print the X_0-Y_0 components of the rotated box.	Segment 4: Print the X_0-Y_0 components of the rotated box.
End Sub	**End Sub**
	Sub zyx(C, psid, thetad, phid) The angles from **Sub main** are used to compute the C matrix. The program then returns to the statement after the Call statement. **End Sub**

The **Call** statement includes a *name* and an *argument list*. The *argument list* contains names of the three angles and the name of the coordinate-transformation matrix (**C**). The **Call** statement sends the values of these angles to the subprogram named **Sub zyx**. This subprogram computes and returns the C matrix. Then the rest of the program continues.

The code used to implement this is shown in the following table. However, for this new program, the **C** matrix itself will be changed. In Chapter 9, the first rotation was about the **Z** axis, the second was about the **Y** axis, and the third was about the **X** axis. In this new program, the order will be reversed.

$$\text{The new } C = \psi_M * \theta_M * \phi_M.$$

Program **xyz** Demonstrating the **Call** Statement

xyz Code	Comments

```Sub main()```
 ``` Dim C(3, 3), x(30), y(30), z(30), xo(30), yo(30), zo(30)```
 	
 ``` psid = Cells(1, 1): thetad = Cells(2, 1): phid = Cells(3, 1)```
 	
 ``` Call xyz(C, psid, thetad, phid)```
 	
 ``` n = Cells(1, 2)```
 ```For i = 1 To n```
 ``` xo(i) = Cells(i, 3) = yo(i) = Cells(i, 4): zo(i) = Cells(i, 5)```
 ``` x(i) = C(1, 1) * xo(i) + C(2, 1) * yo(i) + C(3, 1) * zo(i)```
 ``` y(i) = C(1, 2) * xo(i) + C(2, 2) * yo(i) + C(3, 2) * zo(i)```
 ``` z(i) = C(1, 3) * xo(i) + C(2, 3) * yo(i) + C(3, 3) * zo(i)```
 ```Next i```
 	
 ```For i = 1 To 9```
 ``` Cells(i, 6) = Application.Round(x(i), 2)```
 ``` Cells(i, 7) = Application.Round(y(i), 2)```
 ```Next i```
 	
 ``` Cells(11, 6) = Application.Round(x(11), 2)```
 ``` Cells(11, 7) = Application.Round(y(11), 2)```
 ``` Cells(12, 6) = Application.Round(x(12), 2)```
 ``` Cells(12, 7) = Application.Round(y(12), 2)```
 	
 ``` Cells(14, 6) = Application.Round(x(14), 2)```
 ``` Cells(14, 8) = Application.Round(y(14), 2)```
 ``` Cells(15, 6) = Application.Round(x(15), 2)```
 ``` Cells(15, 8) = Application.Round(y(15), 2)```
 ``` Cells(16, 6) = Application.Round(x(16), 2)```
 ``` Cells(16, 8) = Application.Round(y(16), 2)```
 	
 ``` Cells(18, 6) = Application.Round(x(18), 2)```
 ``` Cells(18, 8) = Application.Round(y(18), 2)```
 ``` Cells(19, 6) = Application.Round(x(19), 2)```
 ``` Cells(19, 8) = Application.Round(y(19), 2)```
 ```End Sub```
	Segment 1: Read in the angles.
	
	 Segment 2: The call statement sends these angles to the subprogram named **Sub xyz**. This subprogram computes and returns the **C** matrix. Then the rest of the program continues.
	
	 Segment 3: Read in the number of vectors used to define the box.
	 For Each Vector (X, Y, and Z components), do the following:
	 • Read in the vector.
	 • Transform the vector.
	 Next Vector
	
	 Segment 4: To project the rotated box onto the X_0-Y_0 plane, print the X-Y components.
	
	 Note:
	 • The points for the front (or visible) part of the box are in rows 1 to 12 and columns 6 and 7. These are plotted as **Series 1** with a solid line.
	 • The points for the back of the box are in rows 14 to 19 and columns 6 and 8. These are plotted as **Series 2** with a dashed line.
	 • The empty rows are for *pen lifting* during plotting.
	 • By altering the print statements, other views can be obtained.

```Sub xyz(C, psid, thetad, phid)```
 ``` psi = psid / 57.3: theta = thetad / 57.3: phi = phid / 57.3```
 ``` C(1, 1) = Cos(theta) * Cos(psi)```
 ``` C(2, 1) = -Cos(theta) * Sin(psi)```
 ``` C(3, 1) = Sin(theta)```
 ``` C(1, 2) = Cos(phi) * Sin(psi) + Sin(phi) * Cos(psi) * Sin(theta)```
 ``` C(2, 2) = Cos(psi) * Cos(phi) - Sin(phi) * Sin(psi) * Sin(theta)```
 ``` C(3, 2) = -Sin(phi) * Cos(theta)```
 ``` C(1, 3) = Sin(psi) * Sin(phi) - Cos(phi) * Cos(psi) * Sin(theta)```
 ``` C(2, 3) = Cos(psi) * Sin(phi) + Cos(phi) * Sin(psi) * Sin(theta)```
 ``` C(3, 3) = Cos(phi) * Cos(theta)```
 ```End Sub```
	The Subprogram:
	
	 The angles from **Sub main** are used to compute the X-Y-Z coordinate-transformation matrix.
	
	 $$C = \psi_M * \theta_M * \phi_M$$
	
	 The program then returns to the statement right after the **Call** statement.
	
	 Note: Sub main and **Sub xyz** must be in the same Code Window.

Important Note: The terms in the coordinate-transformation matrix are stored in the **C** array. The **Dim** statement that declares its size appears only in **Sub main**.

Program xyz Spreadsheet Input and Results							
Angles of Rotation Column 1	Number of Points Column 2	Input Vectors			Output Vectors (X_0-Y_0)		
		X Column 3	Y Column 4	Z Column 5	X_0 Column 6	Y_0 Column 7	Y_0 Column 8
-45	19	4	0	2	0.59	-4.41	
-45		4	0	0	2	-3.41	
45		4	1	0	2.5	-3.27	
		4	1	2	1.09	-4.27	
		4	0	2	0.59	-4.41	
		0	0	2	-1.41	-1	
		0	1	2	-0.91	-0.85	
		0	1	0	0.5	0.15	
		4	1	0	2.5	-3.27	
		4	1	2	1.09	-4.27	
		0	1	2	-0.91	-0.85	
		0	0	2	-1.41		-1
		0	0	0	0		0
		4	0	0	2		-3.41
		0	1	0	0.5		0.15
		0	0	0	0		0

The following is the **Scatter Chart** of the results of **Program xyz**.

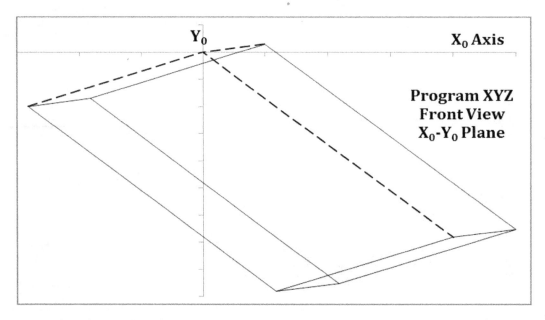

Comparing the results of **Program xyz** with **Program zyx** makes it clear how important the order of rotation is when deriving the coordinate-transformation matrix.

The following table shows the general syntax for using the **Call** statement.

Syntax for a Typical Use of the **Call** Statement

Sub main()
  Dim { arrays used in Sub main }
 	
    { statements }
 	
  Call *name*(argument list)
 	
    { statements }
 	
End Sub

Sub *name*(argument list)
    Dim { arrays used in this subprogram, excluding those in the argument list }
 	
    { statements }
 	
End Sub

Notes: • The argument list contains all of the variables that are transferred *to* and *from*. • There is no limit on the number of **Call** statements or subprograms. • Subprograms can **Call** other subprograms. • Except for the argument list, values of the variables in a subprogram must be reset or recomputed each time the subprogram is entered. • The argument list may be empty. • The calling program and the called program must be in the same Code Window. • Only the programs with empty parentheses are listed in the Macros Window.

In conclusion, the following table contains a small program that illustrates three important points about the **Call** statement.

1) The variables in the argument list are really only ***addresses in memory***. Hence, the *subprograms* may use different names than the names in the **Call** statement. *Of course, there must be a one-to-one correspondence between all of the argument lists.*

2) The values of the argument-list variables can be changed anywhere in the *calling* program or in the *called* program.

3) If an argument list variable requires a **Dim** statement, the **Dim** statement that covers it must appear in the program that contains the **Call** statement.

Program Illustrating **Argument List** Variables	

Sub main()
  Dim a(50)
  a(2) = 0
  Call one(a)
  a(2) = a(2) + 3
  Cells(1, 1) = a(2)
End sub
 	
Sub one(b)
  b(2) = b(2) + 3
  Call two(b)
  b(2) = b(2) + 3
End Sub
 	
Sub two(c)
  c(2) = c(2) + 3
End Sub
	• As their values change, a(2) = b(2) = c(2). This is because these variables reside in the same address. The Dim statement covering these must appear in Sub main(), which is the original *calling* program.
	
	• The final answer is a(2) = 12.

Additional Syntax
•**Exit Sub** This optional statement causes execution to return to the *calling* program, specifically to the statement right after the **Call** statement. If used in the main program, it causes execution to stop. •**End** This optional statement causes execution to stop and can be used anywhere.

Chapter 11: Debugging

Debugging is fun. *Point-and-click menus and windows* make it easy. Execution can be stopped in several ways and at any line of code. Values of variables can be inspected in several ways. Execution can then be continued until the next *stopping point*. A simple program shows all of this. (This chapter may be skipped over until needed.)

The following table shows the listing and description of the program that will be analyzed by *debugging*. The program merely passes a variable *around a loop* between a main program and two subprograms.

The Program Used to Demonstrate Debugging	
Code	**Description**

Sub main()
  For w = 1 To 5
    Call one(w, zDum)
    Cells(w, 1) = zDum
  Next w
End Sub
 	
Sub one(wDum, z)
  x = wDum
  Call two(x, yDum)
  z = yDum
End Sub
 	
Sub two(xDum, y)
  y = xDum
End Sub
	• In Sub main, the For statement starts with w = 1.
	• Call Sub one with w in the argument list.
	• Sub one
	  • wDum is equivalenced to w in the argument list.
	  • x = wDum.
	  • x is passed to Sub two.
	• Sub two
	  • xDum is equivalenced to x.
	  • y = xDum.
	  • y is passed back to Sub one.
	• Sub one
	  • yDum is equivalenced to y.
	  • z = yDum.
	  • z is passed back to Sub main.
	• Sub main
	  • zDum is equivalenced to z.
	  • zDum is printed out.
	• The Next statement then sets w = 2, and execution continues on the second pass.

The first step in *debugging* is to open the Watches Window.

Click Editor. In the View Menu → Watch Window.

Watches will show the values of selected variables as the program executes. For this demonstration, all of the variables in the above program will be put into Watches. The following are the instructions on how to do this.

- Open the Code Window (double-click on its name in the Project Window).
- In the code, put the cursor next to a variable (e.g., w).
- In Debug Menu → Add Watch. The Add Watch Window pops up, and the variable w is already entered. (Options in the Add Watch Window will be discussed later.)
- *Click* OK. The Add Watch Window closes. The variable w now appears in Watches and is *out of context* since the program is not yet executing.
- Put the cursor next to another variable (e.g., zDum). Repeat the process until Watches looks like the following table.

The Watches Window before Execution			
Expression	Value	Type	Context
w	Out of context	Variant/Empty	ThisWorkbook.main
zDum	Out of context	Variant/Empty	ThisWorkbook.main
z	Out of context	Variant/Empty	ThisWorkbook.one
wDum	Out of context	Variant/Empty	ThisWorkbook.one
x	Out of context	Variant/Empty	ThisWorkbook.one
yDum	Out of context	Variant/Empty	ThisWorkbook.one
xDum	Out of context	Variant/Empty	ThisWorkbook.two
y	Out of context	Variant/Empty	ThisWorkbook.two
Note: The Watches Window is not saved when the program file is closed.			

Variables can be added to the Watches Window at any time during *debug*. Now to begin *debugging*.

Open the Code Window, and put the cursor anywhere in Sub main. Select the Debug menu. The focus is now on four commands: Step Into, Step Over, Step Out, and Run To Cursor. We will discuss Step Into first.

- **Step Into:** In the Debug Menu → Step Into . This first Step Into command puts an arrow on line 1 of the code. At the next Step Into command, line 1 will execute, and the arrow will point to line 2. The following two tables show each successive Step Into command and the values of the variables after each step.

This table shows the code line after each Step Into command.

The Code Window	
Step Into *Command Numbers*	**Code Lines**
1	Sub main()
2	For w = 1 To 5
3 and 14	Call one(w, zDum)
12	Cells(w, 1) = zDum
13	Next w
	End Sub
4	Sub one(wDum, z)
5	x = wDum
6	Call two(x, yDum)
10	z = yDum
11	End Sub
7	Sub two(xDum, y)
8	y = xDum
9	End Sub

This table lists the value of the variables *after* each Step Into command.

The Watches Window															
		The Value *after* Each Step Into Command													
	Start	1	2	3	4	5	6	7	8	9	10	11	12	13	14
w	O	E	E	1	1	1	1	1	1	1	1	1	1	1	2
zDum	O	E	E	E	E	E	E	E	E	E	E	1	1	1	1
z	O	O	O	O	E	E	E	E	E	E	E	1	O	O	O
wDum	O	O	O	O	1	1	1	1	1	1	1	1	O	O	O
x	O	O	O	O	E	E	1	1	1	1	1	1	O	O	O
yDum	O	O	O	O	E	E	E	E	E	1	1	1	O	O	O
xDum	O	O	O	O	O	O	O	1	1	1	O	O	O	O	O
y	O	O	O	O	O	O	O	E	E	1	O	O	O	O	O
Notes: • O legend for Out of context, i.e., in a part of the program that is not active • E legend for Empty															

The tables show that after the third Step Into command, line 2 has executed and w = 1. Continue analyzing the above table, or go to Run Menu → Reset.

The Other Options in the Debug Menu

• **Step Over:** When the Debug arrow is pointing to a Call statement (or a Function statement), the Step Over command causes the *debugger* to execute the called program and stop on the statement after the Call.

• **Step Out:** When the Debug arrow is pointing to any statement in a subprogram or function, the Step Out command causes the *debugger* to execute the rest of the subprogram and stop on the statement after the Call. Note that when the Debug arrow is pointing to any statement in the main program, the Step Out command causes the rest of the program to be completed and stop.

• **Run To Cursor:** Put the cursor at the beginning or end of any statement. The Run To Cursor command causes the *debugger* to execute all statements up to the cursor and stop at the cursor.

Viewing Variables with the Cursor

This is another way to see the values of variables. Suppose the Debug arrow is pointing to the following statement: Call one(w, zDum). Hold the *mouse pointer* over the variable w. After a slight delay, a popup will show the value of w. In fact, holding the *mouse pointer* over any variable for a moment will produce a popup showing the value, if it's available.

Debugging by Run To Breakpoint

Another way of *debugging* is to set *breakpoints*. The following table describes how to set *breakpoints*.

Code Window Illustrating Breakpoints

Code	Description

Sub main()
  For w = 1 To 5
    Call one(w, zDum)
    Cells(w, 1) = zDum
  Next w
End Sub
Sub one(wDum, z)
• x = wDum
  Call two(x, yDum)
  z = yDum
End Sub
Sub two(xDum, y)
• y = xDum
End Sub
	• A breakpoint is set by clicking in the gray area in front of a line of code.
	
	• Two breakpoints (bullets) are shown.
	
	• Like a toggle switch, another click will turn it off.
	
	• The program need not be in the debug mode when setting a breakpoint.

With the breakpoints as shown, Run the program. Execution will stop at the statement x=wDum. Values of the variables can be inspected either in Watches or with the *mouse pointer*. Then, Run Menu → Continue causes execution to the next breakpoint. A debugging-session can include using the options from the Debug menu together with run-to-breakpoint. The menus always show the options that are available. When *debugging* is finished, Run Menu → Reset.

Options in the Add Watch Window

Besides variables, the Watches Window can include Arithmetic, Comparative, and Logical expressions (See Chapter 7). The Add Watch Window allows *one* of the following options to be selected for each expression:

- Watch Expression (This is the option that has been used so far in this chapter.)
- Break When Value Is True
- Break When Value Changes

The following are examples of expressions that can be put into the Watches Window. Never mind if they don't make sense.

w	a variable
x + wDum - y * z	an arithmetic expression
y > 3	a comparison expression
w > 3 And zDum > 3	a logical expression

The Immediate Window

This window can display program output via special VBA debug statements that are placed in the code. This window will not be discussed in this book.

Final Note

Back to the oxymoron that *debugging is fun*. When the code malfunctions, VBA automatically stops in the debug mode, points an arrow at the difficult line of code, and allows values to be inspected by hovering the cursor above any variable. And of course, the debug mode can be used as a learning-aide even when there is no malfunction.

References on Debugging

- Roman. "Writing Excel Macros With VBA." O'Reilly, 2002.
- Birnbaum and Vine. "MS Excel VBA Programming For the Absolute Beginner." Course Technology Publishers, 2007.

Chapter 12: The GoSub Statement
with Runge-Kutta Numerical Integration

This chapter shows how a program can be modularized by segmenting the code. The following table shows a demonstration program.

GoSub Demonstration Program	
Code	**Comments**

Sub main()
 	
   a = 10
   GoSub one
   GoSub two
   End
 	
one:
   Cells(1, 1) = a
   Return
 	
two:
   b = 20
   Cells(2, 1) = b
   Return
 	
End Sub
	• GoSub one sends the program to the statement labeled *one*. There, a is printed. Then the Return statement sends the program back to the statement after GoSub one.
	
	• GoSub two sends the program to the statement labeled *two*. There, b is set to 20 and is printed. Then the Return statement sends the program back to the statement after GoSub two.
	
	• End terminates the program. This prevents looping.

The syntax for a statement label: It must be some unique name followed by a *colon*. It must be the first entry on a line. (VBA will reposition it to column 1.) There's no limit on the number of labels.	
Note: The **GoSub** statement may also be used in a subprogram or a function.	

The following example fits into this format.

Example GoSub: The following is a differential equation for a spring-mass-damper system:

$$Mass * \ddot{X} + Damp * \dot{X} + Kspr * X = Kspr * u$$

where **X** is the response to an impulse on **u**, and *Mass, Damp, and Kspr* are constants. The task is to write a program to integrate this equation to get the response of the following:

- the displacement X
- the velocity $\dot{X}$
- the damping force $Damp * \dot{X}$

66

The first step is to convert this equation to a standard form (state variable form).

Let: $Y_1 = X$

Then: $\dot{Y}_1 = \dot{X} = Y_2$

And: $\dot{Y}_2 = \ddot{X} = -(\,Damp*Y_2 + Kspr*(Y_1 - u)\,)\,/\,Mass$

The converted problem is to integrate these two first-order differential equations.

This program will use the Fourth-Order Runge-Kutta integration method. This very popular method is well documented. It is based on approximating the solution with a fourth-order Taylor series. Matthews[*] shows the eleven nonlinear equations with thirteen unknowns that Runge and Kutta solved to yield the four coefficients in their method.

Besides the differential equations and the integrator equations, the program will need the following:
- initial conditions on time and Y(1) and Y(2)
- the integration step size
- stop time
- variables to be output

The program will be designed as follows. It will have a *main* and three *segments*:

- The *main* for the statements directing execution and input/output
- A segment called *runge* for the integrator statements
- A segment called *system* for the equation statements
- A segment called *data* for the statements that specify all the constants

---

[*] Mathews, J., and K. Fink. *Numerical Methods Using Matlab.* Prentice-Hall, 2004.

The following is the block diagram of the program for **Example GoSub**.

The **GoSub data** statement for the constants

⇓

Integrate and gather (or save) the output variables.

For i = 1 To (the number of **dt**s between start and stop)
  Do   (For each **dt**, compute the derivative equations four times)
    GoSub system   (compute the derivatives)
    GoSub runge   (integrate)
  Loop
  After each **dt**, save the output
Next i

⇓

Print out.

⇓

The **End** statement terminates the program.

---

data:
- system constants *Damp*, *Kspr*, *Mass*
- system order n=2
- initial conditions timeh=0, y(1)=0, y(2)=0
- integration data dt=.05, tstop=2, istop = int(tstop/dt),
  where **int** yields the nearest integer in the negative direction
- integrator constants runm, jint
- initial values on the output variables
  - time: timeX(1) = 0
  - displacement: X1(1) = 0
  - velocity: X2(1) = 0
  - damping force: X3(1) = 0

Return

---

system:
- u = impulse weight of 40
- $\dot{y}_1 = y_2$
- $\dot{y}_2 = -(\ Damp * y_2 + Kspr * (y_1 - u)\ )/Mass$

Return

---

runge:
The Runge-Kutta integrator equations

Return

The following table is a listing of the program:

Program for Example GoSub	
Option Base 1 Sub main() Dim timeX(1000), X1(1000), X2(1000), X3(1000), y(10), yo(10), yd(10) Dim runk(10, 4) GoSub data	• The **GoSub data** Statement

For i = 1 To istop
  Do
   GoSub system
   GoSub runge
  Loop While jint <> 1
  timeX(i + 1) = timeh: X1(i + 1) = y(1): X2(i + 1) = y(2)
  X3(i + 1) = y(2) * Damp
Next i
	• Integrate and save the outout variables.

For i = 1 To (istop + 1)
  Cells(i, 1) = timeX(i)
  Cells(i, 2) = Application.Round(X1(i), 4)
  Cells(i, 3) = Application.Round(X2(i), 4)
  Cells(i, 4) = Application.Round(X3(i), 4)
Next i
	• Print out.

End	• The **End** Statement which terminates the program

data:
  Damp = 2: Kspr = 80: Mass = 0.5
  n = 2: timeh = 0: y(1) = 0: y(2) = 0
  dt = 0.05: tstop = 2: istop = Int(tstop / dt)
  runm = Array(1, 0.5, 0.5, 1): jint = 1
  timeX(1) = timeh: X1(1) = y(1): X2(1) = y(2): X3(1) = y(2) * Damp
Return
	• **data: ... Return**

system:
  If i <= 1 Then
    u = 40
  Else
    u = 0
  End If
  yd(1) = y(2)
  yd(2) = -(Damp * y(2) + Kspr * (y(1) - u)) / Mass
Return
	• **system: ... Return**

runge:
  For j = 1 To n
   runk(j, jint) = dt * yd(j)
  Next j
	• **runge: ... Return**

If jint = 1 Then
    tox = timeh
    For j = 1 To n
     yo(j) = y(j)
    Next j
  End If
  jint = jint + 1
  If jint > 1 And jint < 5 Then
    timeh = tox + runm(jint) * dt
    For j = 1 To n
     y(j) = yo(j) + runm(jint) * runk(j, jint - 1)
    Next j
  End If
  If jint = 5 Then
    jint = 1
    For j = 1 To n
     inc = (runk(j, 1) + 2 * runk(j, 2) + 2 * runk(j, 3) + runk(j, 4)) / 6
     y(j) = yo(j) + inc
    Next j
  End If
Return
End Sub
	• System derivatives are computed 4 times for each **dt**. For each **dt**, **runge: ... Return** is entered 5 times.
	
	• jint = 1 initialize integrator.
	• jint = 2 compute first estimate of the y vector.
	• jint = 3 compute second estimate of the y vector.
	• jint = 4 compute third estimate of the y vector.
	• jint = 5 compute fourth estimate and then the weighted average of the y vector. Reset jint = 1

69

The following table is a partial list of the impulse-response output to the spreadsheet.

Impulse Response for Example GoSub			
Time, TimeX(*j*)	Displacement, X1(*j*)	Velocity, X2(*j*)	Damping Force, X3(*j*)
0	0	0	0
0.05	7.23	270.83	542
0.1	17.38	127.13	254
0.15	19.62	-35.04	-70
0.2	14.59	-155.63	-311
.	.	.	.
.	.	.	.
.	.	.	.
1.8	-0.10	-8.82	-18
1.85	-0.46	-5.03	-10
1.9	-0.59	-0.17	0
1.95	-0.49	3.87	8
2	-0.24	5.83	12

The following are Scatter charts of these responses.

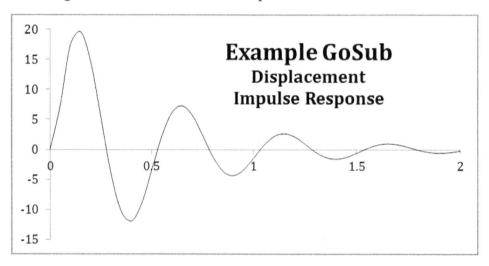

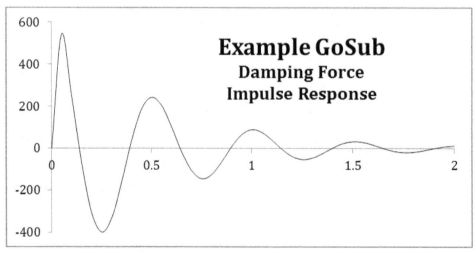

The following is a Scatter chart of the displacement versus velocity. This is called a Phase Plane plot. It is frequently used in the design of autopilots for satellites.

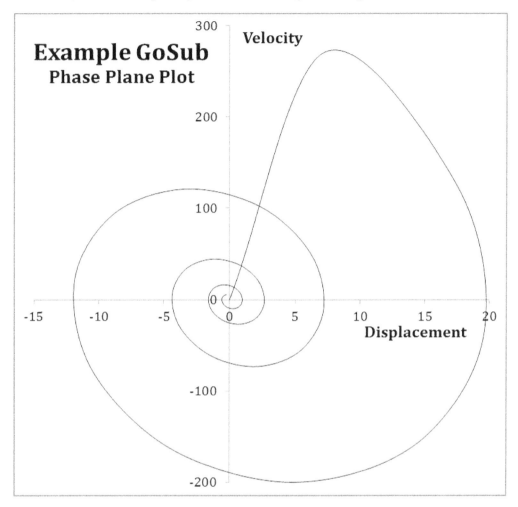

Final Notes:

• The program can easily be adapted to other problems by changing the equations in the segments labeled **data: ... Return** and **system: ... Return**.
• This **GoSub** method of *program segmentation* is used often in the remaining chapters.

Chapter 13: The GoTo Statement
with Sort and Interpolate

This chapter defines the **GoTo** statement. Simply stated, **GoTo** acts like **GoSub** without the **Return**. The following table shows a demonstration program.

GoTo Demonstration Program	
Code	**Comments**

Sub main()
    GoTo one
 	
two:
    Cells(1, 1) = a
    End
 	
one:
    a = 10
    GoTo two
End Sub
	• GoTo one sends the program to the statement labeled one. There, a is set to 10. Then the GoTo two statement sends the program to the statement labeled two.
	
	• At two, a is printed.
	
	• End terminates the program. This prevents looping.

The Syntax for a Statement Label

It must be some unique name followed by a *colon*. It must be the first entry on a line. (VBA will reposition it to column 1.) There's no limit on the number of labels.

Note: The **GoTo** statement may also be used in a subprogram or function.

The following example uses the **GoTo** statement.

Example GoTo: Take a list of paired numbers, Xin(i) and Yin(i). Sort Xin(i) in ascending order.

Unsorted		Sorted	
Xin(i)	Yin(i)	Xin(i)	Yin(i)
9	3	-9	-3
-9	-3	-7	-1
7	1	-5	1
-7	-1	-3	3
5	1	-1	5
-5	1	1	5
3	3	3	3
-3	3	5	1
1	5	7	1
-1	5	9	3

Then by interpolating in this sorted list, find the **y** that corresponds to an *input x*. For this example, use *input x = - 4*.

The following table lists the program for **Example GoTo**. The **GoTo** statement is used in the interpolation segment.

Program for Example GoTo	
Code	**Comments**
| ```
Sub main()
 Dim Xin(100), Yin(100)
 n = Cells(1, 1):    x = Cells(1, 6)
 For i = 1 To n
   Xin(i) = Cells(i, 2):  Yin(i) = Cells(i, 3)
 Next i
 For L = n To 2 Step -1
   For i = 1 To L - 1
     If Xin(i) > Xin(L) Then
       temp = Xin(i)
       Xin(i) = Xin(L)
       Xin(L) = temp
       temp = Yin(i)
       Yin(i) = Yin(L)
       Yin(L) = temp
     End If
   Next i
 Next L
 For i = 1 To n
   Cells(i, 4) = Xin(i): Cells(i, 5) = Yin(i)
 Next i
 If (x < Xin(1)) Or (x > Xin(n)) Then
  Cells(1,7) = " x out of bounds": End
 End If
 For i = 2 To n
   If x <= Xin(i) Then
     m = i - 1
     GoTo st200
   End If
 Next i

st200:
 ydel = (Yin(m + 1) - Yin(m)) * (x - Xin(m)) / (Xin(m + 1) - Xin(m))
 y = Yin(m) + ydel

 Cells(1, 7) = y
End Sub
``` | • **n** is the number of points and **x** *is the **Input***.<br><br>• Unsorted Pair<br><br>• **Sort:**<br><br>  • Sort into ascending order.<br>  • Outer loop runs from bottom up.<br>  • Inner loop runs from top down.<br>  • First pass puts largest number on the bottom.<br>  • Second pass puts second-largest number second last.<br>  • This pattern continues.<br><br>• Print the sorted pair.<br><br>• Check the bounds.<br><br>• **Interpolate:**<br><br>Beginning at the smallest number, when **x** is between $Xin(m)$ and $Xin(m+1)$, the **GoTo st200** statement transfers execution to the statement labeled **st200**.<br><br>• Linear interpolation<br><br>• **y** is the Output that corresponds to *Input x* |

The following is the **Scatter chart** of the sorted input list and the result.

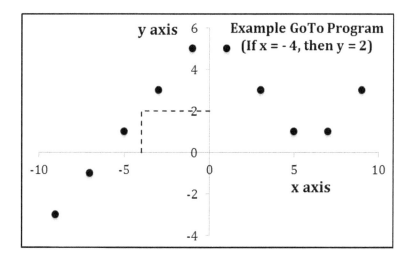
```

Chapter 14: The Newton-Raphson Method

The task of this chapter is to write a program for the Newton-Raphson method of solving nonlinear equality equations. This includes finding the complex roots of polynomials. *No new syntax are introduced in this chapter or in the remainder of the book.*

To illustrate the Newton-Raphson method, assume a single equation with only one variable. The problem is to find **y** such that f(y) = 0. Newton-Raphson is a search method. It starts with an initial guess **y_s** that produces an initial **f_s**. Then a change in **y** (called Δy) is computed from the first-order Taylor series expansion of **f** about **f_s**.

$$f = f_s + \frac{\partial f}{\partial y} \Delta y$$

Since it is desired that f(y) = 0, $\qquad \Delta y = - \left(\frac{\partial f}{\partial y} \right)^{-1} f_s = y - y_s$

This produces a new value for **y** ($y = y_s + \Delta y$), which produces a new value for **f**. This iterative process continues until one of the following occurs:

- Δy gets *small*, which indicates that a solution has been reached.
- $(\partial f / \partial y)$ gets *small*, which indicates that a solution cannot be reached.

or
- the allowed number of iterations has been completed.

If no solution has been reached, it's necessary to start the search over from another initial guess.

These equations and termination criteria are now extended to multiple **f**'s and **y**'s.

$$f_1 = f_{1s} + \frac{\partial f_1}{\partial y_1} \Delta y_1 + \frac{\partial f_1}{\partial y_2} \Delta y_2 + \bullet\bullet\bullet + \frac{\partial f_1}{\partial y_n} \Delta y_n$$

$$\bullet$$
$$\bullet$$
$$\bullet$$

$$f_n = f_{ns} + \frac{\partial f_n}{\partial y_1} \Delta y_1 + \frac{\partial f_n}{\partial y_2} \Delta y_2 + \bullet\bullet\bullet + \frac{\partial f_n}{\partial y_n} \Delta y_n$$

In matrix notation:

$$F = F_s + A * \Delta Y$$

Where:
$$F = \begin{bmatrix} f_1 \\ \bullet \\ \bullet \\ f_n \end{bmatrix}, \; F_s = \begin{bmatrix} f_{s1} \\ \bullet \\ \bullet \\ f_{sn} \end{bmatrix}, \; A = \begin{bmatrix} \frac{\partial f_1}{\partial y_1} & & \frac{\partial f_1}{\partial y_n} \\ & \bullet & \\ & & \bullet \\ \frac{\partial f_n}{\partial y_1} & & \frac{\partial f_n}{\partial y_n} \end{bmatrix} \quad \text{and} \quad \Delta Y = \begin{bmatrix} \Delta Y_1 \\ \bullet \\ \bullet \\ \Delta Y_n \end{bmatrix}$$

Since it is desired that F = 0, then $\Delta Y = - A^{-1} * F_s$.

The search terminates when one of the following occurs:

- All Δy_j get *small.*
- All $(\partial f_i / \partial y_j)$ get *small.*

or - The allowed number of iterations has been completed.

Enhancements like step-size limitation can be added to the Newton-Raphson method. These are not covered in this tutorial.

We will now write a program that computes the **A** matrix. This program will become a part of the Newton-Raphson program.

The **A** matrix is repeated here:

$$A = \begin{bmatrix} \dfrac{\partial f_1}{\partial y_1} & & \dfrac{\partial f_1}{\partial y_n} \\ & \bullet & \\ & & \bullet \\ \dfrac{\partial f_n}{\partial y_1} & & \dfrac{\partial f_n}{\partial y_n} \end{bmatrix}$$

The partial derivatives $\partial f_i / \partial y_j$ will be estimated using the *method of finite differences*.

$$A_{ij} = \frac{\partial f_i}{\partial y_j} = \frac{f_i - f_{si}}{y_j - y_{sj}}$$

Where: - $f_{s1} \rightarrow f_{sn}$ are computed from the first guess (*set point*) $y_{s1} \rightarrow y_{sn}$.
- $y_j = y_{sj} +$ stepd (stepd is the stepsize and is an input constant).

The program that was presented in Chapter 12 included the example problem right in the code. This was done via the **GoSub** code fragments **data: ... Return** and **system: ... Return**. That same method will be used in this program.

Description of the Program to Compute the A Matrix

Description	Code Fragments
• GoSub data to read in $y_1 \rightarrow y_n$ and stepsize [stepd]	Sub df_dy() • GoSub data
• $jA = 0$ • GoSub system to compute $f_1 \rightarrow f_n$ • Save $(f_{s1} = f_1) \rightarrow (f_{sn} = f_n)$ and $(y_{s1} = y_1) \rightarrow (y_{sn} = y_n)$ • Call matrix to disturb $y_1 = y_{s1} + $ stepd	• For $jA = 0$ To n • GoSub system • Call matrix
• $jA = 1$ • GoSub system to compute $f_1 \rightarrow f_n$ • Call matrix to • compute $\dfrac{\partial f_1}{\partial y_1} \rightarrow \dfrac{\partial f_n}{\partial y_1}$ • reset $y_1 \rightarrow y_{s1}$ and disturb $y_2 = y_{s2} + $ stepd • • •	• Next jA • End (to terminate)
• $jA = n$ • GoSub system to compute $f_1 \rightarrow f_n$ • Call matrix to • compute $\dfrac{\partial f_1}{\partial y_n} \rightarrow \dfrac{\partial f_n}{\partial y_n}$ • reset $y_n \rightarrow y_{sn}$	• data: ... Return • system: ... Return End Sub
	• Sub matrix ... End Sub

An example problem for **data: ... Return** and **system: ... Return** will now be defined. This is because it is included in the listing of the program code.

Example NR 1: Compute the **A** matrix for the following two nonlinear equality equations:

$$f_1 = y_2 - 2 * (y_1 - 1)^2 = 0$$
$$f_2 = y_2 - e^{-y_1} = 0$$

data:

The number of equations: N = 2
The perturbation step size: stepd = 0.001
The *set point*: $y_1 = 1$ and $y_2 = 1$
Return

system:

$$f_1 = y_2 - 2 * (y_1 - 1)^2$$
$$f_2 = y_2 - e^{-y_1}$$
Return

76

The following table lists the program that computes the **A** matrix.

Program to Compute the A Matrix	

Sub df_dy()
Dim y(30), ys(30), f(30), fs(30), A(30, 30)
  GoSub data
 	
  For jA = 0 To N
    If jA = 0 Then
      For j = 1 To N
        ys(j) = y(j)
      Next j
    End If
    GoSub system
    If jA = 0 Then
      For i = 1 To N
        fs(i) = f(i)
      Next i
    End If
    Call matrix(N, y, ys, f, fs, jA, stepd, A)
  Next jA
  For i = 1 To N
    For j = 1 To N
        Cells(i, j) = A(i, j)
    Next j
  Next i
  End
data:
  N = 2: y(1) = 1: y(2) = 1: stepd = 0.001
Return
system:
  f(1) = y(2) - 2 * (y(1) - 1) ^ 2
  f(2) = y(2) - Exp(-y(1))
Return
End Sub
	● **GoSub data** for the Initial Guess and the stepsize
	
	● **For** *jA* **= 0 To N**
	
	    ● Save **y***sj* on the first pass.
	
	    ● **GoSub system** to compute **f** from **y**.
	
	    ● Save **f***sj* on the first pass.
	
	    ● **Call matrix** to compute (**A** *ij*).
	
	● **Next** *jA*
	
	●Print out **A**.
	
	●**End** to terminate the program.
	
	●**data** for Example NR 1
	
	●**system** for Example NR 1

Sub matrix(N, y, ys, f, fs, jA, stepd, A)
If jA = 0 Then
    y(1) = ys(1) + stepd
Else
    For i = 1 To N
      A(i, jA) = (f(i) - fs(i)) / stepd
    Next i
    y(jA) = ys(jA)
    If jA < N Then
        y(jA + 1) = ys(jA + 1) + stepd
    End If
End If
End If
End Sub
	If *jA* **= 0 Then**
	  On the first pass, disturb **y** 1.
	Else
	  On the next **N** passes:
	    compute (**A** *ij*) [one column of the **A** matrix per pass],
	    reset last **y**,
	    disturb next **y**.
	
	End If

The above program produced the following results for **Example NR 1**.

The Partial Derivatives Computed at $y_1 = 1$ and $y_2 = 1$					
	Exact	From the Program		Exact	From the Program
$\partial f_1 / \partial y_1$	0	- 0.002	$\partial f_1 / \partial y_2$	1	1
$\partial f_2 / \partial y_1$	0.3679	0.3677	$\partial f_2 / \partial y_2$	1	1

Using code from the *A Matrix* program, we can now write a Newton-Raphson program.

<table>
<tr><td colspan="2" align="center">Program for the Newton-Raphson Method</td></tr>
<tr><td>

```
Option Base 1
Sub main()
Dim Dy(30), y(30), ys(30), f(30), fs(30), A()
 GoSub data
 For iter = 1 To niter
 For jA = 0 To N
   GoSub system
   If jA = 0 Then
     For i = 1 To N
       ys(i) = y(i): fs(i) = f(i)
       Cells(iter, i) = Application.Round(ys(i), 2)
       Cells(iter, i + N) = Application.Round(fs(i), 2)
     Next i
   End If
   Call matrix(N, y, ys, f, fs, jA, stepd, A)
 Next jA
 yes = 0
 For i = 1 To N
   For j = 1 To N
     If Abs(A(i, j)) < Ftol Then yes = yes + 1
   Next j
 Next i
 If yes = N * N Then
   Cells(iter, 2 * N + 2) = "Ftol Stop": End
 End If
 Ainv = Application.MInverse(A)
 For j = 1 To N
   Dy(j) = 0
 Next j
 For j = 1 To N
   For i = 1 To N
       Dy(j) = Dy(j) - Ainv(j, i) * fs(i)
   Next i
   y(j) = ys(j) + Dy(j)
 Next j
 yes = 0
 For j = 1 To N
   If Abs(Dy(j)) < Ytol Then yes = yes + 1
 Next j
 If yes = N Then
   Cells(iter, 2 * N + 2) = "Ytol Stop": End
 End If
Next iter
End
data:
 N = 2: y(1) = 1: y(2) = 1: stepd = 0.001: niter = 40
 ReDim A(N, N): Ftol = 1e-10: Ytol = 0.001
Return
system:
 f(1) = y(2) - 2 * (y(1) - 1) ^ 2: f(2) = y(2) - Exp(-y(1))
Return
End Sub
```

```
Sub matrix(N, y, ys, f, fs, jA, stepd, A)
   Same as in the A matrix program Sub df_dy
End Sub
```
</td><td>

- **A** is dimensioned in **data...Return** when **N** is known.
- **GoSub data**
- **For iter = 1 To niter** (maximum number of iterations)
  - **For jA = 0 To N**

    - Compute the **A** matrix.
    - Print out the results of each iteration.

  - **Next jA**

- **End** if absolute value of all $A_{I,j}$ < Ftol.

- Compute the inverse of **A**.

- Compute the matrix $\Delta Y = -A^{-1} * F_s$.

- Compute the *next guess* matrix $Y = Y_s + \Delta Y$.
  (*Note:* Y becomes Y_s for next iteration.)

- **End** if absolute value of all ΔY_j < Ytol.

- **Next iter**
- **End** the program.
- **data:** (See Example NR 1)
  Number of equations and their constants (if any)
  Initial guess and derivative step size
  Termination criteria (Ftol, Ytol, and niter)
  ReDim A(N, N)
  Return
- **system:** (See Example NR 1)
  Equations that evaluate the *f*'s.
  Return
</td></tr>
<tr><td colspan="2" align="center">*Note:* Ftol and Ytol may need to be changed depending on the problem.</td></tr>
</table>

The following examples demonstrate the use of the Newton-Raphson Program.

Example NR 1: This is the same example that was used in Program df_dy, the program that computes the **A** matrix.

$$f_1 = y_2 - 2 * (y_1 - 1)^2 = 0$$

$$f_2 = y_2 - e^{-y_1} = 0$$

The following is a plot of these equations. The problem is to find the values at the intersections.

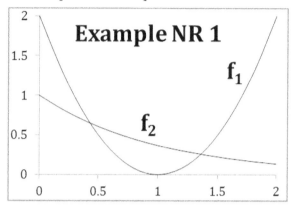

The following table shows the input data. The table also shows that, starting from $Y_1 = 1$ and $Y_2 = 1$, a result was achieved after four iterations. These iterations are plotted in the figure below.

Example NR 1					
Input Data	Results				
	Iteration	Y_1	Y_2	f_1	f_2

data:
  N = 2: y(1) = 1: y(2) = 1: stepd = 0.001
  ReDim A(N, N)
  Ftol = 1e-10: Ytol = 0.001: niter = 40
Return
system:
  f(1) = y(2) - 2 * (y(1) - 1) ^ 2
  f(2) = y(2) - Exp(-y(1))
Return
	start
	1
	2
	3
	4
		1
		2
		1.55
		1.39
		1.36
			1
			0
			0.2
			0.25
			0.26
				1
				-1.98
				-0.4
				-0.05
				0
					0.63
					-0.13
					-0.02
					0
					0

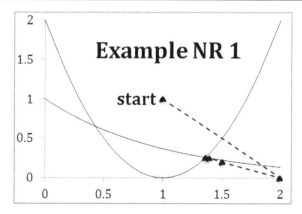

Final Note: The other solution ($Y_1 = .43$ and $Y_2 = .65$) was found starting at ($Y_1 = .75$ and $Y_2 = 1$).

Example NR 2: Find the roots of the following polynomial:

$$f = s^3 + 4*s^2 - 8*s - 8$$

For this problem, **A** is a (1x1) matrix. The Newton-Raphson Program uses the **Minverse** function to compute A^{-1}. When **Minverse** inverts a (1x1), the result is a scalar. To avoid the extra programming steps required to handle this, add a *dummy* equation and a *dummy* variable. Hence, the problem to be solved is this:

Find **y₁** such that

$$f_1 = y_1^3 + 4*y_1^2 - 8*y_1 - 8 = 0$$
$$f_2 = y_2 = 0$$

The following table shows the input data for this example. The table also shows that, starting from ($Y_1 = 0.3$), a result was achieved after three iterations. These iterations are plotted in the figure below and show the *slope-following* characteristic of the Newton-Raphson search.

Example NR 2					
Input Data	Results				
	Iteration	Y_1	Y_2 (*dummy*)	f_1	f_2 (*dummy*)
data: N = 2: y(1) = 0.3: y(2) = 0: stepd = 0.001 ReDim A(N, N) Ftol = 1e-10: Ytol = 0.001: niter = 40 Return system: f(1) = y(1) ^ 3 + 4 * y(1) ^ 2 - 8 * y(1) - 8 f(2) = y(2) Return	start 1 2 3	0.3 -1.58 -0.77 -0.76	0 0 0 0	-10.01 10.69 0.05 0	0 0 0 0

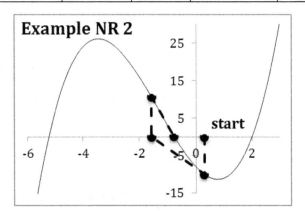

Final Note: The other solutions are as follows:

- ($Y_1 = -5.24$) was found starting at ($Y_1 = -6$).
- ($Y_1 = 2$) was found starting at ($Y_1 = 5$).

Example NR 3: During checkout of the Newton-Raphson program, the following example was contrived. Find the solution to the following system of equations:

$$f_1 = 2^{y_1} + y_2^2 + y_3^2 - y_2 * y_4 - 102 = 0$$

$$f_2 = y_1^{2.718} + y_1 * y_2 + \log_{10}(y_3) + 1^{-y_4} + 6 = 0$$

$$f_3 = y_1^3 - \frac{1}{2^{y_2}} + e^{\ln(y_3)} - y_1 * y_4 - 77 = 0$$

$$f_4 = 10^{\log_{10}(y_1)} + y_2^3 - y_2 * y_3 + \frac{y_4}{10} + 99 = 0$$

The following table shows the input data for this example.

Example NR 3 Input Data
data:
N = 4: y(1) = 1: y(2) = 1: y(3) = 1: y(4) = 1: stepd = 0.001
ReDim A(N, N)
Ftol = 1e-10: Ytol = 0.001: niter = 40
Return
system:
f(1) = 2 ^ y(1) + y(2) ^ 2 + y(3) ^ 2 - y(2) * y(4) - 102
f(2) = y(1) ^ 2.718 + y(1) * y(2) + Application.Log10(y(3)) + 1 ^ (-y(4)) + 6
f(3) = y(1) ^ 3 - 1 / (2 ^ y(2)) + Exp(Log(y(3))) - y(1) * y(4) - 77
f(4) = 10 ^ Application.Log10(y(1)) + y(2) ^ 3 - y(2) * y(3) + y(4) / 10 + 99
Return

The following table shows the results:

Example NR 3 Results								
Iteration	Y_1	Y_2	Y_3	Y_4	f_1	f_2	f_3	f_4
start	1	1	1	1	-99	9	-76.5	100.1
1	1.25	-26.56	41.65	-43.9	1174.5	-22.66	-99002966	-17536.22
2	0.58	-25.12	595.88	-1825.81	309746.15	-4.53	-36407983	-962.68
3	0.43	-23.67	612.34	-15040.16	19338.95	-0.19	-13386048	-177.5
4	0.44	-22.23	547.93	-13438.81	1840.51	0.02	-4921253.3	-51.78
5	0.47	-20.79	478.53	-10969.58	1258.21	0.04	-1808671.9	-35.47
6	0.5	-19.35	413.02	-8770.81	1129.49	0.04	-664215.91	-31.85
7	0.54	-17.92	352.25	-6882.41	986.38	0.05	-243516.94	-29.25
8	0.58	-16.49	296.45	-5287.53	844.98	0.06	-88964.26	-26.53
9	0.64	-15.09	245.97	-3969.86	706.33	0.07	-32269.96	-23.48
10	0.7	-13.74	201.37	-2915.95	566.41	0.08	-11543.6	-19.89
11	0.77	-12.49	163.59	-2114.05	421.39	0.09	-4021.18	-15.59
12	0.85	-11.4	133.86	-1550.63	272.77	0.09	-1327.57	-10.59
13	0.93	-10.59	113.49	-1205.14	134.66	0.07	-384.74	-5.49
14	0.98	-10.14	103.02	-1043.54	37.27	0.03	-76.15	-1.61
15	1	-10.01	100.19	-1002.71	2.79	0	-4.99	-0.13
16	1	-10	100	-1000.01	0.01	0	-0.02	0
17	1	-10	100	-1000	0	0	0	0

Adapting the Newton-Raphson Program to Find Complex Roots of Polynomials

In Chapter 3, polynomials were plotted in order to find their complex roots. In this chapter, the Newton-Raphson method will be used.

For the polynomial $f(s) = c_n s_n + c_{n-1} s_{n-1} + \ldots + c_1 s + c_0$, the following two equations were derived in Chapter 3:

- For the real part of the root, $f_1 = c_0 + \displaystyle\sum_{i=1}^{n} c_i \, r^i \, \cos(i\,\theta)$

- For the imaginary part of the root, $f_2 = \displaystyle\sum_{i=1}^{n} c_i \, r^i \, \sin(i\,\theta)$

By setting $f_1 = 0$ and $f_2 = 0$, we can use the Newton-Raphson search to find the values for r and θ.

The input statements for a polynomial of order **n** are as follows:

data:

The number of equations:	N = 2
The order of the polynomial:	order = n
The polynomial coefficients:	c_n, c_{n-1}, ... , c_0 and Dim c(10)
The first guess:	$y_1 = r$ and $y_2 = \theta * 57.296$
The perturbation step size:	stepd = 0.001
The termination criteria:	F_{tol}, Y_{tol}, niter
The **A** matrix dimension statement:	ReDim A(N, N)

Return

system:

$r = y_1$

$\theta = y_2 / 57.296$

$f_1 = c_0 + \displaystyle\sum_{i=1}^{n} c_i \, r^i \, \cos(i\,\theta)$

$f_2 = \displaystyle\sum_{i=1}^{n} c_i \, r^i \, \sin(i\,\theta)$

Return

Two examples follow:

Example NR 4: Find the roots of the following polynomial: $f(s) = s^3 + s^2 - 2$.

The roots that were found in **Program five of Chapter 3** are as follows:

$$(s_1 = 1), (s_2 = -1 + j), (s_3 = -1 - j)$$

The coefficients are $c_3 = 1$, $c_2 = 1$, $c_1 = 0$, and $c_0 = -2$. For this run, the first guess is $y_1 = 3$ and $y_2 = 100$. In rectangular coordinates, this is (-0.52 + j 2.95).

The following table shows the input data and the results:

Example NR 4					
Input Data	Results				
	Iter.	$y_1\cos(y_{2rad})$	$y_1\sin(y_{2rad})$	f_1	f_2

data:
  N = 2
  Dim c(10)
  order = 3
  c0 = -2: c(1) = 0: c(2) = 1: c(3) = 1
  y(1) = 3: y(2) = 100: stepd = 0.001
  ReDim A(N, N)
  Ftol = 1e-10: Ytol = 0.001: niter = 40
Return
system:
  r = y(1): thetar = y(2) / 57.296
  f(1) = c0: f(2) = 0
  For i = 1 To order
    f(1) = f(1) + c(i) * r ^ i * Cos(i * thetar)
    f(2) = f(2) + c(i) * r ^ i * Sin(i * thetar)
  Next i
Return
	start
	1
	2
	3
	4
	5
	6
	7
		-0.52
		-0.47
		-0.5
		-0.7
		-1.12
		-0.97
		-1
		-1
			2.95
			1.96
			1.3
			0.88
			0.86
			0.98
			1
			1
				3.04
				-0.29
				-1.01
				-1
				-0.39
				-0.16
				0
				0
					-26.46
					-8.08
					-2.52
					-0.64
					0.65
					-0.06
					0
					0

The following is the **Scatter chart** of the results. The **Xs** mark the roots in the first and second quadrants.

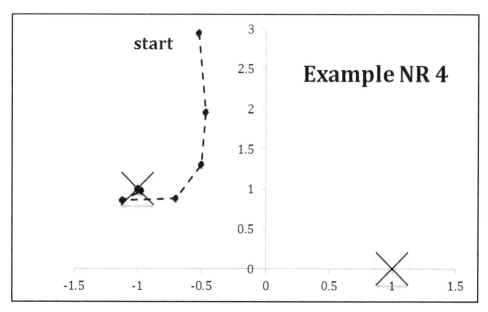

Final Note: The other root (s = 1) was found starting at (Y_1 = 3) and (Y_2 = 0).

Example NR 5: Find the roots: $f = s^7 + c_6 s^6 + c_5 s^5 + c_4 s^4 + c_3 s^3 + c_2 s^2 + c_1 s + c_0$
(The coefficients are given in the table below.)

The first guess is $y_1 = 15$ and $y_2 = 115$. In rectangular coordinates, this is $(-6.34 + j\,13.6)$.

The following table shows the input data and the results:

Example NR 5					
Input Data	Results				
	Iter.	$y_1\cos(y_{2rad})$	$y_1\sin(y_{2rad})$	f_1	f_2

data:
  N = 2
  Dim c(10)
  order = 7
  c0 = -324480: c(1) = 74464: c(2) = 16696
  c(3) = 8695
  c(4) = 2197: c(5) = 109: c(6) = 7: c(7) = 1
  y(1) = 15: y(2) = 115: stepd = 0.001
  ReDim A(N, N)
  Ftol = 1e-10: Ytol = 0.001: niter = 40
Return
system:
  r = y(1): thetar = y(2) / 57.296
  f(1) = c0: f(2) = 0
  For i = 1 To order
    f(1) = f(1) + c(i) * r ^ i * Cos(i * thetar)
    f(2) = f(2) + c(i) * r ^ i * Sin(i * thetar)
  Next i
Return
	start
	1
	2
	3
	4
	5
	6
	7
	8
	9
	10
		-6.34
		-5.24
		-4.25
		-3.39
		-2.65
		-1.99
		-1.23
		-0.3
		-0.47
		-0.41
		-0.4
			13.6
			11.44
			9.46
			7.62
			5.97
			4.6
			3.65
			3.54
			4.06
			3.98
			3.98
				22118644
				7445395
				2722565
				1041548
				316701
				-14134
				-147625
				-160059
				41040
				482
				-7
					183044017
					64294258
					22642752
					7873471
					2673078
					895766
					292256
					10804
					23467
					2347
					1

The following is the **Scatter chart** of the results. The **Xs** mark the roots in the first and second quadrants.

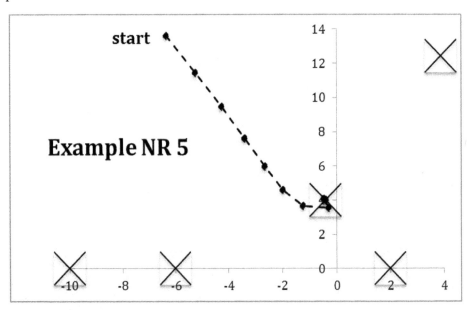

The other roots were found by iterating from other starting points.

Chapter 15: Eigenvalues of General Matrices with Complex Solutions

The subject of this chapter is a program to compute eigenvalues. By definition, eigenvalues (denoted λ) satisfy the following n equations:

$$Ax = \lambda x \qquad \text{(A is a matrix of constants.)}$$

How are the λs found? Rewrite as follows:

$$(A - \lambda I)\, x = 0 \qquad \text{(I is the identity matrix.)}$$

For these equations to have a solution for $x \neq 0$, the coefficient matrix must be singular.

$$\det(A - \lambda I) = 0$$

This is a polynomial equation. The roots are the λs. There is another way to find the λs.

For the moment, assume that the λs are real. We will cover complex λs later. Two matrices (**A** and **B**) are similar (have the same eigenvalues), if for any matrix **T**:

$$T * B = A * T$$

Define:
$$\text{diag}(\lambda_i) = \begin{bmatrix} \lambda_1 & & & & \\ & \lambda_2 & & & \\ & & \bullet & & \\ & & & \bullet & \\ & & & & \lambda_n \end{bmatrix}$$

If $B = \text{diag}(\lambda_i)$, then:
$$T * \text{diag}(\lambda_i) = A * T$$

$$\text{diag}(\lambda_i) = T^{-1} * A * T$$

Hence, the λs can be found by *operating* on **A** with **T**. The **T** that does this is called the matrix of eigenvectors. The problem is that you need to know the λs in order to find **T**.

Rutishauser[*] discovered how to *hunt* for this **T**, or a matrix like **T**, that will *reveal* the λs. This *hunt* is known as the **LR** algorithm. Starting with the matrix **A₀**, the first step is to factor it into a lower triangular matrix (**L₀**) and an upper triangular matrix (**R₀**).

$$A_o = L_o * R_o$$

(We will discuss later how to compute **L₀** and **R₀**.) Since A₀ and ($L_o * R_o$) have the same λs, they are similar. Using **L₀** as the starting **T** matrix:

---

[*] Rutishauser, H. *Solution of Eigenvalue Problems with the LR Transformation.* Nat. Bur. Stand. Applied Math Series, 1958.

$$L_o * A_o = L_o * R_o * L_o$$

$$A_o = L_o^{-1} * L_o * R_o * L_o = R_o * L_o$$

This new matrix, $(R_o * L_o)$, comes from multiplying the factors in *reverse*. It is numerically different but has the same eigenvalues as the original **A$_o$**. The LR algorithm now uses this new matrix as the starting point for the next iteration. This is shown in the following block diagram:

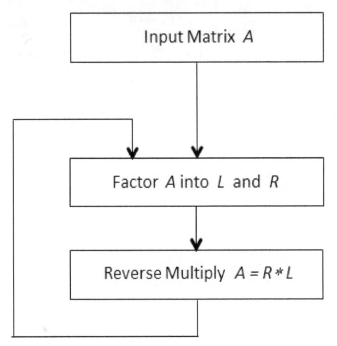

Rutishauser proved that, if you continue this process and there are no numerical difficulties (discussed later), the following will happen. After *m* iterations,

$$A_m = R_m * L_m$$

R_m will remain upper triangular, *but* L_m will approach the identity matrix. That will make $A_m = R_m$ and also upper triangular. An eigenvalue theorem says that, if the λs are real, the elements on the diagonal of an upper triangular matrix are its eigenvalues. *Hence, we have computed the eigenvalues of A$_o$.*

The following table shows a program that implements this LR algorithm. The lower and upper triangular factors are computed using the familiar *Gaussian Elimination* technique. See Matthews[*] for a discussion of this.

---

[*] Matthews, J., and K. Fink. *Numerical Methods Using MATLAB*. Prentice-Hall, 1999.

LR Program Listing	

Option Base 1
Sub LR_main()
Dim A(), L(), R()
N = Cells(1, 1)
ReDim A(N, N), L(N, N), R(N, N)
For i = 1 To N
  For j = 1 To N
    A(i, j) = Cells(i + 1, j)
  Next j
Next i
For iter = 0 To 13
 	
  Cells(iter * (N + 1) + 1 + 1, 3 * N + 3) = iter
    For i = 1 To N
    For j = 1 To N
    Cells(iter * (N + 1) + 1 + i, j) = Application.Round(A(i, j), 2)
    Next j
    Next i
  Call L_R(N, A, L, R)
    For i = 1 To N
    For j = 1 To N
    Cells(iter * (N + 1) + 1 + i, j + 1 * N + 1) = Application.Round(L(i, j), 2)
    Cells(iter * (N + 1) + 1 + i, j + 2 * N + 2) = Application.Round(R(i, j), 2)
    Next j
    Next i
  A = Application.MMult(R, L)
 	
Next iter
End Sub
	• Read in N and A(I, j).
	
	• For iter = 0 To (Niter = 13)
	
	• Call sub L_R(N, A, L, R)
	
	• A ← R * L
	
	• Next iter

Sub L_R(N, A, L, R)
  For i = 1 To N
  For j = 1 To N
  L(i, j) = 0: R(i, j) = 0
  Next j
  L(i, i) = 1
  Next i
  For k = 1 To N - 1
    If Abs(A(k, k)) < 1e-06 Then A(k, k) = Sgn(A(k, k)) * 0.001
  For i = k + 1 To N
    L(i, k) = A(i, k) / A(k, k)
    For j = k + 1 To N
    A(i, j) = A(i, j) - L(i, k) * A(k, j)
    Next j
  Next i
  Next k
  For i = 1 To N
  For j = i To N
  R(i, j) = A(i, j)
  Next j
  Next i
End Sub
	• Subprogram L_R factors **A** into these:
	
	  • **L**, a lower triangular matrix
	
	  • **R**, an upper triangular matrix
	
	(See Mathews for how this is done.)
	
	• Note the *poor man's work-around* for *division by zero.*
	
	• End Sub

Example Demo 1: Use the LR program to verify that the λs of the following matrix are 4, 6, and 12.

$$A = \begin{bmatrix} 6 & 2 & -2 \\ 2 & 6 & -2 \\ -2 & -2 & 10 \end{bmatrix}$$

The following table shows the results:

LR Program Results for Example Demo 1 (*Note:* $A_k = L_k * R_k$ and $A_{k+1} = R_k * L_k$)

Iteration (k)	The A Matrices at Start of Each Iteration (The eigenvalues are $\lambda_1 = 4$, $\lambda_2 = 6$, and $\lambda_3 = 12$ for each of these matrices.)			The L Matrices (lower triangular)			The R Matrices (upper triangular)		
0	6	2	-2	1	0	0	6	2	-2
	2	6	-2	0.33	1	0	0	5.33	-1.33
	-2	-2	10	-0.33	-0.25	1	0	0	9
1	7.33	2.5	-2	1	0	0	7.33	2.5	-2
	2.22	5.67	-1.33	0.3	1	0	0	4.91	-0.73
	-3.00	-2.25	9	-0.41	-0.25	1	0	0	8
2	8.91	3	-2	1	0	0	8.91	3	-2
	1.79	5.09	-0.73	0.2	1	0	0	4.49	-0.33
	-3.27	-2	8	-0.37	-0.2	1	0	0	7.2
3	10.24	3.4	-2	1	0	0	10.24	3.4	-2
	1.02	4.56	-0.33	0.1	1	0	0	4.22	-0.13
	-2.64	-1.44	7.2	-0.26	-0.13	1	0	0	6.67
4	11.10	3.67	-2	1	0	0	11.1	3.67	-2
	0.45	4.23	-0.13	0.04	1	0	0	4.08	-0.05
	-1.72	-0.89	6.67	-0.16	-0.08	1	0	0	6.35
5	11.56	3.82	-2	1	0	0	11.56	3.82	-2
	0.17	4.09	-0.05	0.02	1	0	0	4.03	-0.02
	-0.99	-0.5	6.35	-0.09	-0.04	1	0	0	6.18
6	11.79	3.91	-2	1	0	0	11.79	3.91	-2
	0.06	4.03	-0.02	0.01	1	0	0	4.01	-0.01
	-0.53	-0.26	6.18	-0.04	-0.02	1	0	0	6.09
7	11.9	3.95	-2	1	0	0	11.9	3.95	-2
	0.02	4.01	-0.01	0	1	0	0	4	0
	-0.27	-0.14	6.09	-0.02	-0.01	1	0	0	6.05
8	11.95	3.98	-2	1	0	0	11.95	3.98	-2
	0.01	4	0	0	1	0	0	4	0
	-0.14	-0.07	6.05	-0.01	-0.01	1	0	0	6.02
9	11.98	3.99	-2	1	0	0	11.98	3.99	-2
	0	4	0	0	1	0	0	4	0
	-0.07	-0.03	6.02	-0.01	0	1	0	0	6.01
10	11.99	3.99	-2	1	0	0	11.99	3.99	-2
	0	4	0	0	1	0	0	4	0
	-0.04	-0.02	6.01	0	0	1	0	0	6.01
11	11.99	4	-2	1	0	0	11.99	4	-2
	0	4	0	0	1	0	0	4	0
	-0.02	-0.01	6.01	0	0	1	0	0	6
12	12	4	-2	1	0	0	12	4	-2
	0	4	0	0	1	0	0	4	0
	-0.01	0	6	0	0	1	0	0	6
13	12	4	-2						
	0	4	0						
	0	0	6						

88

By iteration 13, **A** has been triangularized, and the λs are seen on its diagonal. Note that the zeros in most of the matrices are in fact small numbers (e.g., 1. e-20). Hence if the algorithm were to include automatic termination, a convergence criteria would have to account for this.

Example Demo 2: Use the **LR** program to show that the λs of the following matrix are 1, 2, and 5.

$$A = \begin{bmatrix} 1 & -1 & 1 \\ 4 & 6 & -1 \\ 4 & 4 & 1 \end{bmatrix}$$

The following table shows the results:

LR Program Results for Example Demo 2 (*Note:* $A_k = L_k * R_k$ and $A_{k+1} = R_k * L_k$)									
Iteration (k)	The **A** Matrices at Start of Each Iteration (The eigenvalues are $\lambda_1 = 1$, $\lambda_2 = 2$, and $\lambda_3 = 5$ for each of these matrices.)			The **L** Matrices (lower triangular)			The **R** Matrices (upper triangular)		
0	1	-1	1	1	0	0	1	-1	1
	4	6	-1	4	1	0	0	10	-5
	4	4	1	4	0.80	1	0	0	1
1	1	-0.20	1	1	0	0	1	-0.20	1
	20	6	-5	20	1	0	0	10	-25
	4	0.80	1	4	0.16	1	0	0	1
2	1	-0.04	1	1	0	0	1	-0.04	1
	100	6	-25	100	1	0	0	10	-125
	4	0.16	1	4	0.03	1	0	0	1
3	1	-0.01	1	1	0	0	1	-0.01	1
	500	6	-125	500	1	0	0	10	-625
	4	0.03	1	4	0.01	1	0	0	1
4	1	0	1	1	0	0	1	0	1
	2500	6	-625	2500	1	0	0	10	-3125
	4	0.01	1	4	0	1	0	0	1
5	1	0	1						
	12500	6	-3125						
	4	0	1						

The program is diverging. *Division by small numbers* has been encountered. The **LR** algorithm implicitly involves matrix inversion.

Francis[*] avoided matrix inversion by replacing **L** with an *orthogonal matrix*. The inverse of an orthogonal matrix is its transpose. Francis called this the **Q** matrix. $A = Q * R$, where **R** is still upper triangular. This kind of factorization can be achieved by the Householder matrix and is discussed in Hager.[◊] The Francis algorithm is otherwise exactly like the **LR** and is called the **QR**.

---

[*] Francis, J. "The QR Transformation, Parts I and II". *The Computer Journal*, 1961.
[◊] Hager, W. *Applied Numerical Linear Algebra*. Prentice-Hall, 1988.

The following program implements the **QR algorithm:**

QR Program Listing	

Subprogram QR_main
   • Read in N and A(I, j)
   • For iter = 0 To (Niter = 11)
      • call Sub Q_R(N, A, Q, R)
    • A ← R∗Q
   • Next iter
End Sub
 	
Subprogram Q_R factors **A** into:
 	
    • **Q**, a Householder Orthogonal matrix
 	
    • **R**, an upper triangular matrix
 	
    (See Hager for how this is done)
 	
End Subprogram
	Option Base 1
	Sub QR_main()
	Dim A(), Q(), R()
	N = Cells(1, 1)
	ReDim A(N, N), Q(N, N), R(N, N)
	For i = 1 To N
	  For j = 1 To N
	    A(i, j) = Cells(i + 1, j)
	  Next j
	Next i
	For iter = 0 To 11
	  Cells(iter * (N + 1) + 1 + 1, 3 * N + 3) = iter
	For i = 1 To N
	  For j = 1 To N
	  Cells(iter * (N + 1) + 1 + i, j) = Application.Round(A(i, j), 2)
	  Next j
	Next i
	Call Q_R(N, A, Q, R)
	A = Application.MMult(R, Q)
	Next iter
	End Sub ' QR_main

Sub Q_R(N, A, QM, RM)
Dim d(20), AQ(20, 20), Ident(20, 20), vh(), vhT(), H()
ReDim vh(N, 1), vhT(1, N), H(N, N)
 For i = 1 To N
  For j = 1 To N
   QM(i, j) = 0: RM(i, j) = 0: AQ(i, j) = 0: Ident(i, j) = 0
  Next j
   QM(i, i) = 1: Ident(i, i) = 1
 Next i
 k = 0
 For L = 1 To N   '''' Begin Transform
  k = k + 1
  If k = N Then
   d(L) = A(k, L): Exit For
  End If
  sarg = 0
  For i = k To N
   sarg = sarg + A(i, L) ^ 2
  Next i
  s = Sqr(sarg)
  If s = 0 Then
   d(L) = 0: GoTo nextL
  End If
  T = A(k, L): R = 1 / Sqr(s * (s + Abs(T)))
  If T < 0 Then s = -s
  d(L) = -s: A(k, k) = R * (T + s)
  For i = k + 1 To N
   A(i, k) = R * A(i, L)
  Next i
  For j = L + 1 To N
   T = 0
   For i = k To N
    T = T + A(i, k) * A(i, j)
   Next i
   For i = k To N
    A(i, j) = A(i, j) - T * A(i, k)
   Next i
  Next j
nextL: Next L   '''' End Transform
	For i = 1 To N
	  RM(i, i) = d(i)
	Next i
	For i = 1 To N - 1
	  For j = i + 1 To N
	   RM(i, j) = A(i, j)
	  Next j
	Next i
	For j = 1 To N
	  For i = j To N
	   AQ(i, j) = A(i, j)
	  Next i
	Next j
	For j = 1 To N - 1
	  For i = 1 To N
	   vh(i, 1) = AQ(i, j): vhT(1, i) = vh(i, 1)
	  Next i
	  vhvhT = Application.MMult(vh, vhT)
	  For ii = 1 To N
	   For jj = 1 To N
	    H(ii, jj) = Ident(ii, jj) - vhvhT(ii, jj)
	   Next jj
	  Next ii
	  Qtot = Application.MMult(QM, H)
	  For ii = 1 To N
	   For jj = 1 To N
	    QM(ii, jj) = Qtot(ii, jj)
	   Next jj
	  Next ii
	Next j
	End Sub ' Q_R

Example Demo 2 Using the QR Program: The following table shows the results:

Iteration (k)	The A Matrices at Start of Each Iteration (The eigenvalues are $\lambda_1 = 1$, $\lambda_2 = 2$, and $\lambda_3 = 5$ for each of these matrices.)				The Q Matrices (orthogonal)				The R Matrices (upper triangular)		
QR Program Results for Example Demo 2 *(Note:* $A_k = Q_k * R_k$ and $A_{k+1} = R_k * Q_k$)											
0	1	-1	1		-0.17	0.83	-0.53		-5.74	-6.79	-0.17
	4	6	-1		-0.70	-0.48	-0.53		0	-2.63	1.59
	4	4	1		-0.70	0.28	0.66		0	0	0.66
1	5.85	-1.53	6.53		-0.99	0.12	0.08		-5.91	1.32	-6.72
	0.72	1.71	2.45		-0.12	-0.99	-0.03		0	-1.89	-1.67
	-0.46	0.18	0.44		0.08	-0.04	1		0	0	0.90
2	5.16	-1.73	-7.23		-1	0.02	-0.01		-5.16	1.69	7.24
	0.10	1.94	-1.60		-0.02	-1	0.01		0	-1.98	1.47
	0.07	-0.04	0.89		-0.01	0.01	1		0	0	0.98
3	5.03	-1.73	7.33		-1	0	0		-5.03	1.72	-7.33
	0.02	1.99	1.45		0	-1	0		0	-2	-1.42
	-0.01	0.01	0.98		0	0	1		0	0	1
4	5.01	-1.73	-7.34		-1	0	0		-5.01	1.73	7.34
	0	2	-1.42		0	-1	0		0	-2	1.42
	0	0	1		0	0	1		0	0	1
5	5	-1.73	7.35								
	0	2	1.42								
	0	0	1								

The **QR** algorithm converges to the correct solution.

Example Demo 3: Apply the **QR** program to the problem in Example Demo 1 which used the **LR** program. The following table shows the results:

	QR Program Results for Example Demo 3 *(Note: $A_k = Q_k * R_k$ and $A_{k+1} = R_k * Q_k$)*											
Iteration (k)	The **A** Matrices at Start of Each Iteration (The eigenvalues are $\lambda_1 = 4$, $\lambda_2 = 6$, and $\lambda_3 = 12$ for each of these matrices.)				The **Q** Matrices (orthogonal)				The **R** Matrices (upper triangular)		
0	6	2	-2		-0.9	0.36	0.24		-6.63	-4.22	5.43
	2	6	-2		-0.3	-0.92	0.24		0	-5.12	2.56
	-2	-2	10		0.3	0.14	0.94		0	0	8.49
1	8.91	2.31	2.56		-0.93	0.26	-0.25		-9.55	-3.71	-4.82
	2.31	5.09	1.21		-0.24	-0.96	-0.12		0	-4.35	-0.87
	2.56	2.21	8		-0.27	-0.05	0.96		0	0	6.93
2	11.10	1.29	-1.86		-0.98	0.12	0.16		-11.33	-1.8	2.95
	1.29	4.23	-0.34		-0.11	-0.99	0.03		0	-4.06	0.19
	-1.86	-0.34	6.67		0.16	0.01	0.99		0	0	6.27
3	11.79	0.49	1.03		-1	0.04	-0.09		-11.84	-0.66	-1.56
	0.49	4.03	0.06		-0.04	-1	-0.01		0	-4.01	-0.03
	1.03	0.06	6.18		-0.09	0	1		0	0	6.07
4	11.95	0.17	-0.53		-1	0.01	0.04		-11.96	-0.23	0.79
	0.17	4	-0.01		-0.01	-1	0		0	-4	0.01
	-0.53	-0.01	6.05		0.04	0	1		0	0	6.02
5	11.99	0.06	0.26		-1	0	-0.02		-11.99	-0.08	-0.4
	0.06	4	0		0	-1	0		0	-4	0
	0.26	0	6.01		-0.02	0	1		0	0	6
6	12	0.02	-0.13		-1	0	0.01		-12	-0.03	0.2
	0.02	4	0		0	-1	0		0	-4	0
	-0.13	0	6		0.01	0	1		0	0	6
7	12	0.01	0.07		-1	0	-0.01		-12	-0.01	-0.1
	0.01	4	0		0	-1	0		0	-4	0
	0.07	0	6		-0.01	0	1		0	0	6
8	12	0	-0.03		-1	0	0		-12	0	0.05
	0	4	0		0	-1	0		0	-4	0
	-0.03	0	6		0	0	1		0	0	6
9	12	0	0.02		-1	0	0		-12	0	-0.02
	0	4	0		0	-1	0		0	-4	0
	0.02	0	6		0	0	1		0	0	6
10	12	0	-0.01		-1	0	0		-12	0	0.01
	0	4	0		0	-1	0		0	-4	0
	-0.01	0	6		0	0	1		0	0	6
11	12	0	0								
	0	4	0								
	0	0	6								

By iteration 11, **A** has been triangularized, and the λs can be seen on the diagonal. Note that the off-diagonal terms of the final **A** are different than those from the **LR** program.

Complex Eigenvalues

For real matrices, complex eigenvalues come in conjugate pairs. It takes four elements in a matrix of real numbers to yield one complex pair. For example:

$$A = \begin{bmatrix} a & b \\ c & d \end{bmatrix}$$

The eigenvalues of **A** are the roots of:

$$\begin{vmatrix} (a - \lambda) & b \\ c & (d - \lambda) \end{vmatrix} = 0$$

Assume the eigenvalues of a matrix are four real and two complex pairs. The **LR** and **QR** algorithms must iterate until the form of the matrix resembles the following:

$$\begin{bmatrix} x & x & x & x & x & x & x & x \\ & x & x & x & x & x & x & x \\ & & x & x & x & x & x & x \\ & & x & x & x & x & x & x \\ & & & & x & x & x & x \\ & & & & & x & x & x \\ & & & & & x & x & x \\ & & & & & & & x \end{bmatrix}$$

As can be seen, the complex roots show up as *bulges* on the diagonal. Detecting complex roots is a big part of the **LR** and **QR** convergence criteria. The following example demonstrates complex eigenvalues:

Example Demo 4: Apply the **QR** program to the following **A** matrix:

$$A = \begin{bmatrix} 0 & 1 & 0 \\ -6.16 & -2.346 & 0.0027 \\ -242.5455 & -31.5273 & -0.028 \end{bmatrix}$$

This matrix will be discussed later in **Example eig 5**. Its eigenvalues are:

$$\lambda_1 = -0.14, \quad \lambda_2 = -1.12 + j\,2.18, \quad \lambda_3 = -1.12 - j\,2.18.$$

The following table shows the results:

QR Program Results For Example Demo 4			[Note: A_k = Q_k * R_k and A_k+1 = R_k * Q_k]					
Iteration (k)	The **A** Matrices At Start Of Each Iteration (The eigenvalues are $\lambda_1 = -.14$, $\lambda_2 = -1.12+j2.18$, $\lambda_3 = -1.12-j2.18$ for each of these matrices.)			The **Q** Matrices (orthogonal)			The **R** Matrices (upper triangular)	
0	0	1	0	0	0.54	0.84	-242.62	-31.58	-0.03
	-6.16	-2.346	0.0027	0.03	-0.84	0.54	0	1.84	0
	-242.5455	-31.5273	-0.028	1	0.02	-0.01	0	0	0
1	-0.8296	-105.347	-220.8272	-1	-0.05	0	0.83	105.12	220.57
	0.0439	-1.5444	0.9997	0.05	-1	-0.03	0	7.11	10.67
	0.0018	0	0	0	-0.03	1	0	0	-0.14
2	5.2117	-112.2121	216.9874						
	0.3991	-7.446	10.4325						
	-0.0003	0.0046	-0.1397						

At iteration 2, the last row shows $\lambda_1 = -0.14$. After dropping the last row and column, the other 2 λs are the roots of the following equation:

$$\begin{vmatrix} (5.2117-\lambda) & -112.2121 \\ 0.3991 & (-7.446-\lambda) \end{vmatrix} = 0$$

The solution of this equation is $\lambda_2 = -1.12 + j\,2.18$, $\lambda_3 = -1.12 - j\,2.18$.

The QR Algorithm Expanded to Include *Matrix Deflation*

Suppose the following **A** matrix is detected during the iterations:

$$\begin{bmatrix} E & F \\ 0 \cdots 0 & a \end{bmatrix}$$ *Condition 1*

Here, the last row reveals that an eigenvalue has been encountered. The last row and column can be dropped, and the **QR** iterations can continue with **A = E**. This is called matrix deflation.

Now suppose that the following **A** matrix is detected during the iterations:

$$\begin{bmatrix} G & H \\ 0 \cdots 0 & a\; b \\ 0 \cdots 0 & c\; d \end{bmatrix}$$ *Condition 2*

Here, the last two rows reveal a pair of eigenvalues. After computing these λs, the last two rows and columns can be dropped, and the **QR** iterations can continue with **A = G**.

The QR Algorithm Expanded to Include *Shifting*

An eigenvalue theorem says that if **A** has an eigenvalue of λ_1, then one of the eigenvalues of the matrix $(A - \sigma_1 * I)$ will be $(\lambda_1 - \sigma_1)$. This is called *shifting*. If $\sigma_1 = \lambda_1$, then the matrix $(A - \lambda_1 * I)$ will have an eigenvalue of *zero*. When this matrix is factored, the last row of **R** is forced to have all *zeros*. The last row of the reverse multiplication (when **A** is replaced with **RQ**) will also be *zero*. To regain similarity, the *shift* must be added back in. This is done via the statement $A = (A + \lambda_1 * I)$. Hence, the eigenvalue λ_1 will be revealed in the last row of **A**. The following example will show this:

Example Demo 5: This example will use the matrix in **Example Demo 3**:

$$\begin{bmatrix} 6 & 2 & -2 \\ 2 & 6 & -2 \\ -2 & -2 & 10 \end{bmatrix}$$

• Its eigenvalues are 4, 6, and 12. Set shift = $12 * I$.

• Perform the shift $A = (A - 12 * I)$:

$$\begin{bmatrix} -6 & 2 & -2 \\ 2 & -6 & -2 \\ -2 & -2 & -2 \end{bmatrix}$$

• Factor the shifted **A** into **Q** and **R**:

$$Q = \begin{bmatrix} -0.9 & -0.12 & 8 \\ 0.3 & -0.86 & -6 \\ -0.3 & -0.49 & 0 \end{bmatrix} \quad R = \begin{bmatrix} 6.63 & -3.02 & 1.8 \\ 0 & 5.91 & 2.95 \\ 0 & 0 & 0 \end{bmatrix}$$

• Reverse multiply $A = R * Q$:

$$\begin{bmatrix} -7.45 & 0.89 & 71.16 \\ 0.89 & -6.55 & -35.45 \\ 0 & 0 & 0 \end{bmatrix}$$

• To restore similarity, shift back $A = (A + 12 * I)$:

$$\begin{bmatrix} 4.55 & 0.89 & 71.16 \\ 0.89 & 5.45 & -35.45 \\ 0 & 0 & 12 \end{bmatrix}$$

• From the last row, $\lambda_1 = 12$.
• From the *bulge* on the diagonal, the remaining λs are the roots of:

$$\begin{vmatrix} (4.55 - \lambda) & 0.89 \\ 0.89 & (5.45 - \lambda) \end{vmatrix} = 0 \quad \text{which are} \quad \lambda_2 = 4 \text{ and } \lambda_3 = 6$$

With *matrix deflation* and exact *shifting*, the **QR** takes one iteration. On Example Demo 3, without these, the **QR** took eleven iterations.

Of course, exact *shifting* is not feasible. But experience has led to the development of several successful *guessing methods for shifting*.

Francis (previous reference) proposed the following strategy. Eigenvalues are computed from the submatrix in the lower right-hand corner of the **A** matrix.

$$\begin{bmatrix} a_{n-1,n-1} & a_{n-1,n} \\ a_{n,n-1} & a_{n,n} \end{bmatrix} \qquad Guess\ 1$$

Pick the eigenvalue of this submatrix that is closest to $a_{n,n}$. Francis uses this eigenvalue as the *shift* for the start of each **QR** iteration. The *shift* will change on each iteration.

But there is another, perhaps more important, benefit from *shifting*. The **QR** does not diverge like the **LR**, but it can get into a *limit cycle*. Sometimes after several iterations, the **QR** matrices begin to repeat. When this happens, obviously there will be no convergence.

Francis discovered that this *limit cycle* could be interrupted by changing the method of *shifting* during the iteration process. His method is extremely complex and is beyond the scope of this tutorial.

I have discovered a simpler method which is remarkably effective. In fact, it is so effective that I haven't found a single case that makes it fail. But it's heuristic.

If the *first guess* doesn't yield convergence after an arbitrary one hundred iterations, the *guess* is changed. The submatrix used to compute the *shift* becomes:

$$\begin{bmatrix} a_{n-1,n-2} & a_{n-1,n} \\ a_{n,n-2} & a_{n,n} \end{bmatrix} \qquad Guess\ 2$$

The QR Algorithm Expanded to Include the Hessenberg Matrix

There is one final step that has become a part of most **QR** strategies. A Hessenberg Matrix has all *zeros* below the subdiagonal:

$$\begin{bmatrix} x & x & x & x & x & x \\ x & x & x & x & x & x \\ 0 & x & x & x & x & x \\ 0 & 0 & x & x & x & x \\ 0 & 0 & 0 & x & x & x \\ 0 & 0 & 0 & 0 & x & x \end{bmatrix}$$

Since it is *nearly* triangular already, it is common to transform the initial **A** matrix to Hessenberg form before beginning **QR** iterations. Scheid* uses Gaussian Elimination in his method to transform **A** into Hessenberg form.

---

* Scheid, F. *Numerical Analysis* in Schaum's Outline Series. McGraw-Hill, 1988.

We have discussed all of the ingredients needed to write a program. The following is a block diagram of the program. The listing of the code is in Appendix A.1.

Block Diagram of Sub eig

(A program to compute all of the eigenvalues of a general real matrix)

Input the matrix **A** and its size **N**.

⇓

Compute the Hessenberg form of **A**.

⇓

For **iter** = 1 to **NITER** (maximum allowed number of **QR** iterations)

⇓

• shift = *Guess 1* or *Guess 2* • A = A - shift $*I$ • Factor A into Q and R (Sub QR) • A = R$*$Q (reverse multiply) • A = A + shift $*I$ (to restore similiarity)

⇓

Sub Deflate If *Condition 1* is met, one root has been found. If *Condition 2* is met, two roots have been found.

⇓

If roots have been found, reduce **N**.

⇓

If **N** <= 2, Sub eig is successful. Compute last roots and ***STOP***.

⇓

If **iter** < **NITER**, ***next iter***. If not, all roots have not been found. ***STOP***.

We will illustrate the use of this program via a series of examples. The following table contains a listing of a *main* program that reads the **A** matrix from the spreadsheet, calls **Sub eig**, and prints the λ s on the spreadsheet.

Program eig_main	
Code	**Description**

Option Base 1
Sub eig_main()
Dim A(30, 30), WR(30), WI(30)
N = Cells(1, 1)
For i = 1 To N
  For j = 1 To N
    A(i, j) = Cells(i + 1, j)
  Next j
Next i
Call eig(N, A, WR, WI)
For i = 1 To N
  Cells(N + 3 + i, 1) = Application.Round(WR(i), 2)
  Cells(N + 3 + i, 2) = Application.Round(WI(i), 2)
Next i
End Sub
	● Read **N** (the size of the **A** matrix) from the spreadsheet.
	
	● Read the **A** matrix from the spreadsheet.
	
	●Call the program that computes the eigenvalues.
	
	●Print out the eigenvalues $\lambda_i = WR_i + j\, WI_i$.

Sub eig(N, A, WR, WI) See Appendix A.1 for the listing of this program. **End Sub**	●*Note:* Sub eig_main and Sub eig must be in the same Code Window.

Example eig 1: The first example is to find the roots of the following equation:

$$s^3 + s^2 - 2 = 0$$

This polynomial was also used in Chapter 3 (**Program five**) and in Chapter 14 (**Example NR 4**). The roots are (s = 1), (s = -1 + j) and (s = -1 − j).

We will transform this equation into a matrix whose eigenvalues are its roots. The transformation is done as follows. Multiply the equation by the variable **x**.

$$s^3x + s^2x - 2x = 0$$

Let: $\quad\quad y_1 = x$

Then: $\quad\quad sy_1 = sx = y_2$

$$sy_2 = s^2x = y_3$$

$$sy_3 = s^3x = 2x - s^2x = 2y_1 - y_3$$

Writing the last three equations in matrix form:

$$\begin{bmatrix} sy_1 \\ sy_2 \\ sy_3 \end{bmatrix} = \begin{bmatrix} 0 & 1 & 0 \\ 0 & 0 & 1 \\ 2 & 0 & -1 \end{bmatrix} \begin{bmatrix} y_1 \\ y_2 \\ y_3 \end{bmatrix}$$

Rearranging into (A - λ I) y form:

$$\left\{ \begin{bmatrix} 0 & 1 & 0 \\ 0 & 0 & 1 \\ 2 & 0 & -1 \end{bmatrix} - \begin{bmatrix} s & 0 & 0 \\ 0 & s & 0 \\ 0 & 0 & s \end{bmatrix} \right\} \begin{bmatrix} y_1 \\ y_2 \\ y_3 \end{bmatrix} = 0$$

The roots of the initial equation are the eigenvalues of its **A** matrix. The **A** matrix is entered on the spreadsheet as shown in the following table. The table also shows the eigenvalues that are computed by Program **eig_main**. They agree with the roots found in **Example NR 4**.

Example eig 1				
The Input *A* Matrix (N = 3)			Eigenvalues	
			WR(i)	WI(i)
0	1	0	1	0
0	0	1	-1	1
2	0	-1	-1	-1

Example eig 2: This example is to find the roots of the following equation:

$$s^7 + 7 s^6 + 109 s^5 + 2197 s^4 + 8695 s^3 + 16696 s^2 + 74464 s - 324480 = 0$$

This polynomial was used in Chapter 14 (**Example NR 5**). The roots are (s = 2), (s = -6), (s = -10), (s = -.4 + j 3.98), (s = -.4 - j 3.98), (s = 3.9 + j 12.41), (s = 3.9 - j 12.41).

Transforming this equation:

$$s^7 x + 7 s^6 x + 109 s^5 x + 2197 s^4 x + 8695 s^3 x + 16696 s^2 x + 74464 sx - 324480 x = 0$$

Let: $\quad y_1 = x$

Then: $sy_1 = sx = y_2$

$\quad\quad sy_2 = s^2 x = y_3$

$\quad\quad sy_3 = s^3 x = y_4$

$\quad\quad sy_4 = s^4 x = y_5$

$\quad\quad sy_5 = s^5 x = y_6$

$\quad\quad sy_6 = s^6 x = y_7$

$\quad\quad sy_7 = s^7 x = 324480\, y_1 - 74464\, y_2 - 16696\, y_3 - 8695\, y_4 - 2197\, y_5 - 109\, y_6 - 7\, y_7$

In matrix form:

$$\begin{bmatrix} sy_1 \\ sy_2 \\ sy_3 \\ sy_4 \\ sy_5 \\ sy_6 \\ sy_7 \end{bmatrix} = \begin{bmatrix} 0 & 1 & 0 & 0 & 0 & 0 & 0 \\ 0 & 0 & 1 & 0 & 0 & 0 & 0 \\ 0 & 0 & 0 & 1 & 0 & 0 & 0 \\ 0 & 0 & 0 & 0 & 1 & 0 & 0 \\ 0 & 0 & 0 & 0 & 0 & 1 & 0 \\ 0 & 0 & 0 & 0 & 0 & 0 & 1 \\ 324480 & -74464 & -16696 & -8695 & -2197 & -109 & -7 \end{bmatrix} \begin{bmatrix} y_1 \\ y_2 \\ y_3 \\ y_4 \\ y_5 \\ y_6 \\ y_7 \end{bmatrix}$$

This matrix is entered on the spreadsheet as shown in the following table. The table also shows the eigenvalues. They agree with the roots previously found in **Example NR 5**.

Example eig 2								
The Input *A* Matrix (N = 7)							Eigenvalues	
							WR(i)	WI(i)
0	1	0	0	0	0	0	2	0
0	0	1	0	0	0	0	-0.4	3.98
0	0	0	1	0	0	0	-0.4	-3.98
0	0	0	0	1	0	0	-6.01	0
0	0	0	0	0	1	0	-9.99	0
0	0	0	0	0	0	1	3.9	12.41
324480	-74464	-16696	-8695	-2197	-109	-7	3.9	-12.41

Eigenvalues are defined for linear differential equations. It is common practice to analyze nonlinear equations by linearizing them about a *steady state operating condition* (aka, *set point*). These linear equations are then analyzed using the many linear methods available. By choosing more than one set point, conclusions can be made about the behavior of the nonlinear equations throughout their entire *operating region*. As with the Newton-Raphson method, we will now write a program to linearize nonlinear differential equations in order to compute eigenvalues. We will use the following example to demonstrate:

Example eig 3: The following equation is that of a pendulum: $L\ddot{\theta} = -g\sin\theta$, where **L** is the length, **g** is gravitational acceleration, and θ is the swing angle. This equation will be converted into two first-order nonlinear differential equations. Let $Y_1 = \theta$ and $Y_2 = \dot{\theta} = \dot{Y}_1$. Then:

$$\ddot{\theta} = \dot{Y}_2 = -(g/L) * \sin(Y_1)$$

Rewriting these:

$$\dot{Y}_1 = Y_2$$
$$\dot{Y}_2 = -(g/L) * \sin(Y_1)$$

These two equations are linearized by expanding each in a first-order Taylor series:

$$\dot{Y}_1 = \dot{Y}_{1o} + \frac{\partial \dot{Y}_1}{\partial Y_1}\Delta Y_1 + \frac{\partial \dot{Y}_1}{\partial Y_2}\Delta Y_2$$

$$\dot{Y}_2 = \dot{Y}_{2o} + \frac{\partial \dot{Y}_2}{\partial Y_1}\Delta Y_1 + \frac{\partial \dot{Y}_2}{\partial Y_2}\Delta Y_2$$

Since $\Delta\dot{Y}_1 = \dot{Y}_1 - \dot{Y}_{1o}$ and $\Delta\dot{Y}_2 = \dot{Y}_2 - \dot{Y}_{2o}$:

$$\Delta\dot{Y}_1 = \frac{\partial \dot{Y}_1}{\partial Y_1}\Delta Y_1 + \frac{\partial \dot{Y}_1}{\partial Y_2}\Delta Y_2$$

$$\Delta\dot{Y}_2 = \frac{\partial \dot{Y}_2}{\partial Y_1}\Delta Y_1 + \frac{\partial \dot{Y}_2}{\partial Y_2}\Delta Y_2$$

These equations are now linear and can be *Laplace* transformed. $\Delta\dot{Y}_1$ becomes $s\,y_1$, ΔY_1 becomes y_1, and so forth. Putting the transformed equations into matrix form:

$$\begin{bmatrix} s & 0 \\ 0 & s \end{bmatrix}\begin{bmatrix} y_1 \\ y_2 \end{bmatrix} = \begin{bmatrix} \frac{\partial \dot{Y}_1}{\partial Y_1} & \frac{\partial \dot{Y}_1}{\partial Y_2} \\ \frac{\partial \dot{Y}_2}{\partial Y_1} & \frac{\partial \dot{Y}_2}{\partial Y_1} \end{bmatrix}\begin{bmatrix} y_1 \\ y_2 \end{bmatrix} = [A]\begin{bmatrix} y_1 \\ y_2 \end{bmatrix}$$

Example eig 3 (cont.):

In general, an nth-order nonlinear system can be transformed into the form $(A - sI)Y = 0$, where:

$$A = \begin{bmatrix} \dfrac{\partial \dot{Y}_1}{\partial Y_1} & & \dfrac{\partial \dot{Y}_1}{\partial Y_n} \\[2ex] & \bullet & \\ & \bullet \quad \bullet & \\[2ex] \dfrac{\partial \dot{Y}_n}{\partial Y_1} & & \dfrac{\partial \dot{Y}_n}{\partial Y_n} \end{bmatrix}$$

In Chapter 14, a program was written to *compute the A matrix*. Program **df_dy** was written to linearize the vector **f = 0**. In this chapter, we need an identical program to linearize a vector of $\dot{y}$ equations. Program **df_dy** is adapted to compute **A** by simply replacing the **f** equations with $\dot{y}$ equations. Since the example problem is included right in the code, for Example eig 3:

Input to Compute the A Matrix for Example eig 3
data:
The number of equations: N = 2
The derivative stepsize: stepd = .02
The set point: y(1) = 0, y(2) = 0
The constants: (g/L) = 4
Return
system:
$\dot{Y}_1 = Y_2$
$\dot{Y}_2 = -(g/L) * \sin(Y_1)$
Return

Example eig 3 (cont.):

The following is a listing of this program:

Program A_main to Compute the A Matrix	
Code	**Comments**

``Sub A_main()``
``Dim y(100), ys(100), yd(100), yds(100), A(100, 100)``
``GoSub data``
 	
``For jA = 0 To N``
`` If jA = 0 Then``
``  For j = 1 To N``
``   ys(j) = y(j)``
``  Next j``
`` End If``
`` GoSub system``
`` If jA = 0 Then``
``  For i = 1 To N``
``   yds(i) = yd(i)``
``  Next i``
`` End If``
`` Call matrix(N, y, ys, yd, yds, jA, stepd, A)``
``Next jA``
 	
``Cells(1, 1) = N``
``For i = 1 To N``
`` For j = 1 To N``
``  Cells(i + 1, j) = A(i, j)``
`` Next j``
``Next i``
 	
``End``
``data:``
`` N = 2: stepd = 0.02: y(1) = 0: y(2) = 0``
`` grav = 32.176: Length = grav / 4``
``Return``
``system:``
`` yd(1) = y(2)``
`` yd(2) = -(grav / Length) * Sin(y(1))``
``Return``
``End Sub``
 	
``Sub matrix(N, y, ys, yd, yds, jA, stepd, A)``
``If jA = 0 Then``
``   y(1) = ys(1) + stepd``
``Else``
`` For i = 1 To N``
``  A(i, jA) = (yd(i) - yds(i)) / stepd``
`` Next i``
``  y(jA) = ys(jA)``
``  If jA < N Then``
``   y(jA + 1) = ys(jA + 1) + stepd``
``  End If``
``End If``
``End If``
``End Sub``
	This program is identical to Program df_dx in Chapter 14 except for variable name changes:
	
	In Program df_dx, $A = \dfrac{\partial f}{\partial y}$
	
	In this program, $A = \dfrac{\partial \dot{y}}{\partial y}$
	
	The changes made to variable names are: $f(i)$ to $yd(i)$
	                                   $fs(i)$ to $yds(i)$
	
	Printout that will be read by Sub eig_main.
	
	Input data and equations are for Example eig 3.

Example eig 3 (cont.):

To compute the eigenvalues, the matrix from Program A_main is input to Program **eig_main**. The following table shows this input and output for Example eig 3:

Example eig 3		
	The A Matrix	
data:		
N = 2: stepd = 0.02: y(1) = 0: y(2) = 0	0	1
grav = 32.176: Length = grav / 4		
Return	-3.9997	0
	The Eigenvalues	
system:	WR(i)	WI(i)
yd(1) = y(2)		
yd(2) = -(grav / Length) * Sin(y(1))	0	2
Return	0	-2

To check out these results, **Example eig 3** will now be solved manually. Starting with the **A** matrix:

$$\frac{\partial \dot{Y}_1}{\partial Y_1} = 0, \quad \frac{\partial \dot{Y}_1}{\partial Y_2} = 1, \quad \frac{\partial \dot{Y}_2}{\partial Y_1} = -(g/L)*\cos(Y_{1o}) \text{ and } \frac{\partial \dot{Y}_2}{\partial Y_2} = 0.$$

Substituting these partial derivatives into the **A** matrix:

$$\begin{bmatrix} s & 0 \\ 0 & s \end{bmatrix}\begin{bmatrix} Y_1 \\ Y_2 \end{bmatrix} = \begin{bmatrix} 0 & 1 \\ -(g/L)*\cos(Y_{1o}) & 0 \end{bmatrix}\begin{bmatrix} Y_1 \\ Y_2 \end{bmatrix}$$

For the set point: **(g/L) = 4** and $\theta_o = Y_{1o} = 0$.

$$\begin{bmatrix} s & 0 \\ 0 & s \end{bmatrix}\begin{bmatrix} Y_1 \\ Y_2 \end{bmatrix} = \begin{bmatrix} 0 & 1 \\ -4 & 0 \end{bmatrix}\begin{bmatrix} Y_1 \\ Y_2 \end{bmatrix} = [A]\begin{bmatrix} Y_1 \\ Y_2 \end{bmatrix}$$

This checks out **Program A_main**. Rearranging:

$$\begin{bmatrix} -s & 1 \\ -4 & -s \end{bmatrix}\begin{bmatrix} Y_1 \\ Y_2 \end{bmatrix} = 0$$

From the determinant of the above matrix, the eigenvalues are:

$$s^2 + 4 = (s+j2)*(s-j2) = 0$$

This checks out **Program eig_main**.

Example eig 4: Consider the second-order differential equation with nonlinear damping:

$$\ddot{x} = -0.1 * x^2 * \dot{x} - 4 * x$$

Compute the eigenvalues at the set point $x_o = 4$ and $\dot{x}_o = 0$.

Convert the system into two first-order nonlinear differential equations.

Let $Y_1 = x$ and $Y_2 = \dot{x} = \dot{Y}_1$. Then $\dot{Y}_2 = \ddot{x} = -0.1 * Y_1^2 * Y_2 - 4 * Y_1$.

Rewriting these:

$$\dot{Y}_1 = Y_2$$
$$\dot{Y}_2 = -0.1 * Y_1^2 * Y_2 - 4 * Y_1$$

These two equations are put into the code segment **system: … Return** of the program A_main. The set point ($Y_1 = 4$ and $Y_2 = 0$) is put into **data: … Return**. The following table shows these statements as they are appear in A_main. The table also shows the resulting **A** matrix. This matrix is then read by program eig_main, and the table shows the resulting eigenvalues.

Example eig 4		
	The A Matrix	
data: N = 2: stepd = 0.02: y(1) = 4: y(2) = 0 Return	0	1
	-4	-1.6
system:	The Eigenvalues	
yd(1) = y(2)	WR(i)	WI(i)
yd(2) = -0.1 * y(1) ^ 2 * y(2) - 4 * y(1) Return	-0.8	1.83
	-0.8	-1.83

The following is the checkout of these results:

Hand calculating the **A** matrix at $Y_{1o} = 4$ and $Y_{2o} = 0$:

$$A = \begin{bmatrix} \frac{\partial \dot{Y}_1}{\partial Y_1} = 0 & \frac{\partial \dot{Y}_1}{\partial Y_2} = 1 \\ \frac{\partial \dot{Y}_2}{\partial Y_1} = -0.2 * Y_{1o} * Y_{2o} - 4 & \frac{\partial \dot{Y}_2}{\partial Y_2} = -0.1 * Y_{1o}^2 \end{bmatrix} = \begin{bmatrix} 0 & 1 \\ -4 & -1.6 \end{bmatrix}$$

This checks out. Now, we compute the eigenvalues. These are the roots of:

$$s^2 + 1.6 * s + 4 = 0$$

These are (s = -0.8 + j 1.833) and (s = -0.8 - j 1.833). They check out.

105

Example eig 5: Greensite* contains an eleventh-order linear math model of a large launch vehicle. This model is shown in Appendix B. A simplification of that model is used in this example. The following table lists the equations:

Example eig 5 Equations	
$\alpha = \theta + \dfrac{\dot{Z}}{Vel}$	α change in vehicle angle of attack θ change in vehicle angular rotation $\dot{Z}$ change in vehicle lateral velocity Vel vehicle total velocity (constant)
$\delta = -K_D\theta - K_R\dot{\theta}$	δ change in engine angle $\dot{\theta}$ change in vehicle angular rate K_D and K_R are autopilot gains (constants)
$\ddot{\theta} = \mu_\alpha\alpha + \mu_\delta\delta$	$\ddot{\theta}$ change in vehicle angular acceleration μ_α and μ_δ are constants
$\ddot{Z} = -\dfrac{T\text{-}D}{m}\theta - \dfrac{L_\alpha}{m}\alpha + \dfrac{T_c}{m}\delta$	$\ddot{Z}$ change in vehicle lateral acceleration T, D, m, L_α and T_c are constants

The first step is to convert these into first-order equations. The following table shows the conversion variables:

Conversion Variables
$Y_1 = \theta$
$Y_2 = \dot{\theta}$
$Y_3 = \dot{Z}$

Using these conversions, the equations are entered into **system: ... Return** of **A_main**.

system: ... Return	
Equations	Constants
$delta = -K_D * Y_1 - K_R * Y_2$ $alpha = Y_1 + Y_3 / Vel$ $\dot{Y}_1 = Y_2$ $\dot{Y}_2 = mua * alpha + muc * delta$ $\dot{Y}_3 = -tom * Y_1 - aom * alpha + com * delta$	$mua = \mu_\alpha$ $muc = \mu_\delta$ $tom = (T\text{-}D)/m$ $aom = L_\alpha/m$ $com = T_c/m$

---

* Greensite, A. *Analysis and Design of Space Vehicle Flight Control Systems.* Spartan Books, 1970.

Example eig 5 (cont.):

The set point and other data are put into **data: ... Return**.

data: ... Return
• N = 3 the number of first-order differential equations
• stepd = 0.02
• $Y_1 = Y_2 = Y_3 = 0$ the set point (for linear equations)
• the constants in the equations

The following table shows these statements as they appear in A_main. The table also shows the resulting **A** matrix. The **A** matrix is then read by program eig_main. The table shows the eigenvalues:

Example eig 5		
data:	The A Matrix	
N = 3: stepd = 0.02: y(1) = 0: y(2) = 0: y(3) = 0		
vel = 1300: thr = 420000: tc = 340000: aero = 200000	0 1 0	
mass = 5500: mua = 3.5: muc = 4.6: Kd = 2.1: Kr = 0.51	-6.16 -2.35 0.0027	
tom = thr / mass: aom = aero / mass: com = tc / mass	-242.55 -31.53 -0.028	
Return		
system:	The Eigenvalues	
delta = -Kd * y(1) - Kr * y(2)	WR(i)	WI(i)
alpha = y(1) + y(3) / vel		
yd(1) = y(2)	-0.138	0
yd(2) = mua * alpha + muc * delta	-1.118	2.18
yd(3) = -tom * y(1) - aom * alpha + com * delta	-1.118	-2.18
Return		

These eigenvalues are checked out using the following *eigenvalue theorems*.

- The trace of a matrix = the sum of its eigenvalues   Equation eig 1
- The determinant of a matrix = the product of its eigenvalues   Equation eig 2

The following table lists a program that computes the ingredients of these two equations:

Example eig 5 (cont.):

<table>
<tr><th colspan="2">Program eig_check</th></tr>
<tr>
<td>
Option Base 1
Sub eig_check()
 Dim A(), WR(30), WI(30)
 N = Cells(1, 1)
 ReDim A(N, N)
 For i = 1 To N
  For j = 1 To N
   A(i, j) = Cells(i + 1, j)
  Next j
   WR(i) = Cells(N + 3 + i, 1)
   WI(i) = Cells(N + 3 + i, 2)
 Next i
 sum = 0: trace = 0: prod = Application.Complex(1, 0)
 For i = 1 To N
  sum = sum + WR(i)
  trace = trace + A(i, i)
  root = Application.Complex(WR(i), WI(i))
  prod = Application.ImProduct(prod, root)
 Next i
  deter = Application.MDeterm(A)
 Cells(2 * N + 6, 1) = sum: Cells(2 * N + 6, 2) = trace
 Cells(2 * N + 6, 3) = prod: Cells(2 * N + 6, 4) = deter
End Sub
</td>
<td>
● Option Base 1 for MDeterm

● ReDim for MDeterm

● Read ● N [the size of the **A** Matrix]
          ● The **A** Matrix
          ● Its Eigenvalues [WR_i, WI_i]

● Sum of the Eigenvalues
● Trace of the **A** Matrix

● Product of the Eigenvalues

● Determinant of the **A** Matrix

● Print out
</td>
</tr>
</table>

The following table shows that the eigenvalues are correct:

<table>
<tr><th>Eigenvalue Checkout For Example eig 5</th></tr>
<tr><td align="center">Equation eig 1</td></tr>
<tr><td align="center">The Trace of the **A** matrix = -2.3740
The Sum of its Eigenvalues = -2.3739</td></tr>
<tr><td align="center">Equation eig 2</td></tr>
<tr><td align="center">The Determinant of the **A** matrix = -0.8253
The Product of its Eigenvalues = -0.8254</td></tr>
</table>

When these calculations are done directly in Program eig_main, both **Equation eig1** and **Equation eig 2** are satisfied *exactly*.

Note: Throughout the development of Program eig, the results were checked out using these tests.

Example eig 6: A prime method of analysis is to study how a system's eigenvalues vary due to changes in its parameters. By putting the programs A_main and eig_main together in a For ... Next loop and by varying selected parameters on each pass, we can plot the output as a root-locus plot.

The objective of this example is to plot the eigenvalues of Example eig 5 as the autopilot gains (K_D and K_R) vary. In order to make their values change as the program loops, the equations in **system: ... Return** of Example eig 5 are modified:

- $\delta_c = -K_D Y_1 - K_R Y_2$

- $\delta = \delta_c * \text{Groot(iroot)}$ where Groot = Array(0.5, 1, 2). As iroot ranges from one to three in a For ... Next Loop, both autopilot gains will change.

The following is the block diagram of the root-locus program for Example eig 6.

GoSub Data	
⇓	

For iroot = 1 To nroot
  For jA = 0 To N
 	
    GoSub system
 	
    save y_1 , y_2 , $\dot{y}_1$ and $\dot{y}_2$
 	
    GoSub matrix
 	
  Next jA
 	
  Call eig
 	
  Printout
Next iroot
	● For each value of **iroot**, the autopilot gains change.
	
	● In the **jA Loop**, the **A** matrix is computed.
	
	● **Call matrix** has been replaced by **Gosub matrix** (see below).
	
	● The eigenvalues are computed in **Sub eig**.
	
	● Each root is printed in a separate column.
	(Each column becomes a Series for the Scatter chart.)

⇓ ⇑

data: ... Return	To the statements in Example eig 5, add the following:
	    • Groot = Array(0.5, 1, 2)
	    • nroot = 3

system: ... Return	Modify the statements in Example eig 5:
	    • $\delta_c = -K_D Y_1 - K_R Y_2$
	    • $\delta = \delta_c * \text{Groot(iroot)}$

matrix: ... Return	**Sub matrix** has been replaced by **matrix: ... Return**. Otherwise the code is the same. This change is not mandatory.

109

Example eig 6(cont.):

Listing of Root Locus Program for Example eig 6	
| ```
Option Base 1
Sub ex_eig_6_main()
Dim y(30), ys(30), yd(30), yds(30), A(30, 30), WR(30), WI(30)
GoSub data

For iroot = 1 To nroot
 For jA = 0 To N
   GoSub system
   If jA = 0 Then
     For i = 1 To N
       yds(i) = yd(i): ys(i) = y(i)
     Next i
   End If
   GoSub matrix
 Next jA
 Call eig(N, A, WR, WI)
 For i = 1 To N
   aroot = iroot + i + (i - 1) * nroot
   Cells(aroot, 1) = Application.Round(WR(i), 2)
   Cells(aroot, i + 1) = Application.Round(WI(i), 2)
 Next i
Next iroot

End
data:
 nroot = 3: Groot = Array(0.5, 1, 2)
 N = 3: stepd = 0.02: y(1) = 0: y(2) = 0: y(3) = 0
 vel = 1300: thr = 420000: tc = 340000: aero = 200000
 mass = 5500: mua = 3.5: muc = 4.6: Kd = 2.1: Kr = 0.51
 tom = thr / mass: aom = aero / mass: com = tc / mass
Return
system:
 deltac = -y(1) * Kd - y(2) * Kr
 delta = deltac * Groot(iroot)
 alpha = y(1) + y(3) / vel
 yd(1) = y(2)
 yd(2) = mua * alpha + muc * delta
 yd(3) = -tom * y(1) - aom * alpha + com * delta
Return
matrix:
 If jA = 0 Then
     y(1) = ys(1) + stepd
 Else
   For i = 1 To N
     A(i, jA) = (yd(i) - yds(i)) / stepd
   Next i
     y(jA) = ys(jA)
   If jA < N Then
     y(jA + 1) = ys(jA + 1) + stepd
   End If
 End If
Return
End Sub
``` | • GoSub data<br><br>• For iroot = 1 To nroot<br>    • For jA = 0 To N<br><br>        • Compute $A = \dfrac{\partial \dot{Y}}{\partial Y}$<br><br>    • Next jA<br><br>    • Call eig<br><br>    •Print out each root in a separate column.<br><br>• Next iroot<br><br><br>•Note the changes to **data: … Return** compared to Example eig 5.<br><br><br>•Note the changes to **system: … Return** compared to Example eig 5.<br><br><br><br>• **matrix: … Return** |
| ```
Sub eig(N, A, WR, WI)
   See Appendix A.1 for listing.
End Sub
``` | |

Example eig 6(cont.):

The following are the results. The roots are printed in offset columns so that the points can be connected in a scatter chart.

Example eig 6 Results				
Groot	WR(i)	WI(i)		
		First Root	Second Root	Third Root
0.5	-0.49	0		
1	-0.14	0		
2	-0.09	0		
0.5	-0.36		0.96	
1	-1.12		2.18	
2	-2.31		3.22	
0.5	-0.36			-0.96
1	-1.12			-2.18
2	-2.31			-3.22

The eigenvalues for *Groot(2) = 1* match the results in Example eig 5.

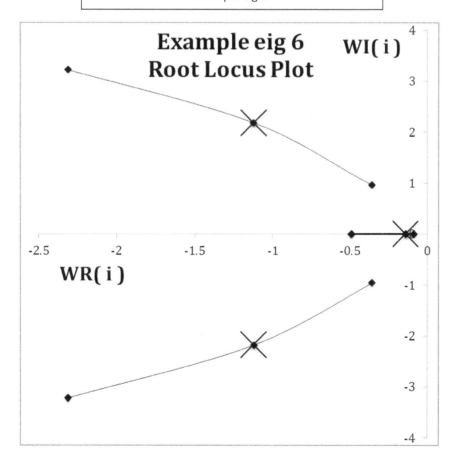

Example eig 7: In Example eig 4, eigenvalues were computed at a set point for this second-order nonlinear differential equation:

$$\ddot{x} = -0.1 * x^2 * \dot{x} - 4 * x$$

This example shows a program that changes this set point as the program loops. The following is the block diagram of the root-locus program for **Example eig 7.**

GoSub data	

For iroot = 1 To 3
  For jA = 0 To N
 	
    If jA = 0 Then
       Yo = Array(0, 4, 5)
       y(1) = Yo(iroot)
       y(2) = 0
       ys(1) = y(1)
       ys(2) = y(2)
    Endif
 	
    GoSub system
 	
Save $\dot{y}_1$ **and** $\dot{y}_2$
 	
    GoSub matrix
 	
  Next jA
 	
  Call eig
 	
  Printout
Next iroot
	• For each value of iroot , the set point changes.
	
	• In the **jA Loop** , the **A** matrix is computed.
	
	• Within this **If ... Then ... Endif**, the set point changes on each value of iroot.
	
	• **Call matrix** has been replaced by **Gosub matrix**.
	
	• The eigenvalues are computed in **Sub eig.**
	
	• Each root is printed in a separate column so as to become a series for the Scatter Chart.

data: ... Return	Compared to Example eig 4, the set point statements are moved inside the **iroot Loop**.
system: ... Return	Compared to Example eig 4, there are no changes.
matrix: ... Return	**Sub matrix** has been replaced by **matrix: ... Return** This change is cosmetic.

Example eig 7(cont.):

<table>
<tr><th colspan="2" style="text-align:center">Listing of Root Locus Program for Example eig 7</th></tr>
<tr><th>Code</th><th>Comments</th></tr>
<tr><td>

```
Option Base 1
Sub ex_eig_7_main()
Dim y(30), ys(30), yd(30), yds(30), A(30, 30), WR(30), WI(30)
GoSub data

For iroot = 1 To 3
  For jA = 0 To N
    If jA = 0 Then
       Yo = Array(0, 4, 5)
       y(1) = Yo(iroot): y(2) = 0
       ys(1) = y(1): ys(2) = y(2)
    End If
    GoSub system
    If jA = 0 Then
      For i = 1 To N
         yds(i) = yd(i)
      Next i
    End If
    GoSub matrix
  Next jA
  Call eig(N, A, WR, WI)
  For i = 1 To N
    aroot = iroot + i + (i - 1) * 3
    Cells(aroot, 1) = Application.Round(WR(i), 2)
    Cells(aroot, i + 1) = Application.Round(WI(i), 2)
  Next i
Next iroot

End
data:
  N = 2: stepd = 0.02
Return
system:
  yd(1) = y(2)
  yd(2) = -0.1 * y(1) ^ 2 * y(2) - 4 * y(1)
Return
matrix:
  If jA = 0 Then
      y(1) = ys(1) + stepd
  Else
    For i = 1 To N
      A(i, jA) = (yd(i) - yds(i)) / stepd
    Next i
      y(jA) = ys(jA)
    If jA < N Then
      y(jA + 1) = ys(jA + 1) + stepd
    End If
  End If
Return
End Sub
```

```
Sub eig(N, A, WR, WI)
    See Appendix A.1 for listing.
End Sub
```
</td><td>

- GoSub data

- For iroot = 1 To 3
    - For jA = 0 To N

        - Note the equations added for the set point.

        - Compute $A = \dfrac{\partial \dot{Y}}{\partial Y}$

    - Next jA

    - Call eig

    - Print out each root in a separate column.

- Next iroot

- Note the changes to **data: ... Return** compared to Example eig 4.

- There are no changes to **system: ... Return** compared to Example eig 4.

- **matrix: ... Return**
</td></tr>
</table>

113

Example eig 7(cont.):

The following are the results. The roots are printed in offset columns so that the points can be connected in a scatter chart.

Example eig 7 Results			
Y_O	WR(i)	WI(i)	
		First Root	Second Root
0	0	2	
4	-0.80	1.83	
5	-1.25	1.56	
0	0		-2
4	-0.80		-1.83
5	-1.25		-1.56

The eigenvalues for $Y_O(2) = 4$ match the results in Example eig 4.

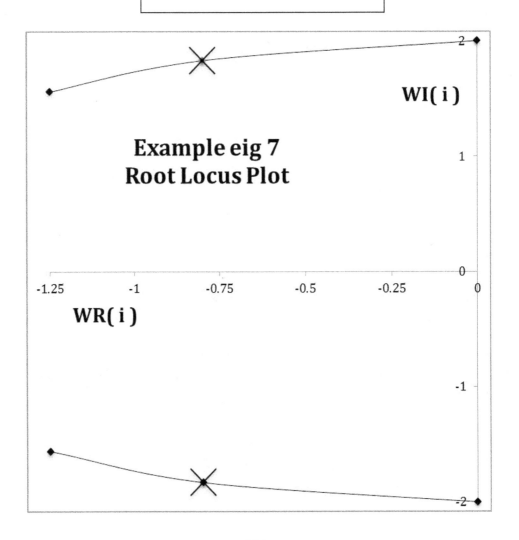

Chapter 16: Differential Equations Converted to State Variable Form

In the last chapter, a program was written to linearize equations in order to compute eigenvalues. In this chapter, this program will be expanded to generate a linear model suitable for computing transfer functions and frequency responses. Chapters 17 and 18 will use this model to compute output transfer functions and frequency responses.

As with the eigenvalue program, input to this program will be first-order nonlinear differential equations. These equations will include a single input and a single output. For illustration, we will use a system defined with one differential equation ($\dot{x}$ is a function of x and an input u):

$$\dot{x} = f_1(x , u)$$

And one output equation (z is a function of x and an input u):

$$z = f_2(x , u)$$

Each equation is expanded in a first-order Taylor series. The following notation is used:

$$\dot{y} = \dot{x} - \dot{x}_0, \quad y = x - x_0, \quad tf_{in} = u - u_0, \quad tf_{out} = z - z_0.$$

$$\dot{y} = \frac{\partial \dot{y}}{\partial y} y + \frac{\partial \dot{y}}{\partial tf_{in}} tf_{in}$$

$$tf_{out} = \frac{\partial tf_{out}}{\partial y} y + \frac{\partial tf_{out}}{\partial tf_{in}} tf_{in}$$

For an nth-order system:

$$
\begin{bmatrix} \dot{y}_1 \\ \bullet \\ \bullet \\ \dot{y}_n \end{bmatrix} =
\begin{bmatrix} \dfrac{\partial \dot{y}_1}{\partial y_1} & & \dfrac{\partial \dot{y}_1}{\partial y_n} \\ & \bullet & \\ & & \bullet \\ \dfrac{\partial \dot{y}_n}{\partial y_1} & & \dfrac{\partial \dot{y}_n}{\partial y_n} \end{bmatrix}
\begin{bmatrix} y_1 \\ \bullet \\ \bullet \\ y_n \end{bmatrix} +
\begin{bmatrix} \dfrac{\partial \dot{y}_1}{\partial tf_{in}} \\ \bullet \\ \bullet \\ \dfrac{\partial \dot{y}_n}{\partial tf_{in}} \end{bmatrix} * tf_{in}
$$

$$
tf_{out} = \begin{bmatrix} \dfrac{\partial tf_{out}}{\partial y_1} & \bullet & \bullet & \dfrac{\partial tf_{out}}{\partial y_n} \end{bmatrix}
\begin{bmatrix} y_1 \\ \bullet \\ \bullet \\ y_1 \end{bmatrix} +
\begin{bmatrix} \dfrac{\partial tf_{out}}{\partial tf_{in}} \end{bmatrix} * tf_{in}
$$

This is called the *state variable form* of the equations. **Y** is the state vector. It is generally written using the following notation:

$$\dot{y} = A * y + B * tf_{in}$$
$$tf_{out} = C * y + D * tf_{in}$$

The partial derivatives in the **ABCD** matrices will be estimated using the *method of finite differences*; they are summarized in the following table:

$A_{ij} = \dfrac{\partial \dot{y}_i}{\partial y_j} = \dfrac{\dot{y}_i - \dot{y}_{si}}{y_j - y_{sj}}$	$B_i = \dfrac{\partial \dot{y}_i}{\partial tf_{in}} = \dfrac{\dot{y}_i - \dot{y}_{si}}{tf_{in} - tf_{ins}}$
$C_j = \dfrac{\partial tf_{out}}{\partial y_j} = \dfrac{tf_{out} - tf_{outs}}{y_j - y_{sj}}$	$D = \dfrac{\partial tf_{out}}{\partial tf_{in}} = \dfrac{tf_{out} - tf_{outs}}{tf_{in} - tf_{ins}}$

The following table shows a block diagram of the program to compute the state variable form. As with previous chapters, this program will include the example problems right in the code. This will be done via the **GoSub** code fragments **data: ... Return** and **system: ... Return**.

Description of the Program to Compute the ABCD Matrices	
Description	**Code Fragments**
• GoSub data to read in $y_1 \rightarrow y_n$, tf_{in} and stepsize [stepd]	

• $jA = 0$ • GoSub system to compute $\dot{y}_1 \rightarrow \dot{y}_n$ and tf_{out}
    • save $(y_{s1} = y_1) \rightarrow (y_{sn} = y_n)$, $tf_{ins} = tf_{in}$
    and $(\dot{y}_{s1} = \dot{y}_1) \rightarrow (\dot{y}_{sn} = \dot{y}_n)$, $tf_{outs} = tf_{out}$
    • GoSub matrix to disturb $y_1 = y_{s1} + \textbf{stepd}$
	• GoSub data
	
	 • For $jA = 0$ To $n + 1$
	
	    • GoSub system

• $jA = 1$ • GoSub system to compute $\dot{y}_1 \rightarrow \dot{y}_n$ and tf_{out}
    • GoSub matrix to compute $\dfrac{\partial \dot{y}_1}{\partial y_1} \rightarrow \dfrac{\partial \dot{y}_n}{\partial y_1}$ and $\dfrac{\partial tf_{out}}{\partial y_1}$
     • reset $y_1 \rightarrow y_{s1}$ and disturb $y_2 = y_{s2} + \textbf{stepd}$
      •
      •
      •
      •
	• GoSub matrix
	
	 • Next jA
	
	 • End (to terminate)
	
	 • data: ... Return
	
	 • system: ... Return
	
	 • matrix: ... Return

• $jA = n$ • GoSub system to compute $\dot{y}_1 \rightarrow \dot{y}_n$ and tf_{out}
    • GoSub matrix to compute $\dfrac{\partial \dot{y}_1}{\partial y_n} \rightarrow \dfrac{\partial \dot{y}_n}{\partial y_n}$ and $\dfrac{\partial tf_{out}}{\partial y_n}$
     • reset $y_n \rightarrow y_{sn}$ and disturb $tf_{in} = tf_{ins} + \textbf{stepd}$	

• $jA = n + 1$ • GoSub system to compute $\dot{y}_1 \rightarrow \dot{y}_n$ and tf_{out}
    • GoSub matrix to compute $\dfrac{\partial \dot{y}_1}{\partial tf_{in}} \rightarrow \dfrac{\partial \dot{y}_n}{\partial tf_{in}}$ and $\dfrac{\partial tf_{out}}{\partial tf_{in}}$
     • reset $tf_{in} = tf_{ins}$	

The following is a listing of the code:

Program to Compute the ABCD State Variable Matrices	
Sub ABCD() Dim y(30), yd(30), ys(30), yds(30), A(30, 30), B(30), C(30) GoSub data	 ● **GoSub data** for the set point

For jA = 0 To N + 1
    If jA = 0 Then
      tfins = tfin
      For j = 1 To N
        ys(j) = y(j)
      Next j
    End If
    GoSub system
    If jA = 0 Then
      tfouts = tfout
      For i = 1 To N
        yds(i) = yd(i)
      Next i
    End If
    GoSub matrix
  Next jA
	● **For** *jA* = **0 to N + 1**
	
	  ● Save y_s and tf_{ins} on first pass.
	
	  ● **GoSub system** to compute $\dot{y}$ and tf_{out}
	
	  ● Save $\dot{y}_s$ and tf_{outs} on first pass.
	
	  ● **Call matrix** to compute the matrices.
	● **Next** *jA*

Cells(1, 1) = N
For i = 1 To N
  For j = 1 To N
    Cells(i + 1, j) = A(i, j)
  Next j
    Cells(i + 1, N + 2) = B(i): Cells(i + 1, N + 4) = C(i)
Next i
    Cells(2, N + 6) = D
End
	
	● Print out the matrices.
	
	● **End** to terminate the program.

data: N = 2: stepd = 0.02: y(1) = 4: y(2) = 0: tfin = 0 Return	● **data** for Example ABCD 1

system:
  u = tfin
  yd(1) = y(2)
  yd(2) = -0.1 * y(1) ^ 2 * y(2) - 4 * y(1) + u
  tfout = y(1)
Return
	
	● **system** for Example ABCD 1

matrix:
  If jA = 0 Then
    y(1) = ys(1) + stepd
  ElseIf jA <= N Then
    For i = 1 To N
      A(i, jA) = (yd(i) - yds(i)) / stepd
    Next i
    C(jA) = (tfout - tfouts) / stepd: y(jA) = ys(jA)
    If jA < N Then
      y(jA + 1) = ys(jA + 1) + stepd
    Else
      tfin = tfins + stepd
    End If
  Else
    For i = 1 To N
      B(i) = (yd(i) - yds(i)) / stepd
    Next i
      D = (tfout - tfouts) / stepd: tfin = tfins
  End If
Return
End Sub
	● First pass *jA* = **0**
	    ● Disturb y_1
	
	● Next **N** passes *jA* = **1 to N.**
	
	  ● Compute $A_{i,jA} = \dfrac{\partial \dot{y}}{\partial y}$ and $C_{jA} = \dfrac{\partial tf_{out}}{\partial y}$.
	  ● Reset y and disturb next y or tf_{in} if *jA* = N.
	
	● Last pass *jA* = **N + 1**
	
	  ● Compute $B_i = \dfrac{\partial \dot{y}}{\partial tf_{in}}$ and $D = \dfrac{\partial tf_{out}}{\partial tf_{in}}$.
	  ● Reset tf_{in}.

Example ABCD 1: Consider the second-order differential equation with nonlinear damping:

$$\ddot{x} = -0.1 * x^2 * \dot{x} - 4 * x + u$$

(*Note: This is the equation used in Example eig 4 and Example eig 7 of Chapter 15.*)

The task is to compute the ABCD matrices at the set point ($Y_1 = 4$ and $Y_2 = 0$).

To prepare this equation for **Program ABCD,** it must first be converted into first-order differential equations. By *letting* $Y_1 = x$, $Y_2 = \dot{x} = \dot{Y}_1$ and by *defining* u = tfin and tfout = x, these equations are listed as follows:

$$u = tfin$$
$$\dot{Y}_1 = Y_2$$
$$\dot{Y}_2 = -0.1 * Y_1^2 * Y_2 - 4 * Y_1 + u$$

And the output equation: $\qquad$ tfout $= Y_1$

These equations are put into the code segment **system: ... Return** of Program ABCD. The set point ($Y_1 = 4$ and $Y_2 = 0$) and the statement tfin = 0 are put into **data: ... Return.** The following table shows these statements as they appear in Program ABCD. The table also shows the resulting **A, B, C,** and **D** matrices.

Example ABCD 1 Input and Output		
data: N = 2: stepd = 0.02: y(1) = 4: y(2) = 0 tfin = 0 Return system: u = tfin yd(1) = y(2) yd(2) = -0.1 * y(1) ^ 2 * y(2) - 4 * y(1) + u tfout = y(1) Return	A Matrix	B Matrix
	$\begin{matrix} 0 & 1 \\ -4 & -1.6 \end{matrix}$	$\begin{matrix} 0 \\ 1 \end{matrix}$
	C Matrix	D Matrix
	$\begin{matrix} 1 & 0 \end{matrix}$	0

Note: The A Matrix agrees with Example eig 4 and Example eig 7.These **ABCD** matrices will be used in Chapters 17 and 18 to compute the transfer function and frequency response.The following table shows the *hand checks* of the matrices.

Example ABCD 1 Hand Check		
A Matrix		B Matrix
$\dfrac{\partial \dot{y}_1}{\partial y_1} = 0 \qquad \dfrac{\partial \dot{y}_1}{\partial y_2} = 1$		$\dfrac{\partial \dot{y}_1}{\partial tf_{in}} = 0$
$\dfrac{\partial \dot{y}_2}{\partial y_1} = -(0.2\,y_{10}y_{20} + 4) = -4 \qquad \dfrac{\partial \dot{y}_2}{\partial y_2} = -0.1y_{10}^2 = -1.6$		$\dfrac{\partial \dot{y}_2}{\partial tf_{in}} = 1$
C Matrix		D Matrix
$\dfrac{\partial tf_{out}}{\partial y_1} = 1 \qquad \dfrac{\partial tf_{out}}{\partial y_2} = 0$		$\dfrac{\partial tf_{out}}{\partial tf_{in}} = 0$

Example ABCD 2: This example computes the ABCD matrices for the following transfer function:

$$\frac{z}{u} = gain * \frac{s + W_n}{s + W_D}$$

To convert this to a first-order differential equation, cross multiply:

$$s\,z + W_D\,z = gain*s*u + gain*W_n*u$$

Gathering terms:

$$s\,z - gain*s*u = gain*W_n*u - W_D\,z$$

Continuing:

$$z - gain*u = \frac{1}{s}(gain*W_n*u - W_D\,z)$$

Because this transfer function has a zero, it's easier to proceed if this equation is put into block-diagram form:

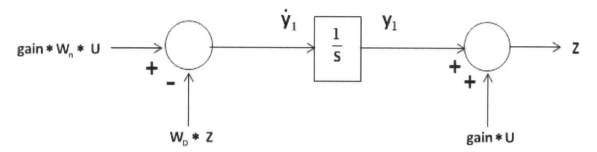

Since 1/S is the Laplace transform for integration, the input to 1/S can be defined as $\dot{y}_1$ and the output as y_1. From the block diagram:

$$\dot{y}_1 = gain*W_n*u - W_D\,z$$
$$z = y_1 + gain*u$$

The input equation is u = **tfin**, and the output equation is **tfout** = z. Summarizing:

$$u = tfin$$
$$z = y_1 + gain*u$$
$$\dot{y}_1 = gain*W_n*u - W_D\,z$$
$$tfout = z$$

These equations are now entered in the **system: … Return** code segment. The **data: … Return** code segment has the equations N = 1, $y_1 = 0$, and tfin = 0, along with values for gain, W_D, and W_n.

Example ABCD 2(cont.):

The following table shows these statements as they appear in **Program ABCD**. The table also shows the resulting ABCD matrices:

Example ABCD 2 Input and Output		
data:	A Matrix	B Matrix
N = 1: stepd = 0.02: y(1) = 0: tfin = 0 gain = 4: Wn = 2: Wd = 3 Return	-3	-4
system:		
u = tfin	C Matrix	D Matrix
z = y(1) + gain * u yd(1) = -Wd * z + gain * Wn * u tfout = z Return	1	4

These ABCD matrices will be used in Chapters 17 and 18 to compute the transfer function and frequency response for this example. The following table shows the *hand checks* of these matrices:

Example ABCD 2 Hand Check	
A Matrix	B Matrix
$\dfrac{\partial \dot{y}_1}{\partial y_1} = -W_D = -3$	$\dfrac{\partial \dot{y}_1}{\partial tf_{in}} = gain * (W_n - W_D) = -4$
C Matrix	D Matrix
$\dfrac{\partial tf_{out}}{\partial y_1} = 1$	$\dfrac{\partial tf_{out}}{\partial tf_{in}} = gain = 4$

Note: Because the input **u** is directly linked to the output **z**, the D Matrix is not equal to zero. That's the reason this example was selected.

Example ABCD 3: This example computes the ABCD matrices for the transfer function of a *damped-cosine* system:

$$\frac{z}{u} = \begin{bmatrix} \omega_n \\ \zeta \end{bmatrix} * \frac{(S + \zeta * \omega_n)}{(S^2 + 2 * \zeta * \omega_n * S + \omega_n^2)}$$

(***Note:*** *This transfer function was used in Example fresp 2 of Chapter 8.*)

To convert this to first-order differential equations, cross multiply.

$$s^2 * z + 2 * \zeta * \omega_n * s * z + \omega_n^2 * z = (\frac{\omega_n}{\zeta}) * s * u + \omega_n^2 * u$$

Gathering terms:

$$s^2 * z = s * (\frac{\omega_n}{\zeta} * u - 2 * \zeta * \omega_n * z) + \omega_n^2 * (u - z)$$

Continuing:

$$z = \frac{1}{s} * \left[\frac{\omega_n}{\zeta} * u - 2 * \zeta * \omega_n * z + \frac{1}{s} * \omega_n^2 * (u - z) \right]$$

Because this transfer function has a zero, it's easier to proceed if this equation is put into block-diagram form:

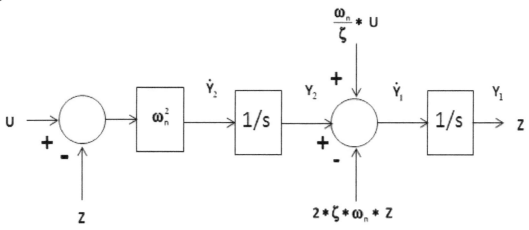

The inputs to the 1/S blocks can be defined as $\dot{y}_1$ and $\dot{y}_2$ and the outputs as y_1 and y_2.

From the block diagram:

$$\dot{y}_1 = y_2 - 2 * \zeta * \omega_n * y_1 + \frac{\omega_n}{\zeta} * u$$

$$\dot{y}_2 = \omega_n^2 * (u - y_1)$$

The input equation is u = tfin, and the output equation is tfout = y_1.

These equations are now entered in the **system: ... Return** code segment. The **data: ... Return** code segment has the equations N = 2, $y_1 = 0$, $y_2 = 0$, and tfin = 0, along with values for ζ and ω_n.

Example ABCD 3(cont.):

The following table shows these statements as they appear in **Program ABCD**. The table also shows the resulting ABCD matrices.

<table>
<tr><td colspan="3" align="center">Example ABCD 3 Input and Output</td></tr>
<tr><td></td><td align="center">A Matrix</td><td align="center">B Matrix</td></tr>
<tr>
<td>
data:
  N = 2: stepd = 0.02: y(1) = 0: y(2) = 0: tfin = 0
  zeta = 0.158: Wn = 12.65
Return
</td>
<td align="center">-3.997   1

-160.02   0</td>
<td align="center">80.06

160.02</td>
</tr>
<tr><td rowspan="2">system:
  u = tfin
  yd(1) = -2 * zeta * Wn * y(1) + y(2) + Wn * u / zeta
  yd(2) = -Wn ^ 2 * y(1) + Wn ^ 2 * u
  tfout = y(1)
Return</td><td align="center">C Matrix</td><td align="center">D Matrix</td></tr>
<tr><td align="center">1   0</td><td align="center">0</td></tr>
</table>

These ABCD matrices will be used in Chapters 17 and 18 to compute the transfer function and frequency response for this example. The following table shows the *hand checks* of these matrices.

<table>
<tr><td colspan="2" align="center">Example ABCD 3 Hand Check</td></tr>
<tr><td align="center">A Matrix</td><td align="center">B Matrix</td></tr>
<tr>
<td>

$\dfrac{\partial \ddot{y}_1}{\partial y_1} = -2\zeta\omega_n = -3.9974 \qquad \dfrac{\partial \ddot{y}_1}{\partial y_2} = 1$

$\dfrac{\partial \ddot{y}_2}{\partial y_1} = -\omega_n^2 = -160.0225 \qquad \dfrac{\partial \ddot{y}_2}{\partial y_2} = 0$

</td>
<td>

$\dfrac{\partial \ddot{y}_1}{\partial tf_{in}} = \dfrac{\omega_n}{\zeta} = 80.063$

$\dfrac{\partial \ddot{y}_2}{\partial tf_{in}} = \omega_n^2 = 160.0225$

</td>
</tr>
<tr><td align="center">C Matrix</td><td align="center">D Matrix</td></tr>
<tr>
<td>

$\dfrac{\partial tf_{out}}{\partial y_1} = 1 \qquad \dfrac{\partial tf_{out}}{\partial y_2} = 0$

</td>
<td>

$\dfrac{\partial tf_{out}}{\partial tf_{in}} = 0$

</td>
</tr>
</table>

Example ABCD 4: This example computes the ABCD matrices for the transfer function of a *damped-sine* system:

$$\frac{z}{u} = \frac{\omega_n^2}{(S^2 + 2 * \zeta * \omega_n * S + \omega_n^2)}$$

*(**Note:** This transfer function was plotted in Example fresp 1 of Chapter 8.
It is also the transfer function of the spring-mass-damper system of Chapter 12.)*

To convert this to first-order differential equations, cross multiply.

$$s^2 * z + 2 * \zeta * \omega_n * s * z + \omega_n^2 * z = \omega_n^2 * u$$

The *Inverse Laplace* transform is: $\ddot{z} + 2 * \zeta * \omega_n \dot{z} + \omega_n^2 z = \omega_n^2 u$

$$\ddot{z} = \omega_n^2 * (u - z) - 2 * \zeta * \omega_n \dot{z}$$

Let $y_1 = z$ and $y_2 = \dot{z}$. Substituting these yields two first-order differential equations:

$$\dot{y}_1 = y_2$$
$$\dot{y}_2 = \omega_n^2 * (u - y_1) - 2 * \zeta * \omega_n * y_2$$

To these, add an input equation, u = tfin, and an output equation, tfout = y_1.

These equations are now entered in the **system: ... Return** code segment. The **data: ... Return** code segment has the equations N = 2, y_1 = 0, y_2 = 0, and tfin = 0, along with values for ζ and ω_n.

The following table shows these statements as they appear in **Program ABCD**. The table also shows the resulting ABCD matrices.

Example ABCD 4 Input and Output		
	A Matrix	B Matrix

data:
  N = 2: stepd = 0.02: y(1) = 0: y(2) = 0: tfin = 0
  zeta = 0.158: Wn = 12.65
Return
system:
  u = tfin
  yd(1) = y(2)
	0 1
	
	-160.02 -3.997
		0
		
		160.02

yd(2) = -2 * zeta * Wn * y(2) + Wn ^ 2 * (u - y(1)) tfout = y(1) Return	C Matrix	D Matrix
	1 0	0

These ABCD matrices will be used in Chapters 17 and 18 to compute the transfer function and frequency response for this example. The following table shows the *hand checks* of these matrices:

Example ABCD 4(cont.):

Example ABCD 4 Hand Check			
A Matrix		**B Matrix**	
$\dfrac{\partial \dot{y}_1}{\partial y_1} = 0$	$\dfrac{\partial \dot{y}_1}{\partial y_2} = 1$	$\dfrac{\partial \dot{y}_1}{\partial tf_{in}} = 0$	
$\dfrac{\partial \dot{y}_2}{\partial y_1} = -\omega_n^2 = -160.0225$	$\dfrac{\partial \dot{y}_2}{\partial y_2} = -2\zeta\omega_n = -3.9974$	$\dfrac{\partial \dot{y}_2}{\partial tf_{in}} = \omega_n^2 = 160.0225$	
C Matrix		**D Matrix**	
$\dfrac{\partial tf_{out}}{\partial y_1} = 1$	$\dfrac{\partial tf_{out}}{\partial y_2} = 0$	$\dfrac{\partial tf_{out}}{\partial tf_{in}} = 0$	

Note: The transfer functions of Example ABCD 3 and Example ABCD 4 have the same denominator. But their **A** matrices are different. This can happen because state variables are chosen, not derived.

In other words, ABCD matrices are not unique. This is discussed further in Chapter 17 on Transfer Functions.

State Variables

Example ABCD 5: The launch vehicle math model of **Example eig 5** is shown in the following block diagram:

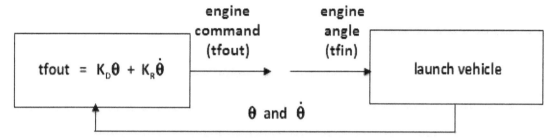

Eigenvalues were computed in **Example eig 5**. Note that the math model has no inputs or outputs.

To add an input and an output so that ABCD matrices can be computed, modify the math model:

The feedback loop has been opened, giving the math model an input (tfin) and an output (tfout). A state variable model of this system can now be computed.

The code segment **system: ... Return** used for Example eig 5 is modified to include tfin and tfout. The following table shows these modifications (*underlined*):

system: ... Return	
Equations	Constants
$tfout = K_D * Y_1 + K_R * Y_2$ alpha = Y_1 + Y_3 / Vel $\dot{Y}_1 = Y_2$ $\dot{Y}_2 = mua * alpha + muc * tfin$ $\dot{Y}_3 = -tom * Y_1 - aom * alpha + com * tfin$	mua = μ_α muc = μ_δ tom = (T-D) / m aom = L_α / m com = T_c / m

The code segment **data: ... Return** is modified by adding the equation tfin = 0 as an initial condition.

125

Example ABCD 5(cont.):

The following table shows all of these input equations and the results from **Program ABCD**:

Example ABCD 5 Input and Output		
	A Matrix	**B Matrix**
data: N = 3: stepd = 0.02: y(1) = 0: y(2) = 0: y(3) = 0: tfin = 0 vel = 1300: thr = 420000: tc = 340000: aero = 200000 mass = 5500: mua = 3.5: muc = 4.6: Kd = 2.1: Kr = 0.51 tom = thr / mass: aom = aero / mass: com = tc / mass Return system: tfout = Kd * y(1) + Kr * y(2) alpha = y(1) + y(3) / vel yd(1) = y(2) yd(2) = mua * alpha + muc * tfin yd(3) = -tom * y(1) - aom * alpha + com * tfin Return	$\begin{matrix} 0 & 1 & 0 \\ 3.5 & 0 & .0027 \\ -112.73 & 0 & -.028 \end{matrix}$	$\begin{matrix} 0 \\ 4.6 \\ 61.82 \end{matrix}$
	C Matrix	**D Matrix**
	2.1 .51 0	0

These ABCD matrices will be used in Chapters 17 and 18 to compute the *open-loop* transfer function and frequency response for this launch vehicle. The following table shows the *hand checks* of these matrices:

Example ABCD 5 Hand Check			
A Matrix			**B Matrix**
$\dfrac{\partial \ddot{y}_1}{\partial y_1} = 0$	$\dfrac{\partial \ddot{y}_1}{\partial y_2} = 1$	$\dfrac{\partial \ddot{y}_1}{\partial y_3} = 0$	$\dfrac{\partial \ddot{y}_1}{\partial tf_{in}} = 0$
$\dfrac{\partial \ddot{y}_2}{\partial y_1} = mua = 3.5$	$\dfrac{\partial \ddot{y}_2}{\partial y_2} = 0$	$\dfrac{\partial \ddot{y}_2}{\partial y_3} = \dfrac{mua}{vel} = .0027$	$\dfrac{\partial \ddot{y}_2}{\partial tf_{in}} = muc = 4.6$
$\dfrac{\partial \ddot{y}_3}{\partial y_1} = -(tom+aom) = -112.73$	$\dfrac{\partial \ddot{y}_3}{\partial y_2} = 0$	$\dfrac{\partial \ddot{y}_3}{\partial y_3} = -\dfrac{aom}{vel} = -.028$	$\dfrac{\partial \ddot{y}_3}{\partial tf_{in}} = com = 61.82$
C Matrix			**D Matrix**
$\dfrac{\partial tf_{out}}{\partial y_1} = K_D = 2.1$	$\dfrac{\partial tf_{out}}{\partial y_2} = K_R = .51$	$\dfrac{\partial tf_{out}}{\partial y_3} = 0$	$\dfrac{\partial tf_{iout}}{\partial tf_{in}} = 0$

Chapter 17: Transfer Functions Computed from the State Variable Form

In the last chapter, a program was written to transform differential equations into *State Variable Form*. In this chapter, a program will be written to compute the output transfer function from this form.

The following is this *State Variable Form*.

$$\dot{x} = A x + B u$$

$$y = C x + D u$$

In this chapter, **u** is a single input, and **y** is a single output. Take the Laplace transform of these equations using the notation $sX(s) = sX$, $Y(s) = Y$ and $U(s) = U$:

$$s X = A X + B U$$

$$Y = C X + D U$$

Since these are single-input, single-output equations, they can be put into the following matrix form:

$$\begin{bmatrix} (sI-A) & 0 \\ -C & 1 \end{bmatrix} \begin{bmatrix} (X/U) \\ (Y/U) \end{bmatrix} = \begin{bmatrix} B \\ D \end{bmatrix}$$

Using *Cramer's rule*, we can solve these equations for the transfer function (Y/U):

$$\frac{Y}{U} = \frac{\begin{vmatrix} (sI-A) & B \\ -C & D \end{vmatrix}}{\begin{vmatrix} (sI-A) & 0 \\ -C & 1 \end{vmatrix}} = \frac{(sI-A)D + BC}{(sI-A)} = [D]\frac{sI - (A - BCD^{-1})}{(sI-A)}$$

This is a ratio of two polynomials. The values of **S** for which the denominator is zero are called ***poles***. The values of **S** for which the numerator is zero are called ***zeros***. When the coefficients of the highest powers of **S** are unity, **D** is called the **Gain**.

The poles of the transfer function are the eigenvalues of the **A** matrix. The zeros of the transfer function are the eigenvalues of the $(A - BCD^{-1})$ matrix.

To demonstrate this, consider the following transfer function:

$$\frac{Y}{U} = [4]\frac{s+2}{s+3}$$

In **Example ABCD 2**, it was shown that $A = [-3]$, $B = [-4]$, $C = [1]$, and $D = [4]$.

- The pole of (Y/U) is the eigenvalue of **A**, which is -3.
- The zero of (Y/U) is the eigenvalue of $(A - BCD^{-1})$, which is (-3 + 4*1/4) = -2.
- The **Gain** of (Y/U) is **D**, which is 4.

This checks out. Now consider the following transfer function:

$$\frac{Y}{U} = [4] \, \frac{1}{s+3}$$

Here, $A = [-3]$, $B = [4]$, $C = [1]$, and $D = [0]$. Since D = 0, the formula for computing the zeros cannot be used. But what about using an *engineering approach* and letting D = 1.0E-6, which is almost zero? Now using the formula, we find that the zero is given by:

$$(A - BCD^{-1}) = (-3 - 4.0E6) \simeq -4.0E6.$$

Since the pole is at -3 and the Gain = D, the transfer function can be written:

$$\frac{Y}{U} = [1.0E\text{-}6] \, \frac{(s+4.0E6)}{(s+3)}$$

In the frequency region of interest, $(s + 4.0E6) \simeq 4.0E6$. Therefore:

$$\frac{Y}{U} = [1.0E\text{-}6] \, \frac{(4.0E6)}{(s+3)} = [4] \, \frac{1}{(s+3)}$$

This is correct. Hence, the *eigenvalue formulas* for computing a transfer function can still be used when D = 0, by approximating **D** with a *small* value. But how *small* is *small* ?

Using Eigenvalues to Compute Zeros When D = 0

To lay some groundwork for this discussion, let's take a look at the following:

$$s\,x = A\,x + B\,u$$

$$x = (s\,I - A)^{-1} B\,u$$

Since $y = C\,x$:

$$y = C\,(s\,I - A)^{-1} B\,u$$

The inverse of a matrix is its adjoint divided by its determinant. The transfer function is:

$$\frac{y}{u} = C \, \frac{adj(s\,I - A)}{|s\,I - A|} \, B$$

This is a ratio of polynomials:

$$\frac{y}{u} = C \, \frac{e_1 s^{k-1} + e_2 s^{k-2} + \bullet\bullet + e_k}{s^k + a_1 s^{k-1} + \bullet\bullet + a_k} \, B$$

Since D = 0, the number of zeros is less than the number of poles. If the number of zeros is exactly *one fewer* than the number of poles, and $e_1 = 1$, then:

$$\frac{y}{u} = C * B \, \frac{s^{k-1} + e'_2 s^{k-2} + \bullet\bullet + e'_k}{s^k + a_1 s^{k-1} + \bullet\bullet + a_k}$$

And: $C * B = c_1 b_1 + c_2 b_2 + \bullet\bullet + c_k b_k$ and is called the Gain of the transfer function.

128

We are looking for a transform that will change the numerator into the form of the *eigenvalue problem*. Let's call this transform the **T** matrix:

$$z = T x \quad \text{or} \quad x = T^{-1} z$$

This is the system equation:

$$\dot{x} = A x + B u$$

It becomes:

$$T^{-1} \dot{z} = A T^{-1} z + B u$$

If we multiply this equation by **T**, we preserve eigenvalues: $T T^{-1} \dot{z} = T A T^{-1} z + T B u$

Or:

$$\dot{z} = \alpha z + T B u \qquad \text{where } \alpha \text{ is similar to } \mathbf{A}.$$

The proof of the following is beyond the scope of this tutorial, but we will show that it works. We will start with the following case:

(the number of zeros) **equals** (the number of poles minus one)

Let's choose:

$$T = \begin{bmatrix} c_1 & c_2 & c_3 & \bullet & \bullet & c_k \\ & 1 & & & & \\ & & 1 & & & \\ & & & \bullet & & \\ & & & & \bullet & \\ & & & & & 1 \end{bmatrix}$$

Because **T** must be inverted, rows and columns of A might have to be interchanged so that $c_1 \neq 0$.

Then:

$$T * B = \begin{bmatrix} c_1 & c_2 & c_3 & \bullet & \bullet & c_k \\ 0 & 1 & 0 & & & 0 \\ 0 & 0 & 1 & & & 0 \\ & & & \bullet & & \\ & & & & \bullet & \\ & & & & & 1 \end{bmatrix} \begin{bmatrix} b_1 \\ b_2 \\ b_3 \\ \bullet \\ \bullet \\ b_k \end{bmatrix} = \begin{bmatrix} \text{Gain} \\ b_2 \\ b_3 \\ \bullet \\ \bullet \\ b_k \end{bmatrix}$$

So far, we have computed the **Gain**. Continuing:

$$\alpha = \begin{bmatrix} c_1 & c_2 & c_3 & \bullet & \bullet & c_k \\ 0 & 1 & 0 & & & 0 \\ 0 & 0 & 1 & & & 0 \\ & & & \bullet & & \\ & & & & \bullet & \\ & & & & & 1 \end{bmatrix} \begin{bmatrix} a_{11} & a_{12} & & & a_{1k} \\ a_{21} & \bullet & & & \\ & & \bullet & & \\ & & & \bullet & \\ & & & & \bullet \\ a_{k1} & & & & a_{kk} \end{bmatrix} \begin{bmatrix} \frac{1}{c_1} & \frac{-c_2}{c_1} & \frac{-c_3}{c_1} & \bullet & \bullet & \frac{-c_k}{c_1} \\ 0 & 1 & 0 & & & \\ 0 & 0 & 1 & & & \\ & & & \bullet & & \\ & & & & \bullet & \\ & & & & & 1 \end{bmatrix}$$

$$\alpha = \begin{bmatrix} \alpha_{11} & \alpha_{12} & & & & \alpha_{1k} \\ \alpha_{21} & \bullet & & & & \\ & & \bullet & & & \\ & & & \bullet & & \\ & & & & \bullet & \\ \alpha_{k1} & & & & & \alpha_{kk} \end{bmatrix}$$

Because of the choice for T, the following is true:

- Column 1 of α can be dropped.
- The eigenvalues of the following matrix are the **zeros** of the transfer function. The elements of this matrix are computed from the remaining columns of α and the $T*B$ matrix.

$$az = \begin{bmatrix} \alpha_{22} - b_2 \dfrac{\alpha_{12}}{\text{Gain}} & \alpha_{23} - b_2 \dfrac{\alpha_{13}}{\text{Gain}} & \bullet \quad \bullet & \alpha_{2k} - b_2 \dfrac{\alpha_{1k}}{\text{Gain}} \\ \alpha_{32} - b_3 \dfrac{\alpha_{12}}{\text{Gain}} & \alpha_{33} - b_3 \dfrac{\alpha_{13}}{\text{Gain}} & & \alpha_{3k} - b_3 \dfrac{\alpha_{1k}}{\text{Gain}} \\ \bullet & & & \\ \bullet & & & \\ \alpha_{k2} - b_k \dfrac{\alpha_{12}}{\text{Gain}} & \alpha_{k3} - b_k \dfrac{\alpha_{13}}{\text{Gain}} & & \alpha_{kk} - b_k \dfrac{\alpha_{1k}}{\text{Gain}} \end{bmatrix}$$

The following example will demonstrate this algorithm:

Example Zeros: This is a greatly simplified math model of a spacecraft with one bending mode:

$$[\dot{x}] = \begin{bmatrix} 0 & 0 & 0 \\ 0 & 0 & 1 \\ 0 & -400 & 0 \end{bmatrix} [x] + \begin{bmatrix} 5 \\ 0 \\ 230 \end{bmatrix} [u] \quad \text{and} \quad [y] = \begin{bmatrix} 1 & 0 & .01 \end{bmatrix} [x]$$

We will compute the zeros two ways.

Method one: Using the formula $C*adj(s\,I - A)*B$:

$$(s\,I - A) = \begin{bmatrix} s & 0 & 0 \\ 0 & s & -1 \\ 0 & 400 & s \end{bmatrix}$$

130

The cofactor matrix:

$$cof(s\,I - A) = \begin{bmatrix} + \begin{vmatrix} s & -1 \\ 400 & s \end{vmatrix} & - \begin{vmatrix} 0 & -1 \\ 0 & s \end{vmatrix} & + \begin{vmatrix} 0 & s \\ 0 & 400 \end{vmatrix} \\ - \begin{vmatrix} 0 & 0 \\ 400 & s \end{vmatrix} & + \begin{vmatrix} s & 0 \\ 0 & s \end{vmatrix} & - \begin{vmatrix} s & 0 \\ 0 & 400 \end{vmatrix} \\ + \begin{vmatrix} 0 & 0 \\ s & -1 \end{vmatrix} & - \begin{vmatrix} s & 0 \\ 0 & -1 \end{vmatrix} & + \begin{vmatrix} s & 0 \\ 0 & s \end{vmatrix} \end{bmatrix}$$

The adjoint matrix:

$$adj(s\,I - A) = \begin{bmatrix} s^2 + 400 & 0 & 0 \\ 0 & s^2 & s \\ 0 & -400s & s^2 \end{bmatrix}$$

Finally:

$$C * adj(s\,I - A) * B = 7.3\,(s + j\,16.55)\,(s - j\,16.55)$$

Method two: Computing the numerator using eigenvalues:

$$T = \begin{bmatrix} 1 & 0 & .01 \\ 0 & 1 & 0 \\ 0 & 0 & 1 \end{bmatrix}$$

$$T * B = \begin{bmatrix} 1 & 0 & .01 \\ 0 & 1 & 0 \\ 0 & 0 & 1 \end{bmatrix} \begin{bmatrix} 5 \\ 0 \\ 230 \end{bmatrix} = \begin{bmatrix} \text{Gain} = 7.3 \\ 0 \\ 230 \end{bmatrix}$$

The **Gain** has been verified. Continuing:

$$\alpha = T\,A\,T^{-1} = \begin{bmatrix} \alpha_{11} & \alpha_{12} & \alpha_{13} \\ \alpha_{21} & \alpha_{22} & \alpha_{23} \\ \alpha_{31} & \alpha_{32} & \alpha_{33} \end{bmatrix} = \begin{bmatrix} 0 & -4 & 0 \\ 0 & 0 & 1 \\ 0 & -400 & 0 \end{bmatrix}$$

Using the equations previously derived for the **az** matrix:

- $az_{11} = \alpha_{22} - b_2 \dfrac{\alpha_{12}}{\text{Gain}} = 0$ • $az_{12} = \alpha_{23} - b_2 \dfrac{\alpha_{13}}{\text{Gain}} = 1$

- $az_{21} = \alpha_{32} - b_3 \dfrac{\alpha_{12}}{\text{Gain}} = -274$ • $az_{22} = \alpha_{33} - b_3 \dfrac{\alpha_{13}}{\text{Gain}} = 0$

Finally: $az = \begin{bmatrix} 0 & 1 \\ -274 & 0 \end{bmatrix}$ from which $(s + j\,16.55)\,(s - j\,16.55)$

131

These are correct. We will now consider the following case:

(the number of zeros) **is less than** (the number of poles minus one)

For this case, $C*B = 0$. Since this is the first element of $T*B$, the first transformation is not enough. We must transform again. From the α matrix of the first pass, we *pull out* the **A** and **C** matrices to be used for the next pass.

$$
\alpha = \begin{bmatrix}
\alpha_{11} & \vdots & \alpha_{12} & \alpha_{13} & \bullet & \bullet & \alpha_{1k} \\
\alpha_{21} & \vdots & \alpha_{22} & \alpha_{23} & & & \alpha_{2k} \\
\alpha_{31} & \vdots & \alpha_{32} & \alpha_{33} & & & \\
\bullet & \vdots & & & \bullet & & \\
\bullet & \vdots & & & & \bullet & \\
\alpha_{k1} & \vdots & \alpha_{k2} & & & & \alpha_{kk}
\end{bmatrix}
$$

From which: $\quad A_{next} = \begin{bmatrix} \alpha_{22} & \alpha_{23} & & & \alpha_{2k} \\ \alpha_{32} & \alpha_{33} & & & \\ & & \bullet & & \\ & & & \bullet & \\ \alpha_{k2} & & & & \alpha_{kk} \end{bmatrix} \quad$ and $\quad C_{next} = \begin{bmatrix} \alpha_{12} & \alpha_{13} & \bullet & \bullet & \alpha_{1k} \end{bmatrix}$

Also: $\quad T*B = \begin{bmatrix} Gain \\ \hline b_2 \\ b_3 \\ \bullet \\ \bullet \\ b_k \end{bmatrix} \quad$ from which $\quad B_{next} = \begin{bmatrix} b_2 \\ b_3 \\ \bullet \\ \bullet \\ b_k \end{bmatrix}$

• Iterations reduce the size of α until $C*B \neq 0$. This indicates that zeros have been found. They are then computed from the resulting **az** matrix. The Gain is $C*B$.
• If a transfer function exists, and $C*B = 0$ when α is a 2x2 matrix, then the transfer function has no zeros. Its Gain is $\alpha_{12}*b_2$.
• This algorithm is implemented in **Program zeros** and is listed in **Appendix A.2**.

The following table lists **Program TF_main**, which does the following:

- reads the ABCD matrices from the spreadsheet
- calls Program zeros to compute transfer function zeros and the value of gain
- calls Program eig (same as in Chapter 15) to compute the poles

<table>
<tr><td colspan="2" align="center">Program TF_main</td></tr>
<tr><td align="center">Code</td><td align="center">Comments</td></tr>
<tr><td>

```
Option Base 1
Sub TF_main()
Dim Ain(30, 30), Bin(30), Cin(30), WR(30), WI(30)
N = Cells(1, 1)
For i = 1 To N
  For j = 1 To N
    Ain(i, j) = Cells(i + 1, j)
  Next j
    Bin(i) = Cells(i + 1, N + 2)
    Cin(i) = Cells(i + 1, N + 4)
Next i
    din = Cells(2, N + 6)
Call zeros(N, Ain, Bin, Cin, din, nz, gain, WR, WI)
If nz = 0 Then
    Cells(N + 5, 5) = " No Zeros"
    Cells(N + 6, 5) = " gain="
    Cells(N + 6, 6) = gain
Else
    Cells(N + 3, 1) = gain
  For i = 1 To nz
    Cells(N + 4 + i, 1) = Application.Round(WR(i), 2)
    Cells(N + 4 + i, 2) = Application.Round(WI(i), 2)
  Next i
End If
Call eig(N, Ain, WR, WI)
For i = 1 To N
  If nz > 0 Then
    Cells(N + 4 + nz + i, 1) = Application.Round(WR(i), 2)
    Cells(N + 4 + nz + i, 3) = Application.Round(WI(i), 2)
  Else
    Cells(N + 4 + 1 + i, 1) = Application.Round(WR(i), 2)
    Cells(N + 4 + 1 + i, 3) = Application.Round(WI(i), 2)
  End If
Next i
End Sub
```

</td><td>

• Read the **A**, **B**, **C** and **D** matrices.

• Call **Sub zeros**.

• **If nz = 0**, then there are no zeros.
  • Print out the **gain**.

• **If nz > 0**, then there are zeros.
  • Print out the **gain**.
  • Print out the **zeros**.

• Call **Sub eig**.

• Print out the **poles**.

</td></tr>
<tr><td>

```
Sub zeros(nmat, Ain, B, C, D, nz, gain, WR, WI)
    See Appendix A.2.
End Sub
```

</td><td>

• **Sub TF_main**, **Sub zeros**, and **Sub eig** are in the same **Code Window**.

</td></tr>
<tr><td>

```
Sub eig(N, A, WR, WI)
    See Appendix A.1.
End Sub
```

</td><td>

• If no transfer function exists, the program will stop in **Sub zeros**.

</td></tr>
</table>

Example tf 1: In Example ABCD 1 (Chapter 16), the ABCD matrices were computed for the following differential equation:

$$\ddot{x} = -0.1 * x^2 * \dot{x} - 4 * x + u$$

The set point is $x_0 = 4$ and $\dot{x}_0 = 0$. The task for this example is to compute the transfer function (x/u) from these matrices.

First, compute the transfer function manually. In Example ABCD 1, the following linear equation was derived:

$$\dot{y}_2 = -4 * y_1 - 1.6 * y_2 + u$$

Since $y_1 = x$, $y_2 = \dot{x}$ and $\dot{y}_2 = \ddot{x}$, the linear equation can be written as follows:

$$\ddot{x} = -4 * x - 1.6 * \dot{x} + u$$

Take the Laplace transform of this equation and rearrange to yield:

$$(s^2 + 1.6 * s + 4) x = u$$

$$\frac{x}{u} = \frac{1}{(s^2 + 1.6 * s + 4)} = \frac{1}{(s + 0.8 + j\,1.83)(s + 0.8 - j\,1.83)}$$

Now to use Program TF_main to compute the transfer function. The following table shows the ABCD matrices. The table also shows the resulting transfer function.

Example tf 1: Transfer Function of (x/u)					
A Matrix	B Matrix	Gain = 1.			
0 1 -4 -1.6	0 1	Numerator Roots		Denominator Roots	
		WR(i)	WI(i)	WR(i)	WI(i)
C Matrix	D Matrix	none	none	-0.8 -0.8	1.83 -1.83
1 0	0				
$\dfrac{\text{tfout}}{\text{tfin}} = \dfrac{x}{u} = [1.]\dfrac{1}{(s + 0.8 + j\,1.83)(s + 0.8 - j\,1.83)}$					

The transfer function checks out. **Note:** The denominator roots agree with the eigenvalues computed in Example eig4.

Example tf 2: In Example ABCD 2 (Chapter 16), the ABCD matrices were computed for the following transfer function:

$$\frac{z}{u} = gain * \frac{s + W_n}{s + W_D}$$

This transfer function has already been computed from its ABCD matrices in the introduction of this current chapter. The purpose here is to verify that the Program TF_main can also compute this transfer function. The following table shows these ABCD matrices and the resulting transfer function.

Example tf 2: Transfer Function of z/u					
A Matrix	B Matrix	Transfer Function Gain = 4			
-3	-4	Numerator Roots		Denominator Roots	
		WR(i)	WI(i)	WR(i)	WI(i)
C Matrix	D Matrix	-2	0	-3	0
1	4				
$$\frac{tfout}{tfin} = \frac{z}{u} = [4]\frac{(s+2)}{(s+3)}$$					

The program checks out.

Example tf 3: In Example ABCD 3 (Chapter 16), the ABCD matrices were computed for the following transfer function:

$$\frac{z}{u} = \begin{bmatrix} \omega_n \\ \zeta \end{bmatrix} * \frac{(S + \zeta * \omega_n)}{(S^2 + 2 * \zeta * \omega_n * S + \omega_n^2)}$$

(This transfer function is for a damped-cosine system and was used in Example fresp 2 of Chapter 8.)

The task for this example is to compute the transfer function from these **ABCD** matrices. The following table shows these matrices and the resulting transfer function:

Example tf 3: Transfer Function of (z / u)						
A Matrix		B Matrix	Transfer Function Gain = 80.06			
-3.997 1		80.06	Numerator Roots		Denominator Roots	
-160.02 0		160.02				
			WR(i)	WI(i)	WR(i)	WI(i)
C Matrix		D Matrix	-2	0	-2	12.49
1 0		0			-2	-12.49
$\dfrac{tfout}{tfin} = \dfrac{z}{u} = [80.06]\dfrac{(s+2)}{(s+2+j\,12.49)(s+2-j\,12.49)}$						

A *hand check* of this result follows. The following equation was derived in the introduction of this chapter, using *Cramer's rule*:

$$\frac{Z}{U} = \frac{\begin{vmatrix} (sI-A) & B \\ -C & D \end{vmatrix}}{\begin{vmatrix} (sI-A) & 0 \\ -C & 1 \end{vmatrix}}$$

The numerator:

$$\begin{vmatrix} (sI-A) & B \\ -C & D \end{vmatrix} = \begin{vmatrix} s+3.997 & -1 & 80.06 \\ 160.02 & s & 160.02 \\ -1 & 0 & 0 \end{vmatrix} = 80.06*(s+1.9988)$$

The denominator:

$$\begin{vmatrix} (sI-A) & 0 \\ -C & 1 \end{vmatrix} = \begin{vmatrix} s+3.997 & -1 & 0 \\ 160.02 & s & 0 \\ -1 & 0 & 1 \end{vmatrix} = (s+2+j\,12.49)*(s+2-j\,12.49)$$

The transfer function checks out.

Example tf 4: In Example ABCD 4 (Chapter 16), the ABCD matrices were computed for the following transfer function:

$$\frac{z}{u} = \frac{\omega_n^2}{(S^2 + 2*\zeta*\omega_n*S + \omega_n^2)}$$

[This transfer function is for a damped-sine system and was used in Example fresp 1 of Chapter 8.

This is also the transfer function of the spring-mass-damper system of Chapter 12.]

The task for this example is to compute the transfer function from these ABCD matrices. The following table shows these matrices and the resulting transfer function.

Example tf 4: Transfer Function of (z / u)				
A Matrix	B Matrix	Transfer Function Gain = 160.02		
0 1	0	Numerator Roots		Denominator Roots	
-160.02 -3.997	160.02	WR(i)	WI(i)	WR(i)	WI(i)
C Matrix	D Matrix	none	none	-2	12.49
1 0	0			-2	-12.49

$$\frac{tfout}{tfin} = \frac{z}{u} = [160.02]\frac{1}{(s+2+j\,12.49)(s+2-j\,12.49)}$$

A *hand check* of this result follows. The following equation was derived in the introduction of this chapter using Cramer's rule:

$$\frac{Z}{U} = \frac{\begin{vmatrix} (sI-A) & B \\ -C & D \end{vmatrix}}{\begin{vmatrix} (sI-A) & 0 \\ -C & 1 \end{vmatrix}}$$

The numerator: $\begin{vmatrix} (sI-A) & B \\ -C & D \end{vmatrix} = \begin{vmatrix} s & -1 & 0 \\ 160.02 & s+3.997 & 160.02 \\ -1 & 0 & 0 \end{vmatrix} = 160.02$

The denominator: $\begin{vmatrix} (sI-A) & 0 \\ -C & 1 \end{vmatrix} = \begin{vmatrix} s & -1 & 0 \\ 160.02 & s+3.997 & 0 \\ -1 & 0 & 1 \end{vmatrix} = (s+2+j\,12.49)*(s+2-j\,12.49)$

The transfer function checks out. **Note:** Example tf 3 and Example tf 4 point out again that ABCD matrices are not unique. The transfer functions of these examples have the same denominator. But their **A** matrices are different because state variables are chosen, not derived.

Example tf 5: In Example ABCD 5 (Chapter 16), the ABCD matrices were computed for a launch vehicle with the autopilot feedback loops open. The task of this example is to compute the open-loop transfer function from these matrices. The following table shows the ABCD matrices along with the resulting transfer function:

Example tf 5: Transfer Function of Engine Command Due to Engine Angle						
A Matrix			B Matrix	Transfer Function Gain = 2.346		
0 1 0			0	Numerator Roots		Denominator Roots	
3.5 0 2.69231E-3			4.6				
-112.72727 0 -2.7972E-2			61.82	WR(i)	WI(i)	WR(i)	WI(i)
C Matrix			D Matrix	-4.1176	0	-1.9134	0
				-0.0642	0	1.8266	0
2.1 0.51 0			0			0.0588	0

$$\frac{\text{tfout}}{\text{tfin}} = \frac{\text{engine command}}{\text{engine angle}} = [2.346]\frac{(s + 4.1176)(s + 0.0642)}{(s + 1.9134)(s - 1.8266)(s - 0.0588)}$$

Note that two of the denominator roots are unstable. They have positive real parts. That's typical for a launch vehicle during the time of flight when it's in the atmosphere. Its like an inverted pendulum.

The roots in the denominator of this transfer function are the eigenvalues of the **A** matrix. Eigenvalue checkout was covered in Chapter 15.

A Method to Check Out the Numerator of Example tf 5

The numerator was computed by Sub zeros. We will check out this program by computing the numerator from the closed-loop-root equation derived in the following figure.

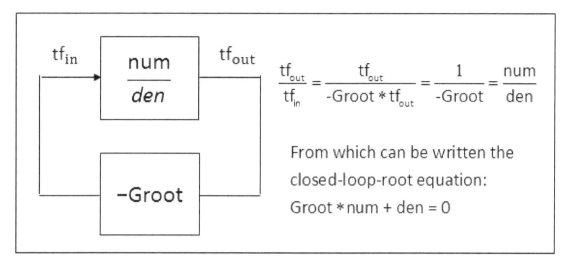

If Groot = Large (e.g., 1.e6), the closed-loop-root equation can be approximated by the following:

$$1.e6 * num \approx 0$$

Substitute the numerator (num) that was computed by Sub zeros:

$$1.e6 * [2.346] * (s + 4.1176)(s + 0.0642) \approx 0 \qquad Equation\ 1$$

Example eig 6 (Chapter 15) used the same launch vehicle math model that was used here in Example tf 5. In Example eig 6, the autopilot feedback loops were closed by setting the following:

engine angle = Groot * engine command

The closed-loop roots were derived for Groot = 0.5, 1, and 2. Rerunning that program with Groot = 1.e6, the roots are as follows:

$$(s + 2345995.8)(s + 4.1176)(s + 0.0642)$$

In the frequency region of interest, the term $(s + 2345995.8)$ can be treated as a gain $[2345995.8]$. Therefore, the roots can be written this way:

$$[2345995.8](s + 4.1176)(s + 0.0642)$$

Since this agrees with *Equation 1*, the numerator is checked out.

Chapter 18:
Frequency Response Computed from the State Variable Form

In Chapter 17, the ABCD state variable matrices were put into the following form:

$$\begin{bmatrix} (sI - A) & 0 \\ -C & 1 \end{bmatrix} \begin{bmatrix} x/u \\ y/u \end{bmatrix} = \begin{bmatrix} B \\ D \end{bmatrix}$$

The output transfer function was computed. In this chapter, a program will be written to compute the output frequency response.

At a particular frequency, the Laplacian variable is written $s_1 = j\,\omega_1$.

$$\begin{bmatrix} (j\omega_1 I - A) & 0 \\ -C & 1 \end{bmatrix} \begin{bmatrix} x/u \\ y/u \end{bmatrix} = \begin{bmatrix} B \\ D \end{bmatrix} \qquad \text{Equation one}$$

At this frequency, Equation one is a system of $n + 1$ equations and $n + 1$ unknowns. In this chapter, we are only interested in the single transfer function y/u.

Using the *three elementary row operations in linear algebra*, Equation one can be transformed into *upper triangular form*.

$$\begin{bmatrix} \times & \times & \times & \times \\ & \times & \times & \times \\ & & \times & \times \\ & & & 1 \end{bmatrix} \begin{bmatrix} x/u \\ \\ y/u \end{bmatrix} = \begin{bmatrix} \times \\ \times \\ \times \\ \boxed{} \end{bmatrix}$$

At $s_1 = j\,\omega_1$, the transfer function y/u has the complex value that is located in the matrix location marked with the rectangle. **Program fresp** in Appendix A.3 implements this transformation.

Equation one is input to Program fresp in the following form:

$$[\, \text{mat} + j\, \text{matw}\,] \begin{bmatrix} x/u \\ y/u \end{bmatrix} = [\text{real} + j\, \text{imag}] \qquad \text{Equation two}$$

The inputs to Equation two are the ABCD matrices and a desired frequency, $s_1 = j$ Win. The following table shows how the matrices mat, matw, real, and imag are formed.

The Matrices Input to Program fresp	
$$\left[\begin{bmatrix}-A & 0 \\ -C & 1\end{bmatrix} + j \begin{bmatrix}\omega_1 I & 0 \\ 0 & 0\end{bmatrix}\right]\begin{bmatrix}x/u \\ y/u\end{bmatrix} = \left[\begin{bmatrix}B \\ D\end{bmatrix} + j \begin{bmatrix}0 \\ 0\end{bmatrix}\right]$$	Equation one
$$\Big[\ [\text{mat}] + j\ [\text{matw}]\Big]\begin{bmatrix}x/u \\ y/u\end{bmatrix} = \Big[[\text{real}] + j\ [\text{imag}]\Big]$$	Equation two

$$\text{mat} = \begin{bmatrix} -A(1,1) & -A(1,2) & & & -A(1,n) & 0 \\ -A(2,1) & \bullet & & & & 0 \\ & & \bullet & & & \bullet \\ & & & \bullet & & \bullet \\ -A(n,1) & & & & -A(n,n) & 0 \\ -C(1,1) & -C(1,2) & \bullet & \bullet & -C(1,n) & 1 \end{bmatrix}$$

$$\text{matw} = \begin{bmatrix} \text{Win} & 0 & & & 0 & 0 \\ 0 & \text{Win} & & & & 0 \\ & & \bullet & & & \bullet \\ & & & \bullet & & \bullet \\ 0 & & & & \text{Win} & 0 \\ 0 & 0 & \bullet & \bullet & 0 & 0 \end{bmatrix}$$

$$\text{real} = \begin{bmatrix} B(1,1) \\ B(2,1) \\ \bullet \\ \bullet \\ B(n,1) \\ D \end{bmatrix} \qquad \text{imag} = \begin{bmatrix} 0 \\ 0 \\ \bullet \\ \bullet \\ 0 \\ 0 \end{bmatrix}$$

The following table shows a listing of Program FR_main, which does the following:
- reads the ABCD matrices from the spreadsheet
- forms the matrices mat, matw, real, and imag
- contains the array of the desired frequencies
- calls Program fresp
- prints out y/u at each desired frequency

Program FR_main

Program FR_main	
| ```
Option Base 1
Sub FR_main()
Dim Ain(30, 30), Bin(30), Cin(30), real(30), imag(30)
Dim mat(30, 30), matw(30, 30)
nomega = 24
omega = Array(0.1, 0.2, 0.5, 0.7, 1, 2, 3, 4, 5, 6, 7, 8, 9, _
        10, 11, 12, 13, 14, 15, 20, 30, 40, 60, 100)
N = Cells(1, 1)
For i = 1 To N
  For j = 1 To N
    Ain(i, j) = Cells(i + 1, j)
  Next j
    Bin(i) = Cells(i + 1, N + 2)
    Cin(i) = Cells(i + 1, N + 4)
Next i
    din = Cells(2, N + 6)
nsize = N + 1


For iomega = 1 To nomega

  Win = omega(iomega)
  For i = 1 To nsize
    For j = 1 To nsize
      matw(i, j) = 0
      mat(i, j) = 0
    Next j
      real(i) = 0
      imag(i) = 0
  Next i
  For i = 1 To N
    For j = 1 To N
      mat(i, j) = -Ain(i, j)
    Next j
      mat(nsize, i) = -Cin(i)
      real(i) = Bin(i)
      matw(i, i) = Win
  Next i
      mat(nsize, nsize) = 1
      real(nsize) = din
  Call fresp(mat, matw, real, imag, nsize)

  amp = Sqr(real(nsize) ^ 2 + imag(nsize) ^ 2)
  ampdb = 20 * Application.Log10(amp)
  phase = Application.Atan2(real(nsize), imag(nsize)) * 57.296
  If (imag(nsize) >= 0) Then
    phase = phase - 360
  End If
  frcol = Application.Max(N + 8, 11)
  Cells(iomega + 1, frcol) = Win
  Cells(iomega + 1, frcol + 1) = Application.Round(phase, 2)
  Cells(iomega + 1, frcol + 2) = Application.Round(ampdb, 2)
  Cells(iomega + 1, frcol + 3) = Application.Round(real(nsize), 2)
  Cells(iomega + 1, frcol + 4) = Application.Round(imag(nsize), 2)

Next iomega
End Sub
``` | • Frequencies at which the response is to be computed. Shown are those used in Example fr 1.<br><br><br><br>• Read in the **ABCD** matrices.<br><br><br><br><br><br>• **For each desired frequency**<br><br>  • **Win** = next value<br><br><br><br><br><br><br>• Form **Equation two**<br><br><br><br><br><br><br>• Call **fresp**<br><br>• amp = $\sqrt{\text{real( nsize )}^2 + \text{imag( nsize )}^2}$<br><br>• phase = $\tan^{-1}($ imag(nsize) / real(nsize) $) * 57.296$<br>  (For plotting, sometimes the value of of phase is adjusted 360 degrees.)<br><br>• Print out.<br><br>• **Next frequency** |
| ```
Sub fresp(A, Aw, B, Bw, nsize)

    See Appendix A.3

End Sub
``` | • Transform Equation two to *upper triangular form*:<br><br>$$\frac{y}{u} = B(\text{ nsize }) + j\, Bw(\text{ nsize })$$ |

Example fr 1: In Example ABCD 1 (Chapter 16), the ABCD matrices were computed for the following differential equation:

$$\ddot{x} = -0.1 * x^2 * \dot{x} - 4 * x + u$$

(*Note: This is the equation used in Example eig 4 and Example eig 7 of Chapter 15.*)

The set point is $x_0 = 4$ and $\dot{x}_0 = 0$. The task is to compute the frequency response from these matrices. The following table shows these matrices and the resulting frequency response:

Example fr 1: Frequency Response of x / u				
A Matrix	B Matrix	Frequency (rps)	Phase(deg)	Amp(db)
0 1 -4 -1.6	0 1	0.1 0.2 0.5 0.7	-2.3 -4.62 -12.04 -17.7	-12.03 -11.98 -11.67 -11.33
C Matrix	D Matrix	• • •	• • •	• • •
1 0	0	30 40 60 100	-176.93 -177.7 -178.47 -179.08	-59.06 -64.07 -71.12 -80
The desired frequencies listed in Program FR_main are as follows: nomega = 24, omega = Array(0.1, 0.2, 0.5, 0.7, 1, 2, 3, 4, 5, 6, 7, 8, 9, 10, 11, 12, 13, 14, 15, 20, 30, 40, 60, 100).				

The following scatter charts are called **Bode plots**. These are semilog plots of the amplitude in decibels and phase in degrees versus frequency in radians per second. The response is that of an underdamped second order.

Note: By selecting the phase(deg) column for the x-axis and the amp(db) column for the y-axis, we will create a **Nichols plot**. (It is not shown.)

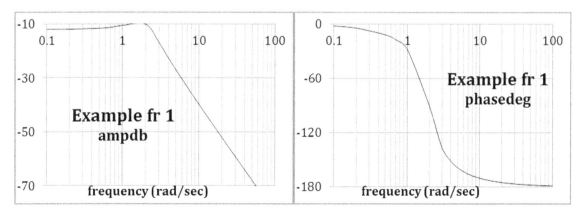

143

Example fr 2: In Example ABCD 2 (Chapter 16), the ABCD matrices were computed for the following transfer function:

$$\frac{z}{u} = gain * \frac{s + W_n}{s + W_D}$$

The task of this example is to compute the frequency response from these matrices. The following table shows these ABCD matrices and the resulting frequency response:

Example fr 2: Frequency Response of z/u				
A Matrix	B Matrix	Frequency (Rad/Sec)	Phase(deg)	Amp(db)
		0.1	0.95	8.53
		0.2	1.9	8.54
		0.5	4.57	8.66
-3	-4	0.7	6.16	8.79
		•	•	•
		•	•	•
C Matrix	D Matrix	•	•	•
		30	1.9	12.02
		40	1.43	12.03
1	4	60	0.95	12.04
		100	0.57	12.04
The desired frequencies listed in Program FR_main are as follows: nomega = 24, omega = Array(0.1, 0.2, 0.5, 0.7, 1, 2, 3, 4, 5, 6, 7, 8, 9, 10, 11, 12, 13, 14, 15, 20, 30, 40, 60, 100).				

The following charts are the **Bode plots** of this frequency response.

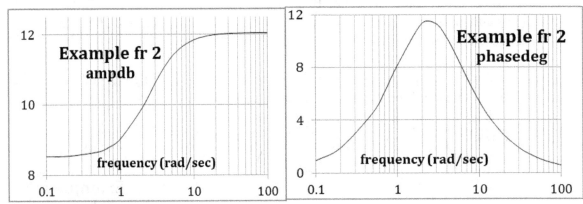

Example fr 3: In Example ABCD 3 (Chapter 16), the ABCD matrices were computed for the following transfer function:

$$\frac{z}{u} = \begin{bmatrix} \omega_n \\ \zeta \end{bmatrix} * \frac{(S + \zeta * \omega_n)}{(S^2 + 2 * \zeta * \omega_n * S + \omega_n^2)}$$

(***Note:*** *This transfer function is for a damped-cosine system and was used in Example fresp 2 of Chapter 8.*)

The task for this example is to compute the frequency response from these ABCD matrices. The following table shows these matrices and the resulting frequency response:

Example fr 3: Frequency Response of z/u				
A Matrix		B Matrix	Frequency (rps)	Phase(deg)	Amp(db)
-3.997　　1		80.06	0.1	2.72	0.01
-160.02　　0		160.02	0.2	5.43	0.05
			0.5	13.33	0.28
			0.7	18.3	0.53
C Matrix		D Matrix	•	•	•
			•	•	•
1　　0		0	•	•	•
			30	-84.61	10.13
			40	-86.52	6.9
			60	-87.92	2.88
			100	-88.82	-1.8
The desired frequencies listed in Program FR_main are as follows: nomega = 24, omega = Array(0.1, 0.2, 0.5, 0.7, 1, 2, 3, 4, 5, 6, 7, 8, 9, 10, 11, 12, 13, 14, 15, 20, 30, 40, 60, 100).					

The following charts are the Bode plots of this frequency response. They agree with those in Example fresp 2 of Chapter 8.

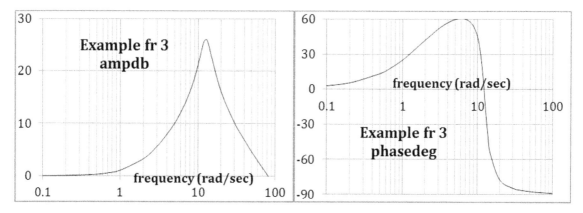

Example fr 4: In Example ABCD 4 (Chapter 16), the ABCD matrices were computed for the following transfer function:

$$\frac{z}{u} = \frac{\omega_n^2}{(S^2 + 2*\zeta*\omega_n*S + \omega_n^2)}$$

(This transfer function is for a damped-sine system and was used in Example fresp 1 of Chapter 8. It is also the transfer function of the spring-mass-damper system of Chapter 12.)

The task for this example is to compute the frequency response from these ABCD matrices. The following table shows these matrices and the resulting frequency response:

Example fr 4: Frequency Response of z/u				
A Matrix	B Matrix	Frequency (rps)	Phase(deg)	Amp(db)
0　　　1 -160.02　　-3.997	0 160.02	0.1 0.2 0.5 0.7 • •	-0.14 -0.29 -0.72 -1 • •	0 0 0.01 0.03 • •
C Matrix	D Matrix	•	•	•
1　　　0	0	30 40 60 100	-170.8 -173.66 -176.01 -177.67	-13.41 -19.14 -26.67 -35.78
The desired frequencies listed in Program FR_main are as follows: nomega = 24, omega = Array(0.1, 0.2, 0.5, 0.7, 1, 2, 3, 4, 5, 6, 7, 8, 9, 10, 11, 12, 13, 14, 15, 20, 30, 40, 60, 100).				

The following charts are the Bode plots of this frequency response. They are the same as those in Example fresp 1 of Chapter 8.

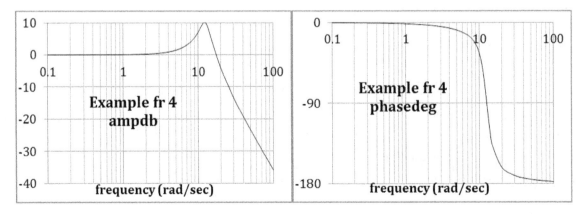

Example fr 5: In Example ABCD 5 (Chapter 16), the ABCD matrices were computed for a launch vehicle with the autopilot feedback loops open. The task of this example is to compute the open-loop frequency response from these matrices. The following table shows the ABCD matrices along with the resulting frequency response.

Example fr 5: Frequency Response of Engine Command Due to Engine Angle					
A Matrix			B Matrix	Frequency (rps)	Real Part	Imaginary Part

A Matrix	B Matrix	Frequency (rps)	Real Part	Imaginary Part
0 1 0 3.5 0 .0027 -112.73 0 -.028	0 4.6 61.82	0.01 0.02 0.03 0.04 • • •	2.85 2.41 1.8 1.16 • • •	0.96 1.78 2.35 2.7 • • •
C Matrix	**D Matrix**			
2.1 .51 0	0	3 8 15 20	-0.78 -0.14 -0.04 -0.02	-0.55 -0.28 -0.15 -0.12

The desired frequencies listed in Program FR_main are as follows: nomega = 21, omega = Array(0.01, 0.02, 0.03, 0.04, 0.05, 0.06, 0.08, 0.09, 0.11, 0.13, 0.16, 0.2, 0.3, 0.5, 1, 1.5, 2, 3, 8, 15, 20).

This frequency response is plotted below as a **Nyquist plot**. It compares exactly to Example fresp 3 in Chapter 8 which was computed using the transfer function in Example tf 5.

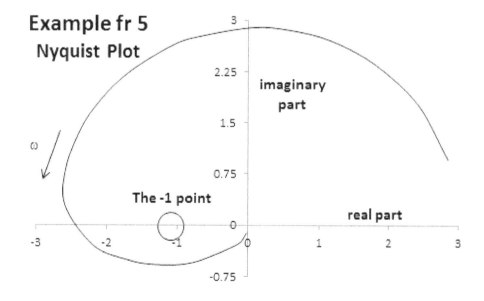

The **Nyquist** plot is used in flight control system stability analyses. D'Azzo[◊] derives and explains the theory behind this plot. The following is a short discussion of this theory, included for interest.

The **ABCD** matrices for this example were computed for a *feedback system* with the *feedback loop* open. Hence, they describe an *open-loop* transfer function. It has two unstable poles (see **Example tf 5**). The **Nyquist Stability Criterion** says that for this system to be *closed-loop stable*, the *open-loop* frequency response must encircle the *minus-one point*, two times in the *counterclockwise* direction as frequency varies from minus infinity to plus infinity.

The above plot is for the positive frequencies. It encircles the *minus-one point*, one time in the *counterclockwise* direction. There is another *counterclockwise* encirclement from the negative frequencies. Hence, with two *counterclockwise* encirclements, the system is *closed-loop* stable. This is verified by the eigenvalues of **Example eig 5**, which are all stable.

[◊] D'Azzo, J., and C. Houpis. *Linear Control System Analysis and Design.* McGraw-Hill, 1988.

Chapter 19: The Simplex Method of Optimization

The *Linear Programming Problem* is defined in the following table.

Given the constant matrices (a, b, and c), find values for x_j for j = 1 to N, that:
• yield the maximum value of: $\qquad$ objective $= \displaystyle\sum_{j=1}^{N} c_j x_j$
• subject to the linear constraints: $\qquad \displaystyle\sum_{j=1}^{N} a_{i,j} x_j \begin{Bmatrix} \le \\ = \\ \ge \end{Bmatrix} b_i \qquad$ for $i = 1$ to L
• and all: $\qquad\qquad\qquad\qquad\qquad\qquad x_j \ge 0$
Note: To minimize a function, maximize its negative.

Dantzig[*] devised the Simplex algorithm to find the solution. Appendix A.4 contains a VBA code of his method. This chapter writes a program that *calls* this code.

The following figure shows a system of linear constraints.

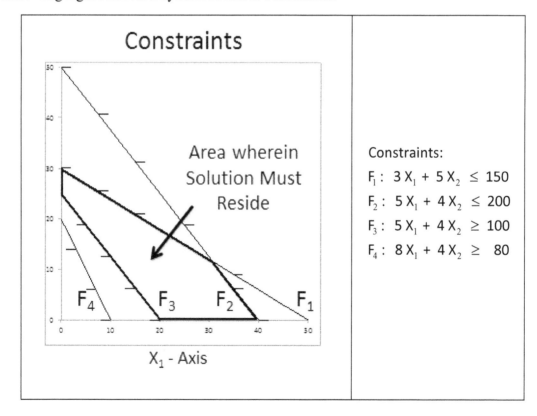

Constraints:

$F_1 :\ 3X_1 + 5X_2 \le 150$

$F_2 :\ 5X_1 + 4X_2 \le 200$

$F_3 :\ 5X_1 + 4X_2 \ge 100$

$F_4 :\ 8X_1 + 4X_2 \ge 80$

---

[*] Dantzig, G. *Linear Programing and Extensions*. Princeton University Press, 1963.

The following figure shows an objective function plotted with the same constraints:

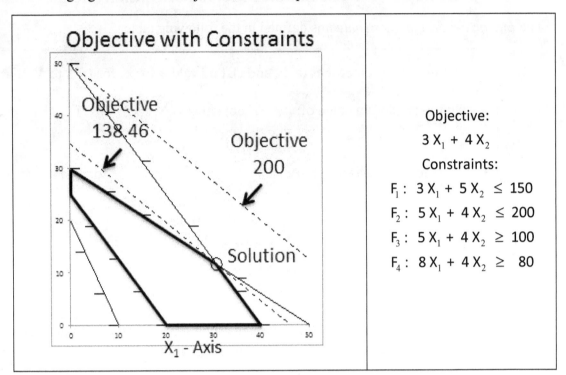

The figure, at right:

Objective:

$$3\,X_1 + 4\,X_2$$

Constraints:

$F_1 : \;\; 3\,X_1 + 5\,X_2 \;\le\; 150$

$F_2 : \;\; 5\,X_1 + 4\,X_2 \;\le\; 200$

$F_3 : \;\; 5\,X_1 + 4\,X_2 \;\ge\; 100$

$F_4 : \;\; 8\,X_1 + 4\,X_2 \;\ge\; \;\; 80$

Because **objective** is linear and because it *sweeps across* the allowed area as it increases in value, the solution must exist at a vertex. Dantzig's Simplex algorithm starts with all values equal to zero and goes in a series of steps, from vertex to vertex, with each step in the direction to increase **objective**.

The spreadsheet input for the program is now described.

- **objective** is to be *maximized*.
- All constraint constants (b_i) must be ≥ 0. (This may require some constraint equations to be multiplied by *minus one.*)
- The constraints must be input in the following order: K1 *less-than-or-equal-to* constraints, K2 *equality* constraints, and K3 *greater-than-or-equal-to* constraints.

Spreadsheet Input Template for Program simp_main							
	Column 1	Column 2	Column 3	Column 4			
Row 1	N	K1	K2	K3			
Row 2							
Row 3		c_1	c_2	•	•	•	c_N
Row 4	b_1	$a_{1\,1}$	$a_{1\,2}$				$a_{1\,N}$
•	b_2	$a_{2\,1}$	$a_{2\,2}$	•			
•	•				•		
•	•					•	
•	b_L	$a_{L\,1}$					$a_{L\,N}$

The following table is a listing of the program:

Program simp_main	
``Sub simp_main()
' maximize objective function of N variables
' subject to matrix of constraint equations (K1+K2+K3)
' important: b(i) must be >= zero
' constraints must be in following order: K1 <= constraints
'   K2 = constraints
'   K3 >= constraints
Dim x(20), f(20), bin(20, 21), cin(21, 1), a(20, 20), b(20), c(20)
Dim i, j, L, N, K1, K2, K3, object
N = Cells(1, 1)
K1 = Cells(1, 2)
K2 = Cells(1, 3)
K3 = Cells(1, 4)
L = K1 + K2 + K3
For j = 1 To N
  For i = 1 To L
    a(i, j) = Cells(i + 3, j + 1)
    b(i) = Cells(i + 3, 1)
  Next i
    c(j) = Cells(3, j + 1)
Next j
For j = 1 To N
  For i = 1 To L
    bin(i, 1) = b(i)
    bin(i, j + 1) = a(i, j)
  Next i
    cin(j + 1, 1) = c(j)
Next j
    cin(1, 1) = 0

Call simplex(bin, cin, x, L, K1, K2, K3, N)

  For i = 1 To L
    f(i) = 0
    For j = 1 To N
      f(i) = f(i) + a(i, j) * x(j)
    Next j
  Next i
    object = 0
For j = 1 To N
    object = object + c(j) * x(j)
Next j

    Cells(L + 5 + 1, 3) = object
For i = 1 To N
    Cells(L + 5 + i, 1) = x(i)
Next i
For i = 1 To L
    Cells(L + 5 + i, 5) = f(i)
Next i
Cells(L + 5, 1) = " variables": Cells(L + 5, 3) = " objective"
Cells(L + 5, 5) = "constraints"
End Sub``` | • Read in: • **N** is the number of variables.

     • **K1** is the number of $\leq$ constraints.
     • **K2** is the number of = constraints.
     • **K3** is the number of $\geq$ constraints.

• Read in the **a**, **b**, and **c** matrices.

• Convert these to inputs for **Sub Simplex**.

• Call **Sub Simplex**.

• Compute the final value of the objective and constants of the constraint equations.

• Print out. |
| ```Sub simplex(bin, cin, x, L, K1, K2, K3, N)

  See Appendix A.4

End Sub``` | • VBA code of Dantzig's *simplex algorithm* |

Example simp 1: The problem that was previously plotted is input to Program simp_main:

Maximize the objective: $3\,X_1 + 4\,X_2$

Subject to the constraints:

$$F_1: \ 3\,X_1 + 5\,X_2 \ \le \ 150$$
$$F_2: \ 5\,X_1 + 4\,X_2 \ \le \ 200$$
$$F_3: \ 5\,X_1 + 4\,X_2 \ \ge \ 100$$
$$F_4: \ 8\,X_1 + 4\,X_2 \ \ge \ 80$$

The following table shows this input and the results. The results agree with the plot.

Example simp 1: Input and Results						
2	2	0	2	Variables	Objective	Constraints
				30.77	138.46	
	3	4		11.54		
150	3	5				150
200	5	4				200
100	5	4				200
80	8	4				292.31

Example simp 2: A constraint to make $X_1 = X_2$ is added to the above example. The following figure shows the graphical solution:

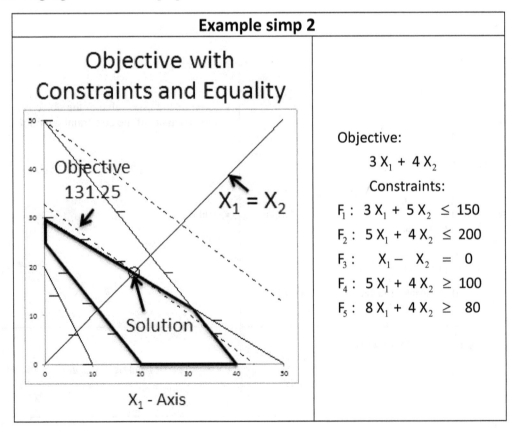

Example simp 2

Objective with Constraints and Equality

Objective 131.25

$X_1 = X_2$

Solution

X_1 - Axis

Objective:

$$3\,X_1 + 4\,X_2$$

Constraints:

$$F_1: \ 3\,X_1 + 5\,X_2 \ \le \ 150$$
$$F_2: \ 5\,X_1 + 4\,X_2 \ \le \ 200$$
$$F_3: \ \ X_1 - \ X_2 \ = \ 0$$
$$F_4: \ 5\,X_1 + 4\,X_2 \ \ge \ 100$$
$$F_5: \ 8\,X_1 + 4\,X_2 \ \ge \ 80$$

This example is input to Program simp_main. The following table shows the input and the results:

Example simp 2: Input and Results						
2	2	1	2	Variables	Objective	Constraints
				18.75	131.25	
	3	4		18.75		
150	3	5				150
200	5	4				168.75
0	1	-1				0
100	5	4				168.75
80	8	4				225

The results agree with the plot.

Solving Linear Equality Equations

The Simplex algorithm can also be used to solve the standard *System of Linear Equality Equations* (**n** *equations* and **n** *unknowns*). To do this, **objective** simply contains zeros. The following examples illustrate this:

Example simp 3: In Chapter 5, the following system of equations was solved in Program lineq 1:

$$x_1 - x_2 + 3x_3 = 4$$
$$x_1 + 2x_2 - 2x_3 = 10$$
$$3x_1 - x_2 + 5x_3 = 14$$

The solution is $x_1 = 2$, $x_2 = 7$, $x_3 = 3$. The following table shows how this problem was input to Program simp_main. The table also shows the results that are correct.

Example simp 3: Input and Results						
3	0	3	0	Variables	Objective	Constraints
				2		
	0	0	0	7	0	
4	1	-1	3	3		4
10	1	2	-2			10
14	3	-1	5			14

Example simp 4: In Chapter 5, the following system of equations was solved in **Program lineq 2:**

$$\begin{bmatrix} 1 & 1/2 & 1/3 \\ 1/2 & 1/3 & 1/4 \\ 1/3 & 1/4 & 1/5 \end{bmatrix}\begin{bmatrix} x_1 \\ x_2 \\ x_3 \end{bmatrix} = \begin{bmatrix} 1 \\ 1 \\ 1 \end{bmatrix}$$

The solution is $x_1 = 3$, $x_2 = -24$, $x_3 = 30$. The following table shows how this problem was input to Program simp_main. The table shows that **no solution exists**.

Example simp 4: Input and Results						
3	0	3	0	Variables	Objective	Constraints
	0	0	0			
1	1	1/2	1/3		No Solution	
1	1/2	1/3	1/4			
1	1/3	1/4	1/5			

The reason for **no solution** is that $x_2 = -24$, and the Simplex algorithm requires that all $x_j \geq 0$. The way to handle this is to bias the variables. Let

$$y_1 = x_1 + 100 \, , \; y_2 = x_2 + 100 \, , \; y_3 = x_3 + 100$$

The transformed problem becomes this:

$$\begin{bmatrix} 1 & 1/2 & 1/3 \\ 1/2 & 1/3 & 1/4 \\ 1/3 & 1/4 & 1/5 \end{bmatrix}\begin{bmatrix} y_1 \\ y_2 \\ y_3 \end{bmatrix} = \begin{bmatrix} 184 + 1/3 \\ 109 + 1/3 \\ 79 + 1/3 \end{bmatrix}$$

The following table shows how this problem was input to **Program simp_main**. The table shows that the answer to the transformed problem is $y_1 = 103$, $y_2 = 76$, $y_3 = 130$.

Example simp 4 transformed: Input and Results						
3	0	3	0	Variables	Objective	Constraints
				103		
	0	0	0	76	0	
184+1/3	1	1/2	1/3	130		184+1/3
109+1/3	1/2	1/3	1/4			109+1/3
79+1/3	1/3	1/4	1/5			79+1/3

The original variables are $x_1 = 103 - 100 = 3$, $x_2 = 76 - 100 = -24$, $x_3 = 130 - 100 = 30$, and the problem is correctly solved.

Chapter 20: The Discrete Fourier Transform

The *discrete Fourier transform* (DFT) is the digital implementation of the *continuous Fourier transform* (CFT). This chapter presents an example showing this. The equations for the DFT are derived in each of the following books:

- Brigham, E. *The Fast Fourier Transform*. Prentice-Hall, 1974.
- Stearns, S. *Digital Signal Analysis.* Hayden Book Co., 1975.
- Matthews, J., and K. Fink. *Numerical Methods Using MATLAB*. Prentice-Hall, 2004.

Given N equally spaced points (x_k), the DFT of these points is as follows:

$$F_n = \frac{1}{N} \sum_{k=0}^{N-1} x_k e^{-j2\pi\frac{n}{N}k} \qquad \text{for } n = 0, 1, \ldots, N-1$$

The DFT can be looked on as the correlation of x_k with the rotating unit phasor:

$$e^{-j\theta} = \cos\theta - j\sin\theta \qquad \text{where } \theta = 2\pi\frac{n}{N}k$$

Substituting this, the DFT can be written in rectangular form:

$$F_n = A_n + j B_n \qquad \text{for } n = 0, 1, \ldots, N-1$$

$$\text{where:} \quad A_n = \frac{1}{N}\sum_{k=0}^{N-1} x_k \cos(2\pi\frac{n}{N}k) \quad \text{and} \quad B_n = \frac{-1}{N}\sum_{k=0}^{N-1} x_k \sin(2\pi\frac{n}{N}k)$$

The DFT can also be described using *amplitude* and *phase vs. frequency*. Corresponding to each value of n, there is a frequency:

$$\omega = 2\pi\frac{n}{\text{Period}}$$

There is also an amplitude (decibels) and phase (degrees):

$$\text{ampdb} = 20 * \text{Log}_{10}(\sqrt{A_n^2 + B_n^2}) \quad \text{and} \quad \text{phase} = \tan^{-1}(B_n/A_n) * 57.296$$

We now make several comments about the DFT:

- The DFT is applicable to aperiodic as well as periodic signals.

- The highest-frequency component in the signal must be sampled *more than twice per cycle*. At this rate, all of its points will be obtained after a finite number of cycles.

- For an aperiodic signal, the samples must cover the *significant nonzero* portions of the signal.

A program to compute the DFT is listed in the following table. Because of sampling, the DFT can be compared to the CFT only at frequencies below the *Nyquist frequency*. This frequency is *one-half of the sampling frequency*, or **N / 2**. (See the references for proof of this.)

Program DFT	

``
Sub DFT()
Dim x(200)
  Ns = Cells(1, 1): Period = Cells(2, 1)
  pie = 4 * Atn(1): Q = 2 * pie / Ns
For k = 0 To (Ns - 1)
  x(k) = Cells(k + 1, 3)
  Cells(k + 1, 4) = k
  Cells(k + 1, 5) = Application.Round(x(k), 4)
Next k
For n = 0 To Ns / 2 - 1
  An = 0: Bn = 0
  For k = 0 To Ns - 1
    An = An + x(k) * Cos(Q * k * n) / Ns
    Bn = Bn - x(k) * Sin(Q * k * n) / Ns
  Next k
  omega = 2 * pie * n / Period
  amp = Sqr(An ^ 2 + Bn ^ 2)
  ampdb = 20 * Application.Log10(amp)
  phase = Application.Atan2(An, Bn) * 57.296
  If Bn >= 0 Then
    phase = phase - 360
  End If
  Cells(n + 1, 6) = n
  Cells(n + 1, 7) = Application.Round(An, 3)
  Cells(n + 1, 8) = Application.Round(Bn, 3)
  Cells(n + 1, 9) = Application.Round(omega, 2)
  Cells(n + 1, 10) = Application.Round(ampdb, 3)
  Cells(n + 1, 11) = Application.Round(phase, 3)
Next n
  Cells(1, 9) = 0.1
End Sub
``
	• *Note:* Option Base 0 (by default) allows all arrays to begin with index "0." This accommodates **n** and k = 0.
	
	• Read X$_k$, N$_S$ and **Period of the Sample.**
	
	• For n = 0 to the *Nyquist frequency*
	
	• Compute An, Bn, omega, ampdb, and phase.
	
	• For plotting (due to Atan2) phase = phase - 360
	
	• Print out.
	
	• Next n
	
	• Initial value of omega for the Bode semilog plots

The following example demonstrates that the DFT is an approximation to the CFT:

Example DFT: The following differential equation was used in **Example GoSub** (Chapter 12):

$$m\,\ddot{x} + d\,\dot{x} + k\,x = k\,u$$

The response of **x** due to an impulse on **u** was computed using a *Runge-Kutta* integrator. The following figure shows this response, sampled at twenty samples per second for a *period* of two seconds.

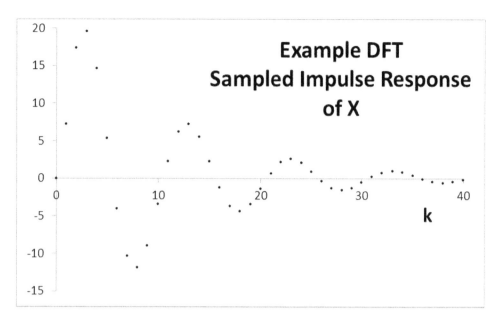

The fundamental question is this: *What does **X** look like in the frequency domain?* To see this, input these forty-one samples of **X** to Program DFT. The following table shows the frequency response that was computed:

Program DFT Spreadsheet								
Input Time Response			Output Frequency Response					
N and Period	k	X_k	n	A_n	B_n	Frequency (rad/sec)	Amplitude (decibels)	Phase (degrees)
41	0	0	0	0.96	0	0 (0.1)	-0.37	0
2	1	7.23	1	1.00	-0.16	3.14	0.12	-9
	2	17.38	2	1.15	-0.43	6.28	1.76	-20
	3	19.62	3	1.40	-1.16	9.42	5.19	-40
	4	14.59	4	-0.38	-3.00	12.57	9.62	-97
	5	5.37	5	-1.48	-0.44	15.71	3.75	-163
	•	•	•	•	•	•	•	•
	•	•	•	•	•	•	•	•
	•	•	•	•	•	•	•	•
	38	-0.59	17	-0.011	0.03	53.41	-30.52	-248
	39	-0.49	18	-0.007	0.02	56.55	-33.70	-251
	40	-0.24	19	-0.004	0.01	59.69	-38.22	-251

Notes: • The sampling frequency is: ω_s = 125.6 rad/sec (20 samples/sec).
• From the differential equation: $\omega_n = \sqrt{k/m}$ = 12.56 rad/sec.
• (ω_s / ω_n) = 10 which satisfies the sample rate requirement.
• The Nyquist frequency is 62.8 rad/sec. Hence, the cutoff is at n = 19.

This frequency response will now be compared to the frequency response of the CFT of the same differential equation.

Frequency Response of the CFT of X

For the CFT, **X** is treated as a continuous signal. We take the *Laplace* transform of its differential equation:

$$m\,s^2 x + d\,sx + k\,x = k\,u \qquad\qquad (m = .5,\ d = 2,\ k = 80)$$

The transfer function of this equation is as follows:

$$\frac{x}{u} = \frac{(k/m)}{s^2 + (d/m)s + (k/m)} = \frac{160}{s^2 + 4s + 160}$$

This transfer function is the same as the one used in **Example fresp 1** (Chapter 8). Its frequency response is plotted in that example.

The following table explains why the CFT of **X** is the same as the frequency response of the above transfer function.

For this Example, Which Is a Damped Sine Wave:

- Since U is an impulse,
  the Laplace Transform of (X/U) is the same as the Laplace Transform of (X).

- From Campbell & Foster[*], for this signal,
  the Fourier Transform of (X) = Laplace Transform of (X) when $s = j\,\omega$.

- Hence,
  the Fourier Transform of (X) = Laplace Transform of (X/U) when $s = j\,\omega$.
  In other words, the frequency response of the CFT of **X** is the same as the frequency response in **Example fresp 1**.

---

[*] Campbell, G., and R. Foster. *Fourier Integrals for Practical Applications*. D. Van Nostrand, 1948.

The following plots compare the frequency response of the CFT of **X** with the frequency response of the DFT of **X**:

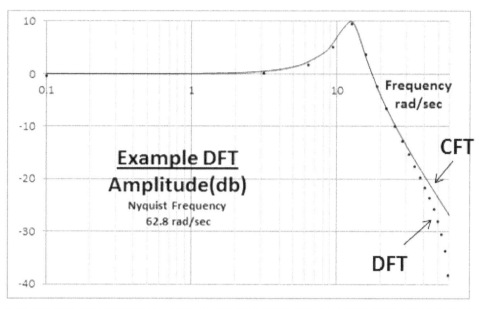

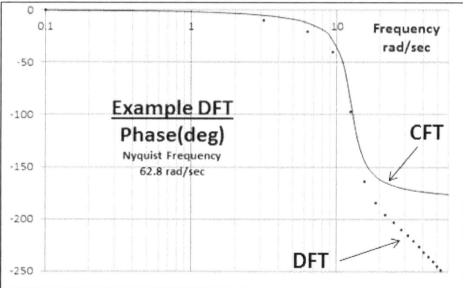

Here are the reasons for the difference between the DFT and the CFT:

- Sampling, which will always introduce some difference.
- Truncation, since the signal was not exactly zero outside the sample period.
- The *time-domain impulse-function* was only an approximation.
- *Runge-Kutta* is an approximate integrator.

Appendix A: Code Listings

A.1: Subprogram eig, which computes eigenvalues

- This subprogram computes the eigenvalues of a general real matrix with complex solutions. A discussion on the theory is in Chapter 15.

- It is called from Programs eig_main in Chapter 15 and TF_main in Chapter 17.

- It implements the algorithm illustrated in the Block Diagram of Sub eig in Chapter 15.

- The inputs and outputs are defined in Chapter 15, along with how it was checked out.

A.2: Subprogram zeros, which computes transfer function zeros

- This subprogram computes the zeros of a transfer function from the state variable form of differential equations. A discussion on the theory is in Chapter 17.

- It is called from Program TF_main in Chapter 17.

- It implements the algorithm that is outlined in Chapter 17.

- The inputs and outputs are defined in Chapter 17, along with how it was checked out.

A.3: Subprogram fresp, which computes frequency responses

- This subprogram computes the frequency response from the state variable form of differential equations. A discussion on the theory is in Chapter 18.

- It is called from Program FR_main in Chapter 18.

- It uses the three elementary row operations in linear algebra to convert a complex matrix to upper triangular form.

- The inputs and outputs are defined in Chapter 18, along with how it was checked out.

A.4: Subprogram simplex, which implements the Simplex algorithm

- This subprogram computes the solution of the general Linear Programming Problem. A discussion on the theory is in Chapter 19.

- It is called from Program simp_main in Chapter 19.

- It implements the Simplex algorithm, documented in *Linear Programming and Extensions*, G. Dantzig, Princeton University Press, 1963.

- The inputs and outputs are defined in Chapter 19, along with how it was checked out.

Subprogram eig Code, Page 1 of 6	Subprogram eig Code, Page 2 of 6

```
Sub eig(npr, Ainput, WR, WI)
Dim Q(), R(), Ahess(), Shift(), Asave(100, 100), A()
N = npr: itype = 0: iroot=0: tol = 1e-05: niter = 500
ReDim Q(N, N), R(N, N), Ahess(N, N), Shift(N, N), A(N, N)
For i = 1 To N
  For j = 1 To N
    A(i, j) = Ainput(i, j)
    Ahess(i, j) = A(i, j)
  Next j
Next i
If N < 3 Then GoTo BOTTOM
Call hess(N, Ahess)
For i = 1 To N
  For j = 1 To N
    A(i, j) = Ahess(i, j)
  Next j
Next i
For iter = 1 To niter              """ BEGIN QR ITERATIONS
 If iter = 100 Then tol = 0.0001
 If iter = 200 Then tol = 0.01
 If iter = 300 Then tol = 0.1
   If iter < 100 Then              " shift begin
     aR = A(N - 1, N - 1): bR = A(N - 1, N)
     cR = A(N, N - 1): dR = A(N, N)
   Else
     aR = A(N - 1, N - 2): bR = A(N - 1, N - 1)
     cR = A(N, N - 2): dR = A(N, N - 1)
   End If
   RAD = dR ^ 2 + aR ^ 2 - 2 * aR * dR + 4 * bR * cR
   If RAD >= 0 Then                """"" two REALs
     WR1 = 0.5 * (dR + aR + Sqr(RAD)): d1 = Abs(WR1 - A(N, N))
     WR2 = 0.5 * (dR + aR - Sqr(RAD)): d2 = Abs(WR2 - A(N, N))
     If d1 < d2 Then
       guess = WR1
     Else
       guess = WR2
     End If
   Else                           """"" one COMPLEX
     WR1 = 0.5 * (dR + aR): WI1 = 0.5 * Sqr(-RAD)
     guess = Sqr(WR1 ^ 2 + WR2 ^ 2)
   End If
   For i = 1 To N
     For j = 1 To N
       Shift(i, j) = 0
     Next j
     Shift(i, i) = guess
   Next i
   For i = 1 To N
     For j = 1 To N
       A(i, j) = A(i, j) - Shift(i, j)
     Next j
   Next i                         " shift end
Call Q_R(N, A, Q, R)
A = Application.MMult(R, Q)
   For i = 1 To N                 """" unshift begin
     For j = 1 To N
       A(i, j) = A(i, j) + Shift(i, j)
     Next j
   Next i                         """"" unshift end
Call deflate(N, A, itype, iroot, WR, WI, tol)
```

```
If itype <> 0 Then               """" Begin "A" Deflate
  If itype = 1 Then
    For i = 1 To N - 1
      For j = 1 To N - 1
        Asave(i, j) = A(i, j)
      Next j
    Next i
    N = N - 1
  Else                           ''' itype = 2
    For i = 1 To N - 2
      For j = 1 To N - 2
        Asave(i, j) = A(i, j)
      Next j
    Next i
    N = N - 2
  End If
  ReDim A(N, N), Q(N, N), R(N, N)
  For i = 1 To N
    For j = 1 To N
      A(i, j) = Asave(i, j)
    Next j
  Next i
  itype = 0
End If                           """"        End "A" Deflate
  If N <= 2 Then Exit For        """"            SUCCESS
Next iter                        """"        End QR Iterations

If N > 2 Then    ' here iroot <> npr, so sub eig has failed
Cells(1, npr + 5) = " Sub eig": Cells(1, npr + 6) = " fails"
Cells(2, npr + 5) = " iter =": Cells(2, npr + 6) = iter
Cells(3, npr + 5) = " iroot =": Cells(3, npr + 6) = iroot
Cells(4, npr + 5) = " WR =": Cells(4, npr + 6) = " WI ="
For i = 1 To iroot
  Cells(4 + i, npr + 5) = WR(i): Cells(4 + i, npr + 6) = WI(i)
Next i
Cells(npr + 4, npr + 2) = iter
For i = 1 To N
  For j = 1 To N
    Cells(npr + 3 + i, j) = A(i, j)
  Next j
Next i
End                              """" Sub eig fails
End If

BOTTOM:    '          compute the last 1 or 2 eigenvalues
  If N = 1 Then                  """"  one REAL
    iroot = iroot + 1: WR(iroot) = A(N, N): WI(iroot) = 0
  Else                           ' N=2 two roots
    aR = A(N - 1, N - 1): bR = A(N - 1, N)
    cR = A(N, N - 1): dR = A(N, N)
    RAD = dR ^ 2 + aR ^ 2 - 2 * aR * dR + 4 * bR * cR
    If RAD >= 0 Then             """"  two REALs
      WR1 = 0.5 * (dR + aR + Sqr(RAD)): WI1 = 0
      WR2 = 0.5 * (dR + aR - Sqr(RAD)): WI2 = 0
    Else                         """"" one COMPLEX
      WR1 = 0.5 * (dR + aR): WI1 = 0.5 * Sqr(-RAD)
      WR2 = WR1: WI2 = -WI1
    End If
    iroot = iroot + 1: WR(iroot) = WR1: WI(iroot) = WI1
    iroot = iroot + 1: WR(iroot) = WR2: WI(iroot) = WI2
  End If                         '     N= 1 or 2
End Sub ' eig
```

Appendix A.1: Subprogram eig

Subprogram eig Code, Page 3 of 6	Subprogram eig Code, Page 4 of 6

```
Sub hess(N, AA)
 LA = N - 1: eps = 2 ^ (-52): T = 0
 For m = 2 To LA
  i = m: x = 0
  For j = m To N
   If Abs(AA(j, m - 1)) > Abs(x) Then
    x = AA(j, m - 1): i = j
   End If
  Next j
  If i <> m Then
   For j = (m - 1) To N
    y = AA(i, j)
    AA(i, j) = AA(m, j)
    AA(m, j) = y
   Next j
   For j = 1 To N
    y = AA(j, i)
    AA(j, i) = AA(j, m)
    AA(j, m) = y
   Next j
  End If
  If x <> 0 Then
   For i = (m + 1) To N
    y = AA(i, m - 1)
    If y <> 0 Then
     AA(i, m - 1) = y / x
     y = AA(i, m - 1)
     For j = m To N
      AA(i, j) = AA(i, j) - y * AA(m, j)
     Next j
     For j = 1 To N
      AA(j, m) = AA(j, m) + y * AA(j, i)
     Next j
    End If
   Next i
  End If
 Next m
 For jj = 1 To N - 2
  For ii = jj + 2 To N
   AA(ii, jj) = 0
  Next ii
 Next jj
End Sub ' hess
```

```
Sub deflate(N, A, itype, iroot, WR, WI, tol)
 ctr = 0
 For j = 1 To N - 1
  If j < N - 1 Then
   If Abs(A(N - 1, j)) < tol Then ctr = ctr + 1  ' on each pass j < N - 1
   If Abs(A(N, j)) < tol Then GoTo NEXTJ
   Exit For                      ' return to QR W/O success
  End If
                                 """ here j = N - 1
  If Abs(A(N, j)) < tol Then      ' begin j = N - 1 checks
   iroot = iroot + 1: WR(iroot) = A(N, N): WI(iroot) = 0 """ one REAL
   itype = 1:  Exit For           ' return to QR to deflate
  End If
  If ctr = N - 2 Then             """ two roots
   aR = A(N - 1, N - 1): bR = A(N - 1, N)
   cR = A(N, N - 1): dR = A(N, N)
   RAD = dR ^ 2 + aR ^ 2 - 2 * aR * dR + 4 * bR * cR
   If RAD >= 0 Then               """ two REALs
    WR1 = 0.5 * (dR + aR + Sqr(RAD)): WI1 = 0
    WR2 = 0.5 * (dR + aR - Sqr(RAD)): WI2 = 0
   Else                           """ one COMPLEX
    WR1 = 0.5 * (dR + aR): WI1 = 0.5 * Sqr(-RAD)
    WR2 = WR1: WI2 = -WI1
   End If
   iroot = iroot + 1: WR(iroot) = WR1: WI(iroot) = WI1
   iroot = iroot + 1: WR(iroot) = WR2: WI(iroot) = WI2
   itype = 2:  Exit For           ' return to QR to deflate
  End If                          ' ctr=N-2
  Exit For                        ''' return to QR W/O success
NEXTJ:
 Next j
End Sub ' deflate
```

162

Subprogram eig Code, Page 5 of 6	Subprogram eig Code, Page 6 of 6
| ```
Sub Q_R(N, A, QM, RM)
Dim d(100), AQ(100, 100), Ident(100, 100), vh(), vhT(), H()
ReDim vh(N, 1), vhT(1, N), H(N, N)
 For i = 1 To N
   For j = 1 To N
     QM(i, j) = 0: RM(i, j) = 0: AQ(i, j) = 0: Ident(i, j) = 0
   Next j
     QM(i, i) = 1: Ident(i, i) = 1
 Next i
 k = 0
 For L = 1 To N          '''' Begin Transform
  k = k + 1
  If k = N Then
    d(L) = A(k, L): Exit For
  End If
  sarg = 0
  For i = k To N
    sarg = sarg + A(i, L) ^ 2
  Next i
  s = Sqr(sarg)
  If s = 0 Then
    d(L) = 0: GoTo nextL
  End If
  T = A(k, L): R = 1 / Sqr(s * (s + Abs(T)))
  If T < 0 Then s = -s
  d(L) = -s: A(k, k) = R * (T + s)
  For i = k + 1 To N
   A(i, k) = R * A(i, L)
  Next i
  For j = L + 1 To N
   T = 0
   For i = k To N
     T = T + A(i, k) * A(i, j)
   Next i
   For i = k To N
     A(i, j) = A(i, j) - T * A(i, k)
   Next i
  Next j
nextL: Next L                '''' End Transform
``` | ```
For i = 1 To N
  RM(i, i) = d(i)
Next i
For i = 1 To N - 1
 For j = i + 1 To N
  RM(i, j) = A(i, j)
 Next j
Next i
For j = 1 To N
 For i = j To N
   AQ(i, j) = A(i, j)
 Next i
Next j
For j = 1 To N - 1
 For i = 1 To N
   vh(i, 1) = AQ(i, j): vhT(1, i) = vh(i, 1)
 Next i
 vhvhT = Application.MMult(vh, vhT)
 For ii = 1 To N
   For jj = 1 To N
     H(ii, jj) = Ident(ii, jj) - vhvhT(ii, jj)
   Next jj
 Next ii
 Qtot = Application.MMult(QM, H)
 For ii = 1 To N
   For jj = 1 To N
     QM(ii, jj) = Qtot(ii, jj)
   Next jj
 Next ii
Next j
End Sub  ' QR
``` |

Subprogram zeros Code 1 of 3	Subprogram zeros Code 2 of 3
| ```
Sub zeros(nmat, Ain, B, C, D, nz, gain, WR, WI)
Dim az(30, 30), ati(30, 30), anew(30, 30), bnew(30), Ann(30, 30)
Dim T(30, 30), TINV(30, 30), tempa(30)
Dim i, j, k, L, NM, nob, noc, nobnew, noanew, temp
For i = 1 To nmat
  For k = 1 To nmat
    Ann(i, k) = Ain(i, k)
  Next k
Next i
For j = 1 To nmat
  For k = 1 To nmat
    T(j, k) = 0: TINV(j, k) = 0
  Next k
Next j
NM = nmat
nob = 0: noc = 0
For k = 1 To nmat
  If B(k) <> 0 Then nob = 1
  If C(k) <> 0 Then noc = 1
Next k
If nob = 0 Then
  Cells(nmat + 5, 1) = "b matrix=0"
  End
End If
If noc = 0 Then
  Cells(nmat + 5, 2) = "c matrix=0"
  End
End If
nz = nmat
If D <> 0 Then
  For i = 1 To nz
    For j = 1 To nz
      az(i, j) = Ann(i, j) - B(i) * C(j) / D
    Next j
  Next i
  gain = D
  GoTo Bot
End If
If nz = 1 Then
  nz = 0: gain = B(1) * C(1)
  GoTo Bot
End If
``` | ```
top:  For k = 1 To nz
        If C(k) <> 0 Then Exit For
        If k = nz Then
          Cells(nmat + 5, 3) = "No Xfer Ftn"
          End
        End If
      Next k
      temp = C(1): C(1) = C(k): C(k) = temp
      temp = B(1): B(1) = B(k): B(k) = temp
      For i = 1 To nz
        tempa(i) = Ann(i, 1): Ann(i, 1) = Ann(i, k): Ann(i, k) = tempa(i)
      Next i
      For i = 1 To nz
        tempa(i) = Ann(1, i): Ann(1, i) = Ann(k, i): Ann(k, i) = tempa(i)
      Next i
      T(1, 1) = C(1): TINV(1, 1) = 1 / C(1)
      For L = 2 To nz
        T(1, L) = C(L): T(L, L) = 1: TINV(1, L) = -C(L) / C(1): TINV(L, L) = 1
      Next L
      For i = 1 To nz
        For j = 1 To nz
          ati(i, j) = 0
          For k = 1 To nz
            ati(i, j) = Ann(i, k) * TINV(k, j) + ati(i, j)
          Next k
        Next j
      Next i
      For i = 1 To nz
        For j = 1 To nz
          anew(i, j) = 0
          For k = 1 To nz
            anew(i, j) = T(i, k) * ati(k, j) + anew(i, j)
          Next k
        Next j
      Next i
      For i = 1 To nz
        bnew(i) = 0
        For k = 1 To nz
          bnew(i) = T(i, k) * B(k) + bnew(i)
        Next k
      Next i
``` |

```
                    Subprogram zeros Code 3 of 3

        If bnew(1) <> 0 Then
          For i = 2 To nz
            For j = 2 To nz
              az(i - 1, j - 1) = anew(i, j) - bnew(i) * anew(1, j) / bnew(1)
            Next j
          Next i
          gain = bnew(1): nz = nz - 1
        Else
          nobnew = 0: noanew = 0
          For L = 2 To nz
            If bnew(L) <> 0 Then nobnew = 1
            If anew(1, L) <> 0 Then noanew = 1
          Next L
          If (nobnew = 0) Or (noanew = 0) Then
            Cells(nmat + 5, 4) = "No Xfer Ftn"
            End
          Else
            For i = 2 To nz
                B(i - 1) = bnew(i): C(i - 1) = anew(1, i)
              For j = 2 To nz
                Ann(i - 1, j - 1) = anew(i, j)
              Next j
            Next i
            nz = nz - 1
            If nz = 1 Then
              nz = 0: gain = bnew(2) * anew(1, 2)
            Else
              GoTo top
            End If
          End If
        End If

Bot:  If nz > 0 Then
         Call eig(nz, az, WR, WI)
      End If

End Sub   ' zeros
```

165

Appendix A.3: Subprogram fresp

Subprogram fresp Code 1 of 2	Subprogram fresp Code 2 of 2

```
Sub fresp(A, Aw, B, Bw, nsize)
Dim ind(30)
nm1 = nsize - 1
For i = 1 To nsize
  ind(i) = i
Next i
For K = 1 To nm1          '   >>>>>>>>>>>   start k Loop
  KP1 = K + 1: Kr = K: Kc = K: BIGA = Abs(A(K, K)) + Abs(Aw(K, K))
  For i = K To nsize
    For j = K To nsize
      BIGT = Abs(A(i, j)) + Abs(Aw(i, j))
      If BIGA < BIGT Then
        BIGA = BIGT: Kr = i: Kc = j
      End If
    Next j
  Next i
If BIGA = 0 Then
  Cells(4, 11) = "Singular Matrix": End
End If
If Kr <> K Then
  For i = K To nsize
    HOLD = A(K, i): A(K, i) = A(Kr, i):     A(Kr, i) = HOLD
    HOLD = Aw(K, i): Aw(K, i) = Aw(Kr, i): Aw(Kr, i) = HOLD
  Next i
    HOLD = B(K):    B(K) = B(Kr):     B(Kr) = HOLD
    HOLD = Bw(K): Bw(K) = Bw(Kr): Bw(Kr) = HOLD
End If
If Kc <> K Then
  For j = 1 To nsize
    HOLD = A(j, K):    A(j, K) = A(j, Kc):    A(j, Kc) = HOLD
    HOLD = Aw(j, K): Aw(j, K) = Aw(j, Kc): Aw(j, Kc) = HOLD
  Next j
    i = ind(K): ind(K) = ind(Kc): ind(Kc) = i
End If
For i = KP1 To nsize
  HOLD = (A(K, i) * A(K, K) + Aw(K, i) * Aw(K, K)) / (A(K, K) ^ 2 + Aw(K, K) ^ 2)
  HOLDW = (Aw(K, i) * A(K, K) - A(K, i) * Aw(K, K)) / (A(K, K) ^ 2 + Aw(K, K) ^ 2)
  A(K, i) = HOLD
  Aw(K, i) = HOLDW
Next i
  HOLD = (B(K) * A(K, K) + Bw(K) * Aw(K, K)) / (A(K, K) ^ 2 + Aw(K, K) ^ 2)
  HOLDW = (Bw(K) * A(K, K) - B(K) * Aw(K, K)) / (A(K, K) ^ 2 + Aw(K, K) ^ 2)
  B(K) = HOLD
  Bw(K) = HOLDW
  For i = KP1 To nsize
    For j = KP1 To nsize
      HOLD = A(i, j) - A(i, K) * A(K, j) + Aw(i, K) * Aw(K, j)
      HOLDW = Aw(i, j) - A(i, K) * Aw(K, j) - Aw(i, K) * A(K, j)
      A(i, j) = HOLD
      Aw(i, j) = HOLDW
    Next j
      HOLD = B(i) - A(i, K) * B(K) + Aw(i, K) * Bw(K)
      HOLDW = Bw(i) - A(i, K) * Bw(K) - Aw(i, K) * B(K)
      B(i) = HOLD
      Bw(i) = HOLDW
  Next i
Next K   '      >>>>>>>>>>>>>>>>>  end k Loop
```

```
If (A(nsize, nsize) = 0) And (Aw(nsize, nsize) = 0) Then
  Cells(4, 11) = "Singular Matrix": End
End If
ns = nsize
den = (A(ns, ns) ^ 2 + Aw(ns, ns) ^ 2)
A(ns, 1) = (B(ns) * A(ns, ns) + Bw(ns) * Aw(ns, ns)) / den
Aw(ns, 1) = (Bw(ns) * A(ns, ns) - B(ns) * Aw(ns, ns)) / den
For i = 1 To nm1
  j = nsize - i: HOLD = 0: HOLDW = 0
  For Kc = 1 To i
    K = nsize + 1 - Kc
    HOLD = HOLD + A(j, K) * A(K, 1) - Aw(j, K) * Aw(K, 1)
    HOLDW = HOLDW + A(j, K) * Aw(K, 1) + Aw(j, K) * A(K, 1)
  Next Kc
    A(j, 1) = B(j) - HOLD: Aw(j, 1) = Bw(j) - HOLDW
Next i
For i = 1 To nsize
  j = ind(i): B(j) = A(i, 1): Bw(j) = Aw(i, 1)
Next i
If (B(nsize) = 0) And (Bw(nsize) = 0) Then
  Cells(4, 11) = "No Xfer Ftn": End
End If
End Sub ' fresp
```

Subprogram simplex Code 1 of 2	Subprogram simplex Code 2 of 2
| ```
Sub simplex(bin, cin, x, L, K1, K2, K3, N)
Dim b(30, 101), c(101, 2), simpX(71)
Dim CQ(101, 2), ZJ(101, 2), ZC(101, 2), NQ(30)
Dim i, j, K, JJ, KK, LL, LN1, XM1, XM2, XX, BIG
BIG = 1e+20
For j = 1 To 101
  For i = 1 To 30
    b(i, j) = 0
  Next i
  c(j, 1) = 0: c(j, 2) = 0
Next j
For j = 1 To N + 1
  For i = 1 To L
    b(i, j) = bin(i, j)
  Next i
  c(j, 1) = cin(j, 1)
Next j
For i = 1 To L
  b(i, N + 1 + i) = 1
Next i
If K3 <> 0 Then
  K = K1 + K2 + 1
  For i = K To L
    b(i, i + N + K3 + 1) = -1
  Next i
End If
K = K2 + K3
If K <> 0 Then
  For i = 1 To K
    c(N + K1 + 1 + i, 2) = -1
  Next i
End If
For i = 1 To L
  NQ(i) = N + i + 1
  CQ(i, 1) = c(N + i + 1, 1)
  CQ(i, 2) = c(N + i + 1, 2)
Next i
JJ = 1 + N + L + K3
TOP: XM1 = BIG:  XM2 = BIG
    For j = 1 To JJ
      ZJ(j, 1) = 0
      ZJ(j, 2) = 0
    Next j
    For i = 1 To JJ
      For j = 1 To L
        ZJ(i, 1) = CQ(j, 1) * b(j, i) + ZJ(i, 1)
        ZJ(i, 2) = CQ(j, 2) * b(j, i) + ZJ(i, 2)
      Next j
      If i <> 1 Then
        ZC(i, 1) = ZJ(i, 1) - c(i, 1)
        ZC(i, 2) = ZJ(i, 2) - c(i, 2)
        If (ZC(i, 2) = 0) Then
          If ((XM1 > ZC(i, 1)) And (XM2 >= 0)) Then
            XM1 = ZC(i, 1): KK = i
          End If
        Else
          If ZC(i, 2) <= XM2 Then
            XM2 = ZC(i, 2)
            If ZC(i, 2) < 0 Then KK = i
          End If
        End If
      End If
    Next i
``` | ```
If ((XM2 < 0) Or ((XM2 >= 0) And (XM1 < 0))) Then
  XM1 = BIG
  For i = 1 To L
    If b(i, KK) > 0 Then
      XX = b(i, 1) / b(i, KK)
      If XX < 0 Then
        Cells(L + 5, 1) = "no solution": Cells(L + 5, 2) = "XX<0": End
      End If
      If XX <= XM1 Then
        XM1 = XX: LL = i
      End If
    End If
  Next i
  If XM1 = BIG Then
    Cells(L + 5, 1) = "no solution": Cells(L + 5, 2) = "XM1=BIG": End
  End If
  XX = b(LL, KK)
  For i = 1 To JJ
    b(LL, i) = b(LL, i) / XX
  Next i
  NQ(LL) = KK: CQ(LL, 1) = c(KK, 1): CQ(LL, 2) = c(KK, 2)
  For i = 1 To L
    If i <> LL Then
      XX = -b(i, KK)
      If XX <> 0 Then
        For j = 1 To JJ
          b(i, j) = b(i, j) + XX * b(LL, j)
        Next j
      End If
    End If
  Next i
  GoTo TOP
End If

LN1 = L + N + 1
For i = 1 To LN1
  simpX(i) = 0
Next i
For i = 1 To L
  simpX(NQ(i)) = b(i, 1)
Next i
j = K3 + K2 + 1
For i = 2 To j
  If simpX(K1 + N + i) <> 0 Then
    Cells(L + 5, 1) = "no solution": Cells(L + 5, 2) = "simpX<>0": End
  End If
Next i
For j = 1 To N
  x(j) = simpX(j + 1)
Next j
End Sub ' simplex
``` |

Appendix B: The Launch Vehicle Example Shown on the Cover

B.1: The Math Model

This is the math model used in **Example eig 5**, expanded to include the following:

- structural bending mode
- fuel slosh mode
- actuator equation
- autopilot filter

B.2: Closed-Loop Eigenvalues

This is Example eig 5 (Chapter 15) with the expanded math model.

B.3: Root Locus Plot as the Autopilot Gains Vary

This is Example eig 6 (Chapter 15) with the expanded math model.

B.4: Open-Loop Transfer Function and Frequency Response from the State Variable Form

This is **Example ABCD 5** (Chapter 16), **Example tf 5** (Chapter 17), and **Example fr 5** (Chapter 18) with the expanded math model.

B.5: Time Response of Vehicle Angle Due to Impulse on Engine Angle

This is **Example GoSub** (Chapter 12) with the spring-mass-damper system replaced with the launch vehicle.

<table>
<tr><td colspan="3" align="center">**Appendix B.1: Launch Vehicle Math Model**
Greensite, A. *Analysis and Design of Space Vehicle Flight Control Systems.* Spartan Books, 1970.
(Note: Since this is a linear model, variables are changes about a set point.)</td></tr>
<tr><td align="center">Closed-Loop Equations</td><td align="center">Variables</td><td align="center">Constants</td></tr>
</table>

Closed-Loop Equations	Variables	Constants
Sensor Outputs $(\theta_T, \dot{\theta}_T)$ $$\theta_T = \theta + \sigma * q$$ $$\dot{\theta}_T = \dot{\theta} + \sigma * \dot{q}$$ Autopilot Command (δ_C) $$\delta_C = -K_D \theta_T - K_R \dot{\theta}_T$$ Vehicle Angle of Attack (α) $$\alpha = \theta + \dot{Z}/\text{Vel}$$ Vehicle Angular Acceleration $(\ddot{\theta})$ $$\ddot{\theta} = \mu_\alpha \alpha + \mu_\delta \delta - \mu_p \Gamma$$ Vehicle Normal Acceleration $(\ddot{Z})$ $$\ddot{Z} = -\frac{T-D}{m}\theta - \frac{L_\alpha}{m}\alpha + \frac{T_C}{m}\delta$$ Engine Angular Acceleration $(\ddot{\delta})$ $$\ddot{\delta} = (\delta_a - \delta)\omega_a^2 - 2\zeta_a \omega_a \dot{\delta}$$ Autopilot Filter Output $(\ddot{\delta}_a)$ $$\ddot{\delta}_a = (\delta_C - \delta_a)\omega_f^2 - 2\zeta_f \omega_f \dot{\delta}_a$$ Vehicle Bending Acceleration $(\ddot{q})$ $$\ddot{q} = -\frac{T_C}{m_{eq}}\delta - 2\zeta_B \omega_B * \dot{q} - \omega_B^2 * q$$ Vehicle Fuel Slosh Angular Acceleration $(\ddot{\Gamma})$ $$\ddot{\Gamma} = -fs_\delta \delta - 2\zeta_{fs}\omega_{fs} * \dot{\Gamma} - \omega_{fs}^2 * \Gamma$$	Vehicle Angle and Rate $\theta, \dot{\theta}$ Bending Displacement and Rate $q, \dot{q}$ Engine Angle Command δ_C Vehicle Normal Velocity $\dot{Z}$ Engine Angle and Rate $\delta, \dot{\delta}$ Engine Actuator Angle and Rate $\delta_a, \dot{\delta}_a$ Fuel Slosh Angle and Rate $\Gamma, \dot{\Gamma}$	Bending Slope $$\sigma = \frac{\partial \theta}{\partial q}$$ Autopilot Gains K_D, K_R Vehicle Velocity Vel Moment Constants μ_α, μ_C, μ_P Force Equation Constants T, D, m, L_α, T_C Engine Damping, Frequency ζ_a, ω_a Autopilot Filter Damping and Frequency ζ_f, ω_f Bending Damping, Frequency and Equivalent Mass $\zeta_B, \omega_B, m_{eq}$ Fuel Slosh Damping, Frequency and Force Constant $\zeta_{fs}, \omega_{fs}, fs_\delta = \frac{\partial \ddot{\Gamma}}{\partial \delta}$

<table>
<tr><td colspan="3" align="center">Modifications to Compute the Open-Loop Transfer Function $\frac{\text{tf}_{out}}{\text{tf}_{in}}$</td></tr>
</table>

Change:	Engine Angular Acceleration $(\ddot{\delta})$ $$\ddot{\delta} = (\text{tf}_{in} - \delta)\omega_a^2 - 2\zeta_a \omega_a \dot{\delta}$$	
Add:	Output Equation $$\text{tf}_{out} = -\delta_a$$	

The following table lists the variables used to convert the launch-vehicle equations to first-order differential equations.

<table>
<tr><td colspan="3" align="center">**Appendix B.1: Launch Vehicle Math Model**
Conversion Variables</td></tr>
<tr><td>$Y_1 = \theta$</td><td>$Y_4 = \delta$</td><td>$Y_8 = q$</td></tr>
<tr><td>$Y_2 = \dot{\theta}$</td><td>$Y_5 = \dot{\delta}$</td><td>$Y_9 = \dot{q}$</td></tr>
<tr><td>$Y_3 = \dot{Z}$</td><td>$Y_6 = \delta_a$</td><td>$Y_{10} = \Gamma$</td></tr>
<tr><td></td><td>$Y_7 = \dot{\delta}_a$</td><td>$Y_{11} = \dot{\Gamma}$</td></tr>
</table>

Appendix B.2: Launch Vehicle Closed-Loop Eigenvalues

data:	Real Part (WR$_j$)	Imaginary Part (WI$_j$)
Dim vel, thr, tc, aero, mass, mua, muc, mup, meq, zb, wb, sigma, zfs, wfs Dim tom, aom, com, comeq, fsd, tzob, wbsq, tzofs, wfsq Dim alpha, delta, deltaa, deltac, thetaTOT, thetadTOT, Wa, Za, Wf, Zf, Kd, Kr		
N = 11: stepd = 0.02: y(1) = 0: y(2) = 0: y(3) = 0: y(4) = 0: y(5) = 0 y(6) = 0: y(7) = 0: y(8) = 0: y(9) = 0: y(10) = 0: y(11) = 0 vel = 1300: thr = 420000: tc = 340000: aero = 200000: mass = 5500 mua = 3.5: muc = 4.6: mup = 0.06: meq = 1590: zb = 0.01: wb = 20 sigma = 0.01: zfs = 0.01: wfs = 5.1: wfsq = wfs ^ 2 tom = thr / mass: aom = aero / mass: com = tc / mass: comeq = tc / meq fsd = 17.9: tzob = 2 * zb * wb: wbsq = wb ^ 2: tzofs = 2 * zfs * wfs Wa = 60: Za = 0.7: Wf = 20: Zf = 0.5: Kd = 2.1: Kr = 0.51 Return	-0.134 -0.952 -0.952 -0.033 -0.033 -0.652 -0.652 -8.623 -8.623 -41.938 -41.938	0 2.58 -2.58 5.09 -5.09 19.50 -19.50 16.47 -16.47 42.95 -42.95

system:
  thetaTOT = y(1) + sigma * y(8)
  thetadTOT = y(2) + sigma * y(9)
  deltac = -thetaTOT * Kd - thetadTOT * Kr
  delta = y(4)
  alpha = y(1) + y(3) / vel
  yd(1) = y(2)
  yd(2) = mua * alpha + muc * delta - mup * y(10)
  yd(3) = -tom * y(1) - aom * alpha + com * delta
  yd(4) = y(5)
  deltaa = y(6)
  yd(5) = (deltaa - y(4)) * Wa ^ 2 - 2 * Za * Wa * y(5)
  yd(6) = y(7)
  yd(7) = (deltac - y(6)) * Wf ^ 2 - 2 * Zf * Wf * y(7)
  yd(8) = y(9)
  yd(9) = -comeq * delta - tzob * y(9) - wbsq * y(8)
  yd(10) = y(11)
  yd(11) = -fsd * delta - tzofs * y(11) - wfsq * y(10)
Return		

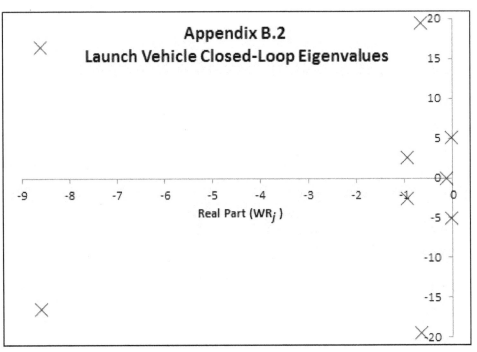

Appendix B.2
Launch Vehicle Closed-Loop Eigenvalues

Appendix B.3: Program to Generate the Locus of Launch-Vehicle Closed-Loop Eigenvalues as the Autopilot Gains Vary

```
Option Base 1
Sub R_L_main()
Dim y(30), yd(30), ys(30), yds(30), A(30, 30)
Dim WR(30), WI(30), omegan(30), zeta(30)
GoSub data
For iroot = 1 To nroot
  For jA = 0 To N
    GoSub system
    If jA = 0 Then
      For i = 1 To N
        yds(i) = yd(i): ys(i) = y(i)
      Next i
    End If
    GoSub matrix
  Next jA
Call eig(N, A, WR, WI)
For i = 1 To N
  omegan(i) = Sqr(WR(i) ^ 2 + WI(i) ^ 2)
  If WI(i) <> 0 Then
    zeta(i) = -WR(i) / omegan(i)
  Else
    If WR(i) <= 0 Then zeta(i) = 1
    If WR(i) > 0 Then zeta(i) = -1
  End If
Next i

' Following sort-on-frequency necessary
' to connect points in Scatter Chart

For L = N To 2 Step -1
  For i = 1 To L - 1
    If omegan(i) > omegan(L) Then
      v1 = omegan(i):        v2 = zeta(i)
      v3 = WR(i):            v4 = WI(i)
      omegan(i) = omegan(L): zeta(i) = zeta(L)
      WR(i) = WR(L):         WI(i) = WI(L)
      omegan(L) = v1:        zeta(L) = v2
      WR(L) = v3:            WI(L) = v4
    End If
  Next i
Next L

For i = 1 To N
  aroot = 4 + N + iroot + i + (i - 1) * nroot
  Cells(aroot, 1) = Application.Round(WR(i), 2)
  Cells(aroot, i + 1) = Application.Round(WI(i), 2)
  Cells(i + 2, 2 * iroot - 1) = Application.Round(zeta(i), 4)
  Cells(i + 2, 2 * iroot) = Application.Round(omegan(i), 2)
Next i
Next iroot

End
```

```
data:
  nroot = 6: Groot = Array(0.5, 0.75, 1, 1.25, 1.5, 2)
  N = 11: stepd = 0.02: y(1) = 0: y(2) = 0: y(3) = 0: y(4) = 0: y(5) = 0
  y(6) = 0: y(7) = 0: y(8) = 0: y(9) = 0: y(10) = 0: y(11) = 0
  vel = 1300: thr = 420000: tc = 340000: aero = 200000: mass = 5500
  mua = 3.5: muc = 4.6: mup = 0.06: meq = 1590: zb = 0.01: wb = 20
  sigma = 0.01: zfs = 0.01: wfs = 5.1: wfsq = wfs ^ 2
  tom = thr / mass: aom = aero / mass: com = tc / mass: comeq = tc / meq
  fsd = 17.9: tzob = 2 * zb * wb: wbsq = wb ^ 2: tzofs = 2 * zfs * wfs
  Wa = 60: Za = 0.7: Wf = 20: Zf = 0.5: Kd = 2.1: Kr = 0.51
Return

system:
  thetaTOT = y(1) + sigma * y(8)
  thetadTOT = y(2) + sigma * y(9)
  deltac = (-thetaTOT * Kd - thetadTOT * Kr) * Groot(iroot)
  delta = y(4)
  alpha = y(1) + y(3) / vel
  yd(1) = y(2)
  yd(2) = mua * alpha + muc * delta - mup * y(10)
  yd(3) = -tom * y(1) - aom * alpha + com * delta
  yd(4) = y(5)
  deltaa = y(6)
  yd(5) = (deltaa - y(4)) * Wa ^ 2 - 2 * Za * Wa * y(5)
  yd(6) = y(7)
  yd(7) = (deltac - y(6)) * Wf ^ 2 - 2 * Zf * Wf * y(7)
  yd(8) = y(9)
  yd(9) = -comeq * delta - tzob * y(9) - wbsq * y(8)
  yd(10) = y(11)
  yd(11) = -fsd * delta - tzofs * y(11) - wfsq * y(10)
Return

matrix:
  If jA = 0 Then
      y(1) = ys(1) + stepd
  Else
    For i = 1 To N
      A(i, jA) = (yd(i) - yds(i)) / stepd
    Next i
      y(jA) = ys(jA)
    If jA < N Then
      y(jA + 1) = ys(jA + 1) + stepd
    End If
  End If
Return
End Sub            ' R_L_main
```

```
Sub eig(N, A, WR, WI)

    SEE APPENDIX A.1

End Sub
```

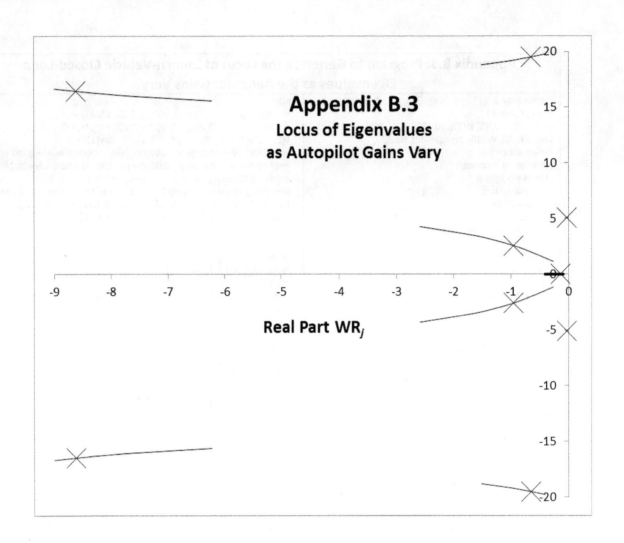

Appendix B.3
Locus of Eigenvalues
as Autopilot Gains Vary

Real Part WR$_j$

Appendix B.4: Open-Loop data_system Equations

data:
```
N = 11: tfin = 0: stepd = 0.02: y(1) = 0: y(2) = 0: y(3) = 0: y(4) = 0
y(5) = 0: y(6) = 0: y(7) = 0: y(8) = 0: y(9) = 0: y(10) = 0: y(11) = 0
vel = 1300: thr = 420000: tc = 340000: aero = 200000: mass = 5500
mua = 3.5: muc = 4.6: mup = 0.06: meq = 1590: zb = 0.01: wb = 20
sigma = 0.01: zfs = 0.01: wfs = 5.1: wfsq = wfs ^ 2
tom = thr / mass: aom = aero / mass: com = tc / mass: comeq = tc / meq
fsd = 17.9: tzob = 2 * zb * wb: wbsq = wb ^ 2: tzofs = 2 * zfs * wfs
Wa = 60: Za = 0.7: Wf = 20: Zf = 0.5: Kd = 2.1: Kr = 0.51
Retun
```

system:
```
thetaTOT = y(1) + sigma * y(8)
thetadTOT = y(2) + sigma * y(9)
deltac = -thetaTOT * Kd - Kr * thetadTOT
delta = y(4)
alpha = y(1) + y(3) / vel
yd(1) = y(2)
yd(2) = mua * alpha + muc * delta - mup * y(10)
yd(3) = -tom * y(1) - aom * alpha + com * delta
yd(4) = y(5)

deltaa = tfin
yd(5) = (deltaa - y(4)) * Wa ^ 2 - 2 * Za * Wa * y(5)
yd(6) = y(7)
yd(7) = (deltac - y(6)) * Wf ^ 2 - 2 * Zf * Wf * y(7)
yd(8) = y(9)
yd(9) = -comeq * delta - tzob * y(9) - wbsq * y(8)
yd(10) = y(11)
yd(11) = -fsd * delta - tzofs * y(11) - wfsq * y(10)

tfout = -y(6)
Return
```

Appendix B.4: Launch Vehicle Open-Loop Transfer Function
(tf_{out} / tf_{in})

Gain = 1807825

Zeros		Poles	
Real Part (WR$_j$)	Imaginary Part (WI$_j$)	Real Part (WR$_j$)	Imaginary Part (WI$_j$)
-0.39	+27.4	-10	+17.32
-0.39	-27.4	-10	-17.32
-0.063	0	1.83	0
-0.0511	+5.12	-1.91	0
-0.0511	-5.12	0.059	0
-4.12	0	-42	+42.85
		-42	-42.85
		-0.2	+20
		-0.2	-20
		-0.051	+5.1
		-0.051	-5.1

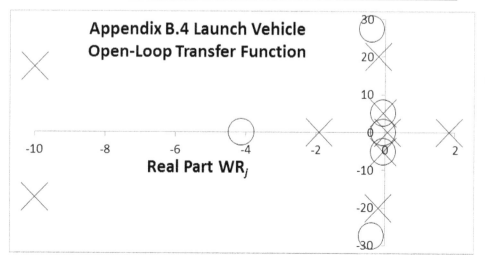

Appendix B.4 Launch Vehicle Open-Loop Transfer Function

Real Part WR$_j$

173

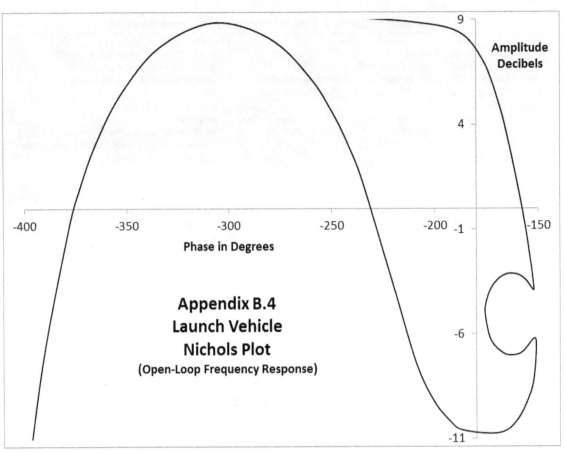

Appendix B.4
Launch Vehicle
Nichols Plot
(Open-Loop Frequency Response)

Amplitude Decibels

Phase in Degrees

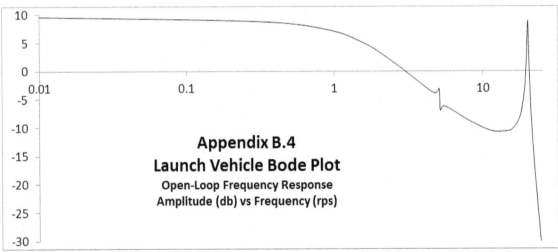

Appendix B.4
Launch Vehicle Bode Plot
Open-Loop Frequency Response
Amplitude (db) vs Frequency (rps)

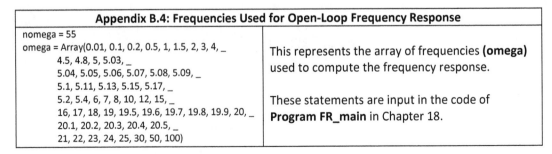

Appendix B.4: Frequencies Used for Open-Loop Frequency Response	

nomega = 55
omega = Array(0.01, 0.1, 0.2, 0.5, 1, 1.5, 2, 3, 4, _
    4.5, 4.8, 5, 5.03, _
    5.04, 5.05, 5.06, 5.07, 5.08, 5.09, _
    5.1, 5.11, 5.13, 5.15, 5.17, _
    5.2, 5.4, 6, 7, 8, 10, 12, 15, _
    16, 17, 18, 19, 19.5, 19.6, 19.7, 19.8, 19.9, 20, _
    20.1, 20.2, 20.3, 20.4, 20.5, _
    21, 22, 23, 24, 25, 30, 50, 100)
	This represents the array of frequencies **(omega)** used to compute the frequency response.
	
	These statements are input in the code of **Program FR_main** in Chapter 18.

Appendix B.5: Time Domain Simulation
Launch Vehicle Angle Response Due to an Impulse on Engine Angle

```
Option Base 1
Sub main()
 Dim timeX(2000), Xt(2000), y(11), yo(11), yd(11), runk(11, 4)
 GoSub data
 For i = 1 To (istop + 1)
   Do
     GoSub system
     GoSub runge
   Loop While jint <> 1
     timeX(i + 1) = timeh
     Xt(i + 1) = thetaTOT
 Next i
 For i = 1 To (istop + 1)
   Cells(i, 1) = timeX(i)
   Cells(i, 2) = Xt(i)
 Next i
 End
data:
   n = 11: timeh = 0: y(1) = 0: y(2) = 0: y(3) = 0: y(4) = 0: y(5) = 0
   y(6) = 0: y(7) = 0: y(8) = 25: y(9) = 0: y(10) = 0: y(11) = 0
   dt = 0.005: tstop = 5: istop = Int(tstop / dt)
   timeX(1) = timeh: Xt(1) = y(1)
   runm = Array(1, 0.5, 0.5, 1): jint = 1
   vel = 1300: thr = 420000: tc = 340000: aero = 200000: mass = 5500
   mua = 3.5: muc = 4.6: mup = 0.06: meq = 1590: zb = 0.01: wb = 20
   sigma = 0.01: zfs = 0.01: wfs = 5.1: wfsq = wfs ^ 2
   tom = thr / mass: aom = aero / mass: com = tc / mass: comeq = tc / meq
   fsd = 17.9: tzob = 2 * zb * wb: wbsq = wb ^ 2: tzofs = 2 * zfs * wfs
   Wa = 60: Za = 0.7: Wf = 20: Zf = 0.5: Kd = 2.1: Kr = 0.51
Return
system:
   If i <= 10 Then
     dimp = 0
   End If
   If i > 10 And i <= 100 Then
     dimp = 100 / 57.296
   End If
   If i > 100 Then
     dimp = 0
   End If
   thetaTOT = y(1) + sigma * y(8)
   thetadTOT = y(2) + sigma * y(9)
   deltac = -thetaTOT * Kd - Kr * thetadTOT
   delta = y(4) + dimp
   alpha = y(1) + y(3) / vel
   yd(1) = y(2)
   yd(2) = mua * alpha + muc * delta - mup * y(10)
   yd(3) = -tom * y(1) - aom * alpha + com * delta
   yd(4) = y(5)
   deltaa = y(6)
   yd(5) = (deltaa - y(4)) * Wa ^ 2 - 2 * Za * Wa * y(5)
   yd(6) = y(7)
   yd(7) = (deltac - y(6)) * Wf ^ 2 - 2 * Zf * Wf * y(7)
   yd(8) = y(9)
   yd(9) = -comeq * delta - tzob * y(9) - wbsq * y(8)
   yd(10) = y(11)
   yd(11) = -fsd * delta - tzofs * y(11) - wfsq * y(10)
Return
runge: ... Return
End Sub
```

- Gather the output after each dt.

- Note the initial conditions on the following:
  - timeh
  - y(8) to simulate vibrations at start

- Note the values for these:
  - dt and tstop
  - timeX(1) and Xt(1)
  - runm and jint

- Impulse on delta

- Closed-loop equations

- See Chapter 12 for runge: ... Return.

175

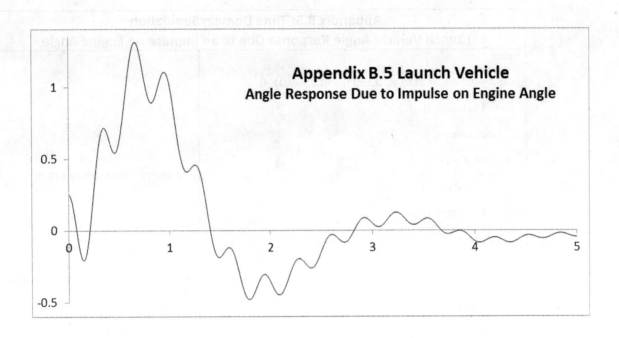

Appendix B.5 Launch Vehicle
Angle Response Due to Impulse on Engine Angle

www.ingramcontent.com/pod-product-compliance
Lightning Source LLC
Chambersburg PA
CBHW080414060326
40689CB00019B/4235